The

CLOCKMAKERS
of
LLANRWST

Pre-Industrial Clockmaking in a
Welsh Market Town

Frontispiece: Clock number 563, c1750.

The

CLOCKMAKERS

of

LLANRWST

Pre-Industrial Clockmaking in a
Welsh Market Town

Colin & Mary Brown

bridge
books
Wrexham

The Clockmakers of Llanrwst
- Pre-Industrial Clockmaking in a Welsh Market Town
© 1993 Colin and Mary Brown

ISBN 1 872424 99 6

This softback edition was
published in Wales in 2002 by
Bridge Books
61 Park Avenue,
Wrexham,
LL12 7AW

CIP date for this book is available
from the British Library

Printed in Great Britain by
MFP
Stretford, Manchester

Contents

Authors' Note:

In the statistical tables included in this book, all percentage figures have been either rounded up or rounded down to the nearest single decimal place. For this reason, the displayed percentages may not add up to exactly 100%.

All measurements in this book are given in Imperial form primarily because this was the measuring system used by the clockmakers of the 18th and 19th centuries. For conversion to metric measurements the scale of 1" = 25.44 mm and 1' = .3048 m should be used.

All Welsh place names used in the text are in their modern, correct spelling (*eg* Llanddoged) except when used in a direct quotation (*eg* Llanddoget).

PREFACE

Tuesday is market-day in Llanrwst. By the time most people are sitting down to eat their breakfasts, the town square is already jammed with market stallholders jostling with each other to get their wares on display before the first customer arrives. On roads throughout the district a motley collection of lorries, Landrovers with trailers and mud-spattered pick-ups converge on the town's smithfield to unload the cattle, sheep and pigs destined to come under the auctioneer's hammer later in the day. Shopkeepers look anxiously at their watches hoping their assistants will not be late, bank managers and solicitors clear their desks and prepare for a busy day and the publicans check that new kegs are connected up to their beer taps. By ten o'clock the streets are jammed with traffic and the pavements are full of jostling shoppers, farmers and tradesmen.

Go into the streets of Llanrwst on just such a day, stop any group of people and ask "Who was Watkin Owen?" and someone is bound to say, "That's easy, he was Llanrwst's old clockmaker". Indeed, the chances are that at least one member of the group will have a grandfather clock made by Watkin Owen ticking away at home. It is unlikely that there is anywhere else in the kingdom where the reputation and handiwork of an 18th century clockmaker retains to this day such universal recognition and affection as it does in the Conwy Valley in the heart of North Wales.

In point of fact, Watkin Owen had a father who was, if anything, an even finer clockmaker though not as prolific, and a younger brother and son who continued his business after he had gone. This remarkable family of a father, two sons and a grandson produced fine clocks in this remote market town for nearly a century and this book is mainly about them and our wonderful heritage of their clocks. There were other clock makers and clock retailers in the town and we have included them in our story, but in this part of North Wales clockmaking in the 18th and early 19th century was entirely dominated by the Owens of Llanrwst.

As our researches progressed something else began to emerge which we had not expected and which provided our book with a further theme. We were not, as we soon realised, dealing with a family of local craftsmen producing distinctively Welsh clocks in remote North Wales, cut off from mainstream clockmaking in England. Instead, we were seeing the same highly organised and integrated pre-industrial clockmaking that was the norm throughout most of the kingdom.

Our friends Alun Davies and Rees Pryce have written a splendid book on Samuel Roberts, a clockmaker more or less contemporary with the first Owen, who practised his craft in Llanfair Caereinion, 40 miles south east of Llanrwst. They show Samuel Roberts to have been very much an individualistic craftsman working in relative isolation and producing the greater part of his clocks in his own workshop. Though he undoubtedly had connections with other clockmakers operating in the Welsh Marches, he was, nevertheless, highly self-sufficient, engraving his own dials and stamping his own personality on his clocks. In Llanrwst the clockmakers worked in a different context. They seem to have been an integral part of an inter-dependent network of masters and apprentices, specialist suppliers and engravers, wholesalers and sub-contractors. Their products followed technical and stylistic fashions that were to be found not just in Llanrwst but in Cheshire, Lancashire and elsewhere. We began to realise that this applied not just to Llanrwst makers but to most other clockmakers in 18th century North Wales. As to the extent of this interdependence and the nature of this proto-industrialisation, the reader will have to draw his own conclusions. We, for our part, have felt it important to demonstrate that the rural craftsman clockmaker, as typified by Samuel Roberts, may not have been typical in North Wales, certainly after the middle of the 18th century.

This book came about very much by accident. A business man from the East Midlands, whose family had owned a home in the Conwy valley for nearly 50 years, went into a Llanrwst antique shop and bought a grandfather clock from the lady proprietor. The clock was signed by John Owen of Llanrwst and the ensuing discussion about who John Owen was and when the clock was made developed into a 10-year collaboration during which more than 30,000 miles were driven to photograph more than six hundred clocks, and countless hours were spent in archive rooms and libraries. The end result of all this activity had to be a book, not just to justify the effort expended, but also to repay all those friendly and hospitable people who had welcomed us into their homes to examine their beloved clocks. We hope that there will be something of interest in these pages for the antiquarian horologist, the local historian and the clock owner. We realise the risks involved in trying to write for such disparate interests, not least the danger of satisfying none. If at the end of the day, however, all our new friends who showed us their clocks, and in some cases lent them to us, consider the exercise to have been worthwhile then we will be well satisfied.

Whilst the friendly hospitality and unstinting co-operation that we received from so many owners of Llanrwst clocks will always be uppermost in our memories, there were also plenty of other people and institutions without whose enthusiastic assistance this book could never have been written, and of whose contributions we would like to make due acknowledgement

The Archivist and all his staff at the Clwyd County Record Office in Ruthin were infinitely patient and helpful over the years, as were their colleagues at Hawarden. Rather less frequently pestered by us but no less helpful was the Assistant County Archivist of Gwynedd, Gareth Haulfryn Williams and his staff at Caernarfon. Gareth Haulfryn Williams himself had already done much research into the first Watkin Owen of Gwydir and our collaboration with him on this subject was particularly fruitful.

At the Library of the University College of North Wales in Bangor, the National Library of Wales at Aberystwyth and at the Lincolnshire County Record Office in Lincoln our requests were always dealt with promptly and efficiently and many helpful suggestions and contributions were provided by the resident staff. Our thanks go to all these keepers of Llanrwst archives with the hope that much more material about the town will be discovered and entrusted to their keeping. In this same category we must include Mr P B Grimes of the Grimsthorpe and Drummond Castle Trust Ltd, who most kindly gave us access to a very considerable volume of material which is still kept at Grimsthorpe Castle in Lincolnshire where the young Mary Wynn went as a bride way back in 1678.

We were fortunate enough to trace several descendants of the old clockmakers and received generous help from them. To Mr R Idloes Owen of Bangor we owe much of our information about Griffith Owen, his great grandfather. Mr Owen himself is an experienced and meticulous family historian and we are grateful to him for allowing us to reproduce the Griffith Owen family tree that he has compiled. Mr W Scriven Williams, son of Owen Williams, late clockmaker and jeweller of Llanrwst, provided us with much of our information about his father.

Mr Bob Lundy, one of Watkin Owen's direct descendants, was just as helpful and generous. He checked much of our research into his family's history and provided us with the family tree of Griffith Owen of Liverpool, Watkin's eldest son. Not only did he provide us with much valuable information but his mere presence as a very real and alive individual helped to provide substance to our researches into a family which, until his arrival, had always seemed shadowy and elusive.

Even with all this assistance our genealogical research in Wales quite often ran into problems for reasons that we will explain in more detail later on. When in difficulty we were in the habit of seeking assistance from Mrs Beryl Morgan Jones of Wrexham. Beryl is not only an experienced researcher but a considerable expert on the Welsh clockmakers. We would feel a good deal less confident about the genealogical information contained in these pages if it were not for the many hours that she spent, on our behalf, in various archive offices supplementing and checking our own findings.

Many people have helped us to locate Llanrwst clocks, not least the staff of local newspapers and periodicals who gave our clock survey plenty of coverage. It seems invidious therefore to single out individuals for mention, but three names stand out amongst all our clock-sleuths. Mr John Owen of Plas Tirion, Mr Jack Hughes of Cwmllanerch and Mr Gwyn Davies of Hafod-y-wern were outstanding for the persistence with which they tracked down so many fine clocks for us and we are most grateful to them. No less successful in this way were Mrs Mary Jones of Denbigh and the late Mr John Williams of Four Crosses who ensured that many clocks in their areas were brought to our attention, and Mr Carl Goldberg of Manchester who found us the wonderful Titley clock.

Several antique dealers were equally diligent on our behalf, amongst them Mr Geoff Collins of Snowdonia Antiques, Llanrwst who can usually be relied upon to have good Llanrwst clocks in his showroom and Mr Michael Thompson who found a number of clocks for us in the south of England.

Mr George Hadfield, a specialist dealer in clocks, not only found us clocks but he also took a personal interest in our project from its inception. In particular, George was always quick to de-bunk all our more pretentious theories. We will always owe him a debt of gratitude for keeping our feet firmly on the ground.

Mr Brian Loomes who has done more than any other person to popularise the subject of long-case clocks and their makers could have been forgiven for looking askance at our first faltering efforts in his own specialist field: instead, he gave us every encouragement and much sound advice and also found us some lovely Llanrwst clocks.

Mr Llyr Gruffydd, then the curator of Oriel Eryri in Llanberis, staged a wonderful exhibition of Llanrwst clocks and found us dozens of new clocks as a result. It was a great pleasure working with him and his staff. The exhibition was seen by Mr Nicholas Moore, at that time curator of the Grosvenor Museum in Chester, who staged much the same exhibition a year later with similar results, a wonderful boost to our efforts. Mr Moore also helped us with the identification of watch-case makers.

Very early in our researches it became apparent that only a detailed study of the innards of the clocks would enable us to draw any significant conclusions about their manufacture. This presented us with a problem because our repair and restoration skills were then very limited and clock owners could not be expected to entrust their heirlooms to anyone that might do them damage. That is how our friend and mentor, Adrian Dolby, came upon the scene and played such a vital role in our story. Adrian is a gifted and experienced professional restorer of fine clocks who was himself not in a position to do the work for us but he did find the time to teach us to do it for ourselves. He proved to be an exacting but marvellous tutor to whom alone we owe such competence that we possess in the workshop. It was typical of him that, unhesitatingly, he passed on to us the important know-how that has taken him so many years, and much anguish, to acquire. He himself has a particular interest in watches and examined most of those that we came across in our survey. The technical conclusions drawn in these pages about Llanrwst watches and about the Watkin Owen bracket clock are mostly his. We owe him a huge debt of thanks.

Very early in our project we were to meet two people who have since made a very special contribution to this project, Dr Rees Pryce of the Open University in Wales and Mr Alun Davies, Assistant Keeper in the Department of Buildings and Domestic Life at the Welsh Folk Museum, St Fagans. They were already well into their own research project concerned with another 18th century clockmaker in Wales, Samuel Roberts of Llanfair Caereinion, and in 1985 the results of their work was published in a fascinating book which we frequently quote from in the pages that follow. When we arrived on the scene Rees Pryce already had thoughts of following his work on Samuel Roberts by a similar project on the Owens of Llanrwst. He could have been forgiven for being very dubious indeed about our ability and qualifications to do justice to the Llanrwst clockmakers. It was typical of him, however, that he soon passed the subject over to us and set about giving us every possible assistance and encouragement as he has continued to do to this day.

Alun Davies, in addition, was able to bring to our support the full weight and reputation of the Welsh Folk Museum. The Museum publicly endorsed our efforts and, amongst other things, made public appeals for information on our behalf and assisted in many other significant ways. To be able to claim the backing of the Welsh Folk Museum gave to our project a credibility that it could never have otherwise achieved. Not only are we exceedingly grateful for all their help, but it is our sincerest wish that everyone at St Fagans should conclude that this modest book is an adequate return for all their efforts on our behalf.

Much closer to home we would like to salute the magnificent contribution made by our secretaries, Ann Page and Karen Walker, who have laboured long and hard at their word processors deciphering with uncanny skill our notes and tapes with total disregard to their normal working hours and, we suspect, their families waiting patiently at home. We are not only very grateful to them, but also to Messrs En-tout-cas plc for turning a Nelsonian eye to this radical departure from their normal duties.

Finally to our brother and brother-in-law, Garth Brown, a special expression of our gratitude. He became embroiled in the project at a very early date and allowed his life to be disrupted by it. Indeed, he became an expert in recording the clocks, and rarely complained!

To all these people we are immensely grateful and no less so to many others whom the limitations of space prevent us from mentioning by name. If ever there was a book which was the result of a team effort, it was this one.

A word about the format of this book. In Part One the first chapter paints an historical sketch of Llanrwst, the market town in which the clockmakers worked and lived. The subsequent nine chapters tell the stories of their lives and describe the clocks that they produced and which have survived to this day. Part Two may appeal more to the researcher, the antiquarian horologist, and to people who have an interest in the technical details of Llanrwst clocks. It describes not just the clocks but the methods we employed for our survey and lists many of our statistical findings. We hope all our readers will find sufficient to interest them.

Finally some information for future researchers about the whereabouts of the Llanrwst archives or, rather, those we located. We hope there is much more material still to be found.

The Llanrwst archives are scattered far and wide. The largest collection of documents is located at the Clwyd County Record Office in Ruthin. Here the extensive church records are kept including the parish registers, the bishop's transcripts, the vestry minutes and accounts, and tithe or *maes* rolls. There is much other material at Ruthin including the Quarter Session rolls which, we have to confess, we did not examine to any significant extent. Anyone looking for a magnum opus to occupy them for a few years would earn the undying gratitude of researchers by transcribing them! Also at Ruthin are the 19th century census enumerators' books. These, like the parish registers, are on micro film.

There is another branch of the Clwyd County Record Office at Hawarden, but we found little original material relating to Llanrwst there.

The library of the University College of North Wales at Bangor also contains a significant volume of Llanrwst archives. In particular, it has been the repository for the Mostyn papers, which contain many documents and deeds relating to Llanrwst.

Gwydir, although it was in the ecclesiastical parish of Llanrwst, was actually located in the administrative county of Caenarfonshire, so there is some material relating to it in the Gwynedd Archive Office in Caernarfon.

The National Library of Wales at Aberystwyth, a wonderful but vast establishment, has much for the researcher interested in Llanrwst, but it can be a rather lengthy process gaining access to all of the material. This implies no criticism of the indexing nor of the helpfulness of the staff - merely that it is a very large and busy place indeed. We recommend a reconnaissance visit to work out the geography and the systems. In the library are the probate records of the ancient North Wales dioceses, including St Asaph, and documents and deeds from many large families and houses, with many references to Llanrwst scattered through them. Here, also, are the majority of the original documents comprising the marvellous Wynn Papers, an abundant source of information about Llanrwst and its environs. In this instance we recommend a new researcher to obtain access to a copy of the *Calendar of the Wynn Papers* in which all the documents are summarised and, hardly less important, all are instantly legible unlike many of the originals.

Another abundant store of Llanrwst documents is to be found in Lincoln Castle, where the Lincolnshire County Record Office is housed. Here, the Ancaster Papers contain much material relating to the Gwydir Estate which the Willoughby d'Eresby family acquired by marriage in the later 17th century. Not all the Gwydir Estate papers have found their way to Lincoln Castle, however; an equally large collection is still in Grimsthorpe Castle, a few miles from Lincoln and the ancestral seat of the Willoughby d'Eresby family. Access may be obtained to them by bona fide researchers by applying to the Grimsthorpe Estate Office. The documents at Grimsthorpe have not yet been catalogued. Incidentally the Gwydir Estate Rentals are to be found mostly at Lincoln and Grimsthorpe, but there are odd ones at Caernarfon and Bangor.

We were lucky enough to unearth a considerable cache of documents relating to the Titley family in Lancashire, copies of which should be lodged at Bangor in the not-too-distant future.

Still further away in London is the Public Record Office where the probate records of the Prerogative Court of Canterbury are housed. Most Llanrwst area wills will be found in Aberystwyth in the probate records of the dioceses of St Asaph or Bangor, but if the testator was leaving properties in more than one diocese, the will may be in the Canterbury probate records at the PRO. This is where we found the will of the first Watkin Owen of Gwydir.

Colin & Mary Brown
Leicester
1993

CHAPTER I
Llanrwst in the 18th Century

The small market town of Llanrwst lies on the eastern edge of the Snowdonia National Park in what is now the county of Gwynedd but which was, until recently, Denbighshire. The town is built entirely on the east bank of the River Conwy, 12 miles due south of the point where the river enters the Irish Sea. Across the river, barely a mile away, the densely wooded foothills of the Carneddau range rise steeply from the valley floor. The great hogsback of Carnedd Llewellyn, second in height only to Snowdon itself and snow covered for long periods in the winter, is visible from several parts of the town. Behind Llanrwst, to the east, gentler field-covered hills climb steadily towards the bleak moorland of Hiraethog and Denbigh. Only down the valley towards the sea is the encircling barrier of hills and mountains broken.

The valley bottom is wide, flat and lush, dotted with farms that have been there for centuries. Through it runs the river Conwy, flowing quietly with only occasional rapids, its deeper pools now and then disturbed by the splash of sea-trout and salmon. The river's source is in the boggy moors of the Migneint near the village of Ysbyty Ifan where its waters are stained brown by the peat through which it flows. From there it enters a series of rocky gorges through which it plunges nearly a thousand feet to the village of Betws-y-coed, a few miles south of Llanrwst. Here it is joined by its two main tributaries, the Llugwy and the Lledr both of which have their origin high in the mountains of Snowdonia.

The Vale of Conwy at Llanrwst offers today's visitor a scene of great beauty and peacefulness and, over time, in this it has changed but little. The first tourists to visit the area during the last quarter of the 18th century and the opening years of the 19th saw a very similar scene. Perhaps the most enthusiastic was the Reverend Bingley who visited the area in 1798 and again in 1801. He wrote:

> The road now led us into the luxuriant Vale of Llanrwst, where the gay tints of cultivation once more beautified the landscape, for the fields were coloured with the rich hues of ripened corn and green meadows. Many gentlemen's seats interspersed around gave an air of civilisation to this valley. We had not enjoyed the beauties of this prospect long, before we entered the gloomy woods of Gwydir which afforded a fine contrast to the luxuriance of the vale. The Conwy runs at a little distance from the road, and the silvery reflection of its water through the dark foliage of the trees, gave an additional interest to the scene. On emerging from hence, we had again the same open vale in which the town of Llanrwst, now before us, formed a conspicuous feature; and the extensive landscape, thus completed, heightened by the dreary rocks bounding it on each side, has been justly admired by all the lovers of nature, as one of the finest scenes her pencil ever traced. [1]

Perhaps the "gentlemen's seats" are not so much in evidence now; some are demolished and others are hidden entirely by trees, but otherwise Bingley could have been writing today.

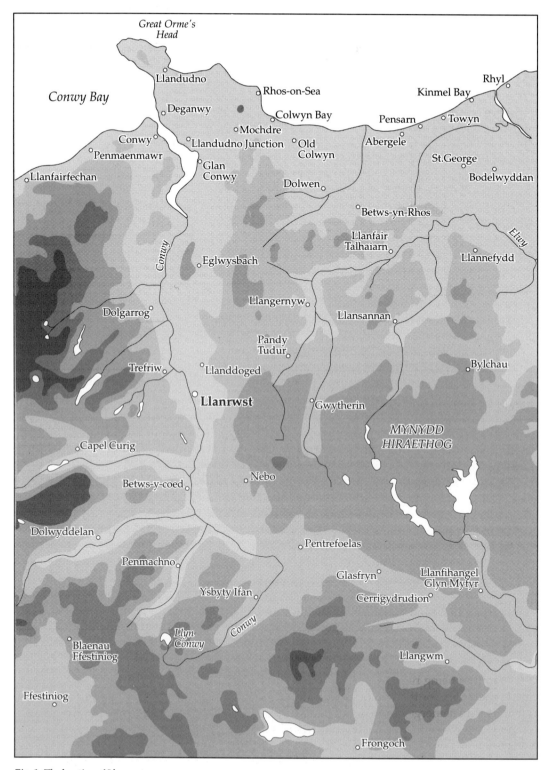

Fig. 1: The location of Llanrwst.

Provincial clockmaking dates from the earliest years of the 18th century and by this time Llanrwst was already an important town. It was, first and foremost, a market town serving a large, widely dispersed rural community. Its catchment area was as much delineated by the unyielding landscape of the district, as by travelling distances or the presence of other markets. Roads and pathways over the higher mountain ranges were few and frequently impassable so the natural tendency was to go to market the easy way - downhill! Thus, Llanrwst was frequented not just by the inhabitants of the valley villages such as Betws-y-coed, Trefriw, Dolgarrog, Llanbedr and Eglwysbach, but also by villagers from the upland settlements of Capel Garmon, Ysbyty Ifan, Pentrefoelas, Penmachno, Capel Curig, Maenan, Dolwyddelan and several others.

More than to any other factor, however, Llanrwst owed it standing as a regional centre to its strategic location within the communications network of the area. In particular, it offered excellent river crossings, the easiest, safest and cheapest for most travellers. When the Conwy is low, it is readily fordable at the town; a few hours rain in the nearby mountains, however, and the river becomes a raging, muddy torrent and is an impassable barrier to any traveller. In 1636, the problem was overcome by the building of the fine stone bridge of three arches that still stands to this day.

Crossings below the town were much more difficult. The river soon becomes tidal and expands into a wide estuary offering very real hazards to anyone trying to cross. There were to be no more bridges until well into the 19th century and anyone wishing to cross below Llanrwst had no alternative but to use the ferries lower downstream at Tal-y-cafn or Conwy, inconvenient at the best and, in the case of Conwy, frequently unpleasant and sometimes dangerous. So the easy crossing at Llanrwst brought all kinds of travellers funnelling through the town, local farmers going to market, cattle drovers with their herds of small black cattle destined for the markets of England and wealthy landowners going on horseback to visit relatives or to conduct their business affairs in Chester, Shrewsbury or London.

The travellers had little in the way of roads to assist their passage. In the 17th and early 18th century, roads in general were rarely more than unpaved, muddy tracks and Welsh roads were, by general consent, even worse. Certainly, journeys by coach were never easy. If they had to be undertaken then, usually, the passengers were elderly or women-folk unable or unwilling to ride on horseback, and it was always wise to send workmen on ahead to ensure the road was passable. In 1666, Sir Richard Wynn of Gwydir commented that his coach was holding up remarkably well despite the rotten pavements between Gwydir and Caermelwr. [2] It may be thought that this involved a long journey but, in reality, the two houses were in full view of each other and a mere mile of road separated them.

To the rest of the country, North Wales was a very remote place indeed - so much so that the Wynns of Gwydir frequently had great difficulty finding wives for their sons, the girls' families being reluctant to agree to so total a separation from their daughters. [3] It says much, therefore, for the vigour and enthusiasm of the gentry of North Wales that they had played such an energetic role in affairs of state in London which they conducted with such successs. A visit to London meant an arduous and sometimes dangerous journey on horseback that frequently took several days.

Llanrwst enjoyed another great asset; the river Conwy was navigable all the way from the sea to the town. Today, however, the only boat a modern visitor is likely to see is a motor-boat towing a water-skier on the estuary below Tal-y-cafn, a fact which requires some explanation. Throughout the 17th and 18th centuries the Conwy was passable to sea-going boats of 30 to 50 tons burthen as far as Tal-y-cafn, six miles downstream of Llanrwst. At this point the river narrowed and their way upstream was barred by a rocky reef. Cargoes had to be unloaded at Tal-y-cafn and transferred to carriers' wagons or placed in shallow-draught boats that could make their way, not without difficulty, to Llanrwst itself. The Gwydir estate had a quay well above the bridge and frequently loaded timber from a field called Lletty Cla still further upstream. 4 In the early years of the 19th century the reef above Tal-y-cafn was dynamited allowing larger vessels to dock at Trefriw within easy reach of the town.

This channel of communication guaranteed Llanrwst's importance, enabling vital raw materials and manufactured goods to be imported into the town; lime for sweetening the acid land and for building, coal to fuel the blacksmith's forge and the rich man's hearth and supplies and provisions of every sort to stock the shops. Equally important was the ease with which the produce of the region could be sent out to distant markets: timber, tan bark and lead ore were among the earlier exports with slate and agricultural produce following later.

A third reason for the pre-eminence of Llanrwst was the presence, a bare half mile from the town, of Gwydir, the seat of perhaps the most influential and successful of all aristocratic families living in northern Wales, the Wynns of Gwydir.

The Wynns had come originally from Eifionydd in Caernarfonshire but, in the years following the Wars of the Roses, family feuding had become so bloody that Maredudd ap Ieuan moved to Dolwyddelen where he lived first in the castle and then in the house which he built nearby at Penamnen. Things were hardly more peaceful here, however, for he soon found himself under constant attack by brigands and cut-throats who dominated the district from their base in Ysbyty Ifan. Maredudd ap Ieuan quelled the brigands and then moved to Gwydir where his descendants were to flourish and increase in wealth and influence for more than one hundred and fifty years, adding greatly to the importance of Llanrwst in the process.

Geographically Gwydir was in the county of Caernarfon and the Wynns frequently sat in Parliament representing that county. Gwydir itself, however, was a township of the parish of Llanrwst and this was actually located in Denbighshire. To complete the confusion Caernarfonshire was in the diocese of Bangor whilst Llanrwst was in the diocese of St Asaph. This situation did, however, allow the Wynns considerable flexibility.

The best known of all the Wynns of Gwydir was Sir John Wynn, 1st Baronet (1553-1627). He was a vigourous and ambitious man who added greatly to the family's fame and fortune, extending their holdings to nearly thirty thousand acres. Most of the land on the Caernarfonshire bank of the river from Trefriw to Betws-y-coed and then along the Lledr to remote Dolwyddelan belonged to the Wynns. In Denbighshire, they owned approximately half of Llanrwst town itself and many adjoining farms. This, together with landholdings further afield, gave the family an annual income in excess of three thousand pounds a year in rents alone.

In addition to the aggrandisement of his family fortunes, Sir John involved himself and his family in public affairs. He himself was High Sheriff of Caernarfonshire and then Merioneth and for a short time he sat in Parliament. He was a member of the influential (and infamous) Council of the Marches which met at Ludlow and was, of course, a local

Justice of the Peace. He grabbed at every available public office, both in London and in North Wales, and his successors at Gwydir did just the same.

As befitted his station in the community, Sir John greatly improved the fabric and furnishings of his mansion at Gwydir. In fact he built himself a second mansion, Gwydir Ucha (or Upper Gwydir) perched on a small plateau a hundred feet above the lower house. From then on the family seemed to move from one to the other but on no particularly systematic basis. Perhaps the upper house was lighter and quieter and, being newer, it was more convenient and fashionable as a family residence. The much grander lower house, the remnants of which today are known as Gwydir Castle, probably would have been used more for entertaining and for local government and family business. Certainly, it was sumptuously furnished with ornately carved panelling and furniture, much of which was made by estate craftsmen.

Sir John was a man of good education and wide interests. He assisted in the publication of a Welsh dictionary and wrote *The History of the Gwydir Family* - the latter more intended perhaps, to enhance the prestige of the family than to record historical fact regarding his pedigree.

Llanrwst derived direct benefit from the presence within its boundaries of such an influential and wealthy family. The estate generated business and employment in no small way and attracted a constant flow of visitors from all levels of society. The Wynns built the first Town Hall in what was then called Bryn-y-botten, now known as Ancaster Square. They endowed several local charities providing, *inter alia*, support for widows, endowments for the church and apprenticeships for poor boys. [5] Sir John had built a new almshouse which he called the Jesus Hospital and founded a fine Free School. [6]

Sir John Wynn died in 1627 and was succeeded by his son Sir Richard Wynn, the 2nd baronet. Llanrwst and Gwydir saw little of him, however, as he spent most of his time at the court of King Charles where he was a Gentleman of the Bedchamber and treasurer to Queen Henrietta Maria. He visited his estates occasionally and built a fine family chapel on to Llanrwst church in 1633.

Sir Richard Wynn died in 1649 and was succeeded by his younger brother Owen. In Sir Richard's absence, Owen Wynn had already established himself at Gwydir and was managing the family estates. He married Grace, niece of Archbishop Williams, Lord Keeper of the Seal, a wealthy and influential woman in her own right. He, in turn, was succeeded in 1660 by his son, the second Sir Richard Wynn. He, too, followed the same pattern, sitting as a member of Parliament and moving regularly between London and Gwydir. He married Sarah, daughter of Sir Thomas Myddleton, Bart of Chirk Castle and settled down to lead a busy private and public life - much like his father and grandfather before him.

The Wynns were not the only major landowners in Llanrwst and its district. The Mostyn family had, for many years, possessed large estates in the valley but on the Denbighshire bank of the river. Most of that part of Llanrwst which was not Wynn property belonged to the Mostyns. Their total estates in Wales were to become even larger than the Wynn's, so much so that even today some of the older folk in Llanrwst remember a saying:- "Mae Mistar, ar Mistar Mostyn," which, loosely translated, means, "Even Mr Mostyn has a master". There was a fundamental difference, however, in the relative influence of the two families in the Conwy valley, because the Mostyns were absentee landlords - their seat at Mostyn being a full 30 miles away, near Holywell in Flintshire. The

Mostyn lands in the valley were administered by agents and the owners were much more likely to come to Llanrwst to visit their friends and relatives, the Wynns, than to involve themselves in estate affairs.

So, for more than a hundred years, the Wynns of Gwydir reigned supreme in the Vale of Conwy, and Llanrwst shared in their prestige and their prosperity.

Then suddenly all was changed. In November 1674 Sir Richard Wynn of Gwydir, 4th Baronet, died without leaving a male heir. His daughter Mary was now an heiress of thirty thousand acres, three fine houses [7] and an income amounting to no less than three thousand pounds per annum. She was the immediate target for every eligible young man in North Wales and many from further afield. In those days a good marriage was an excellent way of bolstering the family fortunes. They all reckoned, however, without Lady Grace Wynn, Mary's redoubtable grandmother. She organised a grand funeral for her son in Chester, paid off his quite staggering debts [8] and then set about arranging the best possible marriage for her grand-daughter. The Welsh suitors failed to meet with the approval of Lady Grace and in 1678 Mary Wynn was married to Robert Bertie, Baron Willoughby D'Eresby, Earl of Lindsey, who shortly was to become 1st Duke of Ancaster and Lord High Chamberlain. [9] The wedding took place in Westminster Abbey and Mary Wynn left the valley to take up residence in her husband's principal seat at Grimsthorpe in Lincolnshire.

Suddenly the Wynns, who had wielded such influence over Llanrwst and the surrounding countryside, were no longer there. They were replaced by a small army of agents and estate managers who descended on the Gwydir estates and proceeded to rationalise them on behalf of the now remote owner. The rents had tended to be paid in kind, and included a very strange selection of commodities such as oatmeal, wild honey and black lace; these were converted by the agents into cash payments. Farming activities on the estate were restricted and old farm machinery sold for scrap. Much of the home-farm itself was let. New revenue-earning activities were started up, including a systematic exploitation of the estate woodlands. [10]

Gareth Haulfryn Williams has given an interesting account of this interlude.[11] He concludes that the agents carried out their task conscientiously and logically, and that in no way could they have been accused of asset stripping or exploitation. They were efficient estate managers and merely wished to assure themselves that their master's new Welsh properties were as effectively managed as were his estates in England. It is satisfactory to note that, in the end, it was one of the Welsh agents who had been resident at Gwydir at the time of Sir Richard's death who was left in charge of the Welsh estate. His name was Watkin Owen and he will feature in our story again.

By comparison with the first three quarters of the 17th century, when the affairs of Llanrwst seemed to be vital and fast moving, the next 75 years appear to have been a period of relative stagnation. To some extent this may be a misleading impression. The Wynns left behind them a marvellous record of their prosperous years at Gwydir[12], whereas, once they were gone, documentation of any kind about Llanrwst and its inhabitants is scanty, at least until 1750. The parish registers record births, marriages and deaths; a few estate rentals have survived along with just a few letters and documents.

In all probability it was nevertheless a period of little change. The first stirrings of what were to become the agricultural and industrial revolutions were to be felt late in Llanrwst. Even the new turnpike roads were not to reach the town until 1777. Also, it has to be said

Fig 2: Mary Wynn,
wife of the 1st Duke of Ancaster.
Painting by Sir Peter Lely.
[Trustees of the Grimsthorpe &
Drummond Castle Trust Ltd]

that the town must have felt the effects of its land and properties being substantially in the hands of absentee landlords. The Ancaster and Mostyn estates, would, by 1700, have accounted for more than two thirds of all the holdings in Llanrwst and its environs. There were still some free-holdings it is true. The largest belonged to the Wynns of Berthddu (who do not appear to have been related to the Wynns of Gwydir) but even they, in due course, married into the Mostyn family and their lands were swallowed up, leaving only relatively few, smaller holdings in the ownership of independent landowners.

So, for the first three quarters of the 18th century, the stewards and agents of the large estates were the most influential men in the district. The Duke of Ancaster's agents usually lived at Gwydir itself and were men of substance in their own right. They appear to have been competent, conscientious men, serving their employers and the tenantry to the best of their ability. But these were not great men, who attracted friends and business to the district: they were not in a position to innovate or take initiatives. They did not embellish the town with newer and larger public buildings or endow new charities nor did they build themselves fashionable new houses. Rather, the tendency was always towards conservatism and the status quo. This situation was not helped by the infrequency with which the owners themselves visited their Conwy valley estates - especially the Ancasters, who lived in far-off Lincolnshire. Certainly they did not use their houses in the valley

19

sufficiently to warrant modernisation and re-furnishing. The Gwydir mansions were let to a series of tenants including some of the agents, and were never to recover their former glory. By 1740 Upper Gwydir was full of old and broken furniture and rotten hangings[13]; before the end of the century it was substantially demolished. [14] The lower house was also occupied by tenants but its fabric was kept in reasonable order as the agents' account books show; and later in the century Baroness Willoughby D'Eresby even ordered improvements to be carried out and the road from the house to the town to be rebuilt.[15]

Therefore, it is not an overstatement to say that for the hundred years following the death of Sir Richard Wynn in 1674, the town and valley of Llanrwst were substantially owned by absentee landlords, inhabited by tenants and administered by agents. Yet it would be far from the truth to conclude that it was a subservient tenantry eking out a meagre living in an infertile land. The clockmakers who worked in Llanrwst throughout the second half of the 18th century sold expensive clocks in remarkable numbers and to do this they needed an extensive and reasonably well-to-do clientele. We need to look back in history, therefore, to the origins of the men who supported perhaps the most successful and prolific family of clockmakers in the whole of Wales.

When Henry Tudor ascended the English throne in 1485, it was hardly surprising that many of his countrymen should have accompanied him to London and flourished under his patronage. Throughout the 16th and early 17th centuries the gentry and petty gentry of North Wales prospered; they regularly held offices at court, sat in Parliament and were involved in the law, the universities, the church and commerce. As they prospered, their families at home in Wales did likewise, building themselves fine houses and extending their estates.

After the Civil War, however, there were radical changes. Wealth and land began to be concentrated in the hands of a mere handful of premier families and the rest of the gentry and petty gentry went into inexorable decline. Professor A H Dodd wrote:

> . . . so for the causes of this growing gulf between greater and lesser gentry we must look beyond the Civil War into economic factors common in the whole country and still imperfectly understood. In those days of pre-scientific agriculture on the one hand and on the other of growing luxury in every direction, it was becoming increasingly difficult to live as a gentleman from land owning only, without some of those extraneous aids which only the wealthy could command; lucrative matches, good jobs under the government, overseas investments and the like. The smaller gentry, eager to follow suit, fell to mortgaging their slender resources until, too often, they lost their freeholds and sank into the class of tenant farmers - hence, in part, the number of farmhouses dotted around the country which bear unmistakable marks of old gentry residences. [16]

and again,

> In this decline of stately homes into humdrum farmhouses the effects of the concentration of wealth are most obvious to the eye. The age of the Tudors had seen the proliferation of manor houses as junior branches of the family hived off for themselves; the processes now brought into reverse.

We have seen exactly this process earlier in this chapter. The Wynns of Gwydir steadily acquired the land of their neighbours and then, suddenly, were swallowed up themselves. So were the Wynns of Berthddu. Therefore, many of the tenants who paid rent each year in Llanrwst to the agents of Ancaster and Mostyn, were descended from leading local

Fig 3: Gwydir Tenancies in the Llanrwst district, 1775
(Taken from the Gwydir Estate Rental, 1775 in the Lincolnshire Record Office)

Annual Rents £	No of Tenants	%
0 - 10	140	57
10 - 20	64	26
20 - 30	26	11
30 - 40	11	4
40+	5	2
Total	246	100

NB: The 246 tenancies were in the parishes of Llanrwst (excluding the town itself) Llanddoged, Llansaintffraid, Llanfair Talhaiarn, Gwytherin, Dowyddelan, Penmachno, Trefriw, Llanrhychwyn, Aber, Dwygyfylchi, Eglwys Rhos, Llanbedr & Caerhun and Betws-y-coed.

families. They had lost the freehold of their family holdings, but they were still men of some substance, far removed from peasant farmers or artisans. Figure 3 is compiled from the Gwydir Estate Rental for 1775 and shows the holdings ranked by the amount of the annual rent. It has been said that a well-to-do shopkeeper or craftsman in an 18th century market town would do very well to earn an income of £40 to £60 [17] per annum and this helps to put the rents paid in the Conwy valley into perspective.

Llanrwst town served a rural community where most people earned their livings from the produce of the land, woods and rivers. The estate rentals give us good insight as to the occupations of the tenantry, both in the town and the surrounding countryside. They are supplemented by a series of parish maes or tithe rolls covering the period of 1750 - 1820. [18] As with the rentals, these give the names of the holdings of the gentry, farmers and smallholders and the professions of people living and working in the town itself. The greater part of the income of the farmers and small holders was derived from their livestock. Much of the land was poor and rocky and unsuitable for growing crops; only along the valley bottom and on the more gently rising farmlands to the east and south east of the town was the land fertile enough for arable crops to be a realistic proposition. On the higher, more exposed holdings the cultivated fields were small and rocky, producing barely sufficient foodstuff for the farmer and his family, let alone his livestock, which was more often turned out onto the hillsides to fend for itself. The acid soils needed lime and manure and the climate was a constant hazard. Hay and cereals had to be harvested late in North Wales and a wet summer would often prevent the harvest altogether or destroy it before it could be gathered in. Hay was a universal crop because, without it, livestock could not be overwintered and had to be slaughtered. Cereals, too, were important, usually oats, but on the better land, wheat and barley. Turnips and potatoes were the most common root crops, but, occasionally, vegetables such as cabbages and peas were grown for the table. [19] But, in addition, there were more unusual crops because, in the 18th century, a relatively remote rural community had to be substantially self sufficient. So, flax was grown to be turned into coarse linen and ropes, and hops for the locally-brewed beer. Another more reliable harvest was provided by the river Conwy. In spring the smelt, a small fish whose flesh tastes of cucumber, swarmed up the river in great numbers. They were much prized and the Wynns used to send jars of pickled smelt to their relations and friends. In early June, the sea trout, or *sewin*, arrived in great abundance and were followed a month later by the river's native salmon. [20] All these provided food for the district and employment for the men who caught them. Many early visitors to Llanrwst comment on the number of fishermen in their coracles on the river. Estates and houses that owned the river-banks installed traps of various kinds to intercept the fish on their way up to their spawning grounds.

Sometimes more unusual fish were captured. In 1612, Sir John Wynn caught a young porpoise in one of his traps and made it into two large pasties. Reading between the lines, Sir John was clearly rather dubious about the whole thing, but solved the problem in part by sending one of the pasties to his son at Llanfrothen in Caernarfonshire. It was high summer and Llanfrothen was a long way from Gwydir so Sir John sent with it the fatherly advice to re-cook the pastie if there were any doubt about its condition on arrival! [21]

The farms and holdings around Llanrwst were much better suited to the rearing of cattle and sheep than the cultivation of crops. The sure-footed mountain sheep and small, native, black cattle were the mainstay of the community and the basis of whatever prosperity it achieved. Wool and cloth had long been a major export from Wales, and there were always a few weavers in the town and fulling-mills in the adjoining countryside involved in this trade. In the Conwy valley, however, cloth was not of major importance as an export, being produced as much for domestic consumption as for shipping to England. Rather it was woollen stockings for which the district was widely renowned, ranking second only to Bala in their production. Most of the community seemed to have been involved in knitting them and so low were the prices paid at the fairs that the poorer families had to spend most of their waking hours with knitting needles in their hands.

The Reverend Evans, visiting Llanrwst in 1798, was most impressed. He arrived on market day and wrote:

> Few men are to be seen; the business being conducted by women; and we could not refuse admiring the spirit of the industry manifest on these occasions. No person is idle - no hand in pockets, or in fold, is seen, but both the buyer and the seller are employed in knitting; and hundreds may be seen going and returning, earning their subsistence as they walk along.
>
> How different is this from the manufacturing poor in England, where attendance on a fair, or market, is a general pretext for squandering and idleness. Indeed economy, as well as industry, the two grand hinges on which the happiness and comfort of the lower classes in society turn, may be learned from all the movements of this people. [22]

The ladies of Llanrwst knitting in the market that day would probably have been astonished at this assessment.

Scarcely less important than the sheep to the local economy were the cattle. There was a long tradition of exporting these, usually at the yearling stage, to be fattened and slaughtered in the English lowlands, especially the midlands and south east. The difficult drive to these distant markets was undertaken by the famous cattle-drovers, who were among the most important and well-to-do men in the community. They travelled from farm to farm buying the cattle from the farmers who had reared them and these were further supplemented by animals bought in local markets and fairs. They usually drove herds of from fifty to several hundred head following traditional routes. Before embarking on their journey, the cattle were fitted with iron shoes to prevent their feet from being damaged by the long arduous journey, much of it over rocky terrain.

So important to the Welsh economy and community life were these drovers that they were required by law to obtain licences from the local magistrates before practising their calling and, because they were men of proven honesty and good standing, they were entrusted with many additional tasks. They were tough and travelled in parties so that they were more than a match for footpads along the way. This made them ideal for carrying business documents and valuables to London, because safe conduct was assured. The postal services of the time were much less reliable. Thus, Watkin Owen, his Grace of Ancaster's high-steward at Gwydir, regularly entrusted substantial sums in gold to a drover for delivery to his employer in London. A typical entry in his accounts would be:

> September 11th, 1685.
>   Ready money pd. Hugh Roberts drover to b. paid unto my Lord Willoughby at London 10th 8br. 85, wch were pd. as per my Lord's receipt dated 9th, 8br 1685 £50 0s 0d. [23]

Owen's meticulous practice of recording both the agreed delivery date and the actual delivery date shows that the journey time to London was usually about four weeks. At the end of their journeys, the drovers would sell their herds, making their own profits in the process; and would then return home having executed various commissions for their customers, once again carrying letters, documents and valuables.

Their cattle were, for long, the largest single source of revenue to Welsh farmers large and small. Scarcely less important to the local community however, and especially to Llanrwst itself, was the tanning of skins and the production of leather goods. For hundreds of years a large tannery stood in the town on the river bank immediately adjacent to the churchyard. In addition there were one or more lesser establishments. The surrounding oak woods produced top-quality tan bark in abundance; and the output of the tanneries provided employment for a whole hierarchy of craftsmen and labourers in the town. First, came the curriers who took the raw leather from the tanners and prepared it for all its many and varied uses - the curriers were skilled men and in the first rank of the town's craftsmen. Next, came the saddlers and harness makers who made the heavy harness for the wagons and sledges which were the main means of moving heavy or bulk-goods locally. Most numerous of all the town's leather workers were the boot and shoe makers (then known as corvisers), closely followed in numbers by the glovers.

If the leather trade was perhaps the leading employer within the town itself, woodworking and furniture-making ran a close second. The Conwy valley had long been renowned for the richness and luxuriance of its woodlands, especially those on the steep hillsides behind Gwydir. One of the first actions of the Duke of Ancaster's managers after the acquisition of his Welsh estates, was to initiate systematic exploitation of these woodlands. The task was entrusted to Watkin Owen and some of his detailed accounts for this operation have survived. [24] He supplied tan-bark, sawn timber, barrel staves, laths and an abundance of other timber products to all parts of North Wales, Cheshire and, by sea, to Liverpool. The estate continued to supply forestry products in considerable quantity well into the 19th century.

In the early 18th century, navy department agents were scouring the land for massive oak timbers and planks for building new fighting ships and it was inevitable that Gwydir's oaks should attract their attention, but all negotiations for felling them were to no avail. [25] Finally, in 1745, a contract was signed with John Gorrell and John Park, timber merchants of Liverpool, authorising them to extract oak, elm and ash to the value of £4810 0s 0d. The purchasers were given no less than nine years to cut and clear the timber and to ship it down the river to Liverpool. [26]

The Duke of Ancaster's woodlands must have been considerably depleted by this operation so replanting was carried out systematically over the ensuing years. A tree nursery was established adjacent to the bridge on the Caernarfonshire bank of the river and seedlings were purchased from Liverpool. Fences and walls were repaired and the wild goats were shot to prevent them damaging the young trees. It is fashionable today to castigate the Forestry Commission for introducing conifer plantations to the valley, so it is interesting to note that in 1781 the estate made payments for the planting of fir trees. Subsequently larch and spruce were added to the range of trees.

The valley woodlands, therefore, provided regular employment, and their produce provided the raw materials for many craftsmen in country and town alike - foresters, sawyers, joiners, carpenters and furniture-makers.

From the earliest time there seems to have been a tradition of furniture making in the town. Many of the finest pieces of carved oak furniture at Gwydir were reputed to have been made by the estate's own craftsmen: local craftsmen would also have been responsible for all work-a-day domestic furniture used in big house and humble cottage alike. For the more prestigious pieces the district began, at an early date, to develop its own forms and styles. In the 17th century the familiar court-cupboard, or *cwpwrdd deuddarn*, was succeeded by the three tier court-cupboard, or *cwpwrdd tridarn*, which may have been confined to a relatively small area of central North Wales with Llanrwst at its centre. These were followed in the 18th century by very fine dressers bearing distinctively local characteristics that make it possible to identify Llanrwst dressers today. Whilst these items were produced throughout much of Wales, those from the Llanrwst area were amongst the most distinctive.

Because, in the 18th century, trade was slow and difficult and rural communities had to achieve something approaching self-sufficiency, all the other more usual craftsmen and tradesmen were to be found in Llanrwst. There were blacksmiths to shoe the horses and cattle, and to make things in metal. There were masons, slaters, thatchers, carpenters and glaziers to build the houses. Tailors and hatters, millers and bakers, shopkeepers and merchants were all found in the town. There were publicans, grooms and ostlers, brewers and barbers, gardeners and fishermen and, of course, labourers in ever increasing numbers. Higher up the social scale there were, by the second half of the century, two doctors, an attorney and several clergymen. Law and order was kept by a constable and His Majesty's dues collected by an excise-man. More unusually there were harp makers and harp players, usually blind, [27] to entertain visitors at the local inns. Llanrwst was in no way special; rather it was a typical market town serving a typical rural community.

In spite of its relative importance Llanrwst was never to be granted a charter to make it a borough and therefore never had its own mayor, alderman and civil administration. Instead, such civil matters as required to be attended to were dealt with by the Justices of the Peace and by the church wardens and vestry. [28] On the latter fell the responsibility for caring for the poor and insane, for raising militia to serve in the army and, surprisingly, for controlling vermin. In Llanrwst foxes were usually the problem and substantial sums were

Fig 4: Llanrwst Parish Church, c1830 by Henri Gastineau.
The Gwydir Chapel is in the foreground.

paid by the church wardens for their extermination. Foxes were more scarce in villages, such as Dolwyddelan, located higher up in the mountains, and ravens accounted for most of the bounty payments.

The ancient parish church in Llanrwst, dedicated to St Grwst, stood on the banks of the Conwy between the Eagles Inn and the tannery. It was rather a small and plain building, although it contained a fine, carved rood-screen and attached to it was the family chapel built by the first Sir Richard Wynn. Like most churches in northern Wales it had two aisles, but no tower or other grander architectural embellishments.

Sir John Wynn, who seems to have spent most of his days disputing with clerics - whether they were the Bishops of Bangor and St Asaph or the local rector - had cause to complain about Llanrwst church too. In 1605 he wrote one of his more conciliatory letters to the Bishop of St Asaph which started as follows (the more fastidious reader may prefer not to read this extract):

> My very good Lo: itt is soe that the pishe [29] church of Llanrwst (beinge not great, and the pishe lardge) is soe pestered wth contynuall burialls (for whoe is he, be he never soe meane, that must not lye wthin the doores?) that the aere wthin is become pestylenciall, and soe noysome, that, for a moneth space and more, most of the better sorte of the pishe refuse to come there, and those that came hardlie able to abyde hitt. [30]

During the 18th century the church wardens and vestry rarely made any significant additions or alterations to the building, contenting themselves with repairing the roof, windows and woodwork and whitewashing the walls. In 1747, the vestry minutes do however, reveal one moment of excitement which, as in Sir John's case, was of a somewhat malodorous nature. The workers from the adjoining tannery had taken to hanging their hides on the yew trees in the churchyard to dry! Obviously, mere complaints had not brought an end to this unsavoury practice, because the vestry meeting resolved that, in future, offending hides would be thrown into the river. Whether they had to resort to such extreme measures, we shall never know. The responsibilities of the vestry even extended to the provision of public conveniences in the town. It is surprising to find that this euphemism for public lavatories appears to be more than 200 years old, as this extract from the vestry minutes of 1754 records:

> Whereas the churchyard is not kept in that decent and clean manner it should and no publick conveniences for the poor and other Inhabitants of Llanrwst as is usual in populous places, it is now ordered by the unanimous consent of this vestry that a proper and convenient Necessary House be built on the churchyard wall next the river - the expense of which is expected to be raised by a voluntary contribution. [31]

If the first half of the 18th century saw little change in Llanrwst, the same cannot be said for the period from about 1765 onwards. The population of the whole parish was less than one thousand in 1700, but a hundred years later it was two thousand five hundred, [32] and much of this growth took place in the second half of the century. Natural increase of the population was augmented by an influx of people settling in the town including a number of people who appear to have been of higher social standing whose names began to appear regularly in the records. [33]

Among the first of these gentlemen immigrants was the Reverend John Royle, a Lincolnshire cleric who succeeded John Williams as the Duke of Ancaster's agent at Gwydir. He settled with his family at Gwydir and lived there until his death in the late 1780s. He had three sons Samuel, James and Charles who set up their own houses in the town. The Moulsdales, natives of Derbyshire, became proprietors of the Eagles Inn and settled in the town. From Denbigh came Peter Titley, a surgeon and apothecary. He opened an apothecary's shop in the town square and practised as doctor and surgeon. He also began building up a significant land holding in the town and in the surrounding countryside. Interestingly, he acquired a number of town properties from the Mostyn estate, which seems to have divested itself of most of its holdings within the town itself by the end of the century. Another man who built up a considerable estate in the district at this time was the Reverend John Ellis of Cyffdy, a small manor house situated about a mile from town.

All these men and a number more, who settled in Llanrwst during the first three decades of the 19th century, formed a new and increasingly influential upper class in the town. Whilst not supplanting the big estates altogether, they had the advantage of living in the town and undoubtedly took over from the agents as leaders of local society and they were prominent in the town's day-to-day affairs.

Another development that was to have a major effect was the arrival in 1777 of the new turnpike road from Shrewsbury. There had already been a gradual improvement in communications with the outside world. Carriers left each week from Chester for Ruthin, Llanrwst and Pwllheli, but in spite of the invaluable service that they provided to the town, they continued to rely on pack horses. The arrival of the new turnpike road meant that wheeled vehicles had access to the town. This opened the way to wagons and coaches

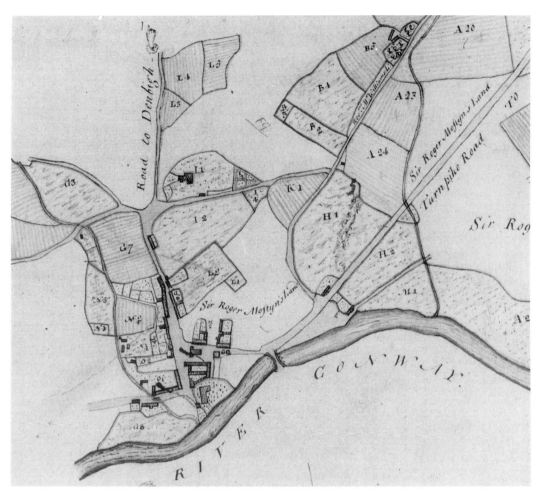

Fig 5: A street map of Llanrwst from the Gwydir Estate Atlas, c1785.
With the exception of the church, only Gwydir Estate buildings are shown.
(Trustees of the Grimsthorpe & Drummond Castle Trust Ltd)

from England via Shrewsbury, and suddenly Llanrwst was very much less isolated. A few years later the Irish Mail which had traditionally travelled to Holyhead via Chester and Conwy, changed its route to avoid the notorious ferry at Conwy. It did this by following the turnpike route from Shrewsbury to Llanrwst, crossing the river by the town bridge and then travelling down the Caernarfonshire side of the valley to Conwy. Suddenly, Llanrwst was very much on the map and the town's coaching inn, The Eagles, began to prosper. In a few years, however, further road improvements, which culminated in the completion of Telford's new road to Holyhead, allowed the Irish Mail to take a new, much shorter and speedier route and Llanrwst was by-passed.

What impressions of Llanrwst and the Conwy valley would be gained by a 20th century time-traveller who went back to the town of 1790? He might be impressed as much by the similarities he observed as by the more obvious differences. Certainly the scenery would be familiar; although there would be more oak trees and fewer conifers on the hillsides, less cultivated land on the valley floor and smaller fields. Otherwise, the views would be much the same. So too would be the farms, all standing where they do today and, moreover, bearing the same names.

He would be surprised, also, to realise that the basic layout of the town was familiar. Figure 5 shows the earliest map of Llanrwst town that we have been able to locate. It comes from the fine book of maps of the Gwydir estate prepared in about 1785. [34] The turnpike road from Shrewsbury is shown entering the town from the north east: this arrived over the high ground to the east of the valley through what is now the hamlet of Nebo, not by the present valley floor route from Betws-y-coed. Bridge Street, Denbigh Street and Ancaster Square are shown much as they are today, as is the road running north toward the coast, now Station Road. It has to be remembered, however, that this plan comes from an estate map intended to delineate the Gwydir holdings and most other buildings are not shown. Thus, the large block of land near the town centre described as "Sir Roger Mostyn's Land" would have been occupied by many buildings as would have been the plot immediately adjacent to the bridge where the Eagles Inn then stood as it does today.

Our 20th century time visitor to old Llanrwst, however, would have been much more struck by the differences that he saw in the town. He would be surprised to find that at least half of the buildings had thatched roofs, of wheat straw too, which must have been rather short-lived in so wet a climate. Many of the buildings would have been very small with tiny windows; the great winter gales kept the towns' glaziers busy and at that time glass was costly. Moreover, the time traveller would have needed to wear a pair of wellington boots to walk through the streets. Apart from the usual crude methods of disposing of household waste, the 18th century town had no purpose-built cattle market and livestock was sold in the streets on market and fair days. The pig market was in Stryd-y-moch (literally 'the street of the pigs'), later to be called Little Bridge Street and known today as Station Road. Cattle, horses and sheep were to be found in Bridge Street, Stryd-y-pwll ('Street of the pool') - which is now Denbigh Street - and the town square. The latter would then be packed with market stalls on market days and the ground floor of the town hall was occupied by stalls and small shops. Regrettably this building has been demolished to make way for 20th century traffic.

As the Reverend Evans reported in 1798:

> We entered the town on the market day, Tuesday; and were not a little entertained at the variety of articles that might be purchased in it. The adjacent towns and villages do not abound with shops of every description as in England; the market day therefore is the time for buying in supplies for the week; and the market is filled with the luxuries as well as the necessaries of life. [35]

Scarcely less busy than the town square would have been the Eagles Inn displaying much more red brick then than it does now. Its courtyard would be full of bustling valley-dwellers who had come to sell their produce and to buy provisions at the market. Mingling with them would be a few English tourists demanding horses and guides to visit the local beauty spots. Adding to the confusion one might see the Chester carrier handing over packages to local businessmen and receiving letters and commissions from them whilst through it all struggled the ostlers and grooms, making preparations for the arrival of the Irish Mail later in the day.

Numerous other inns and public houses would have been doing a roaring trade and the streets would be thronged with people either on horseback or on foot trying to find a way through the clusters of livestock standing patiently there as their owners haggled vociferously with would-be purchasers. Everywhere there would be Welsh voices speaking their native tongue but the English visitors would find plenty of people who spoke English too, certainly most of the town's businessmen and more important shop-keepers. [36] All public and official notices would also be in English.

Our visitor would certainly be able to observe the townswomen washing their clothes in the river just above the bridge and the many fishermen in their coracles on a river which must then have been considerably deeper than it is today. He would not have been surprised by the congestion on the bridge itself: two wagon drivers nose-to-nose at the apex arguing about who should give way, the whole situation aggravated, perhaps, by an ancient resident of the town demonstrating how easily the bridge could be made to shake, to a bemused group of tourists.

Then, suddenly in the afternoon, it would begin to rain - heavy squally rain blowing down the valley. There would be a scramble in the market place as stall-holders struggled to cover their wares. An English voice, perhaps, would be heard at the Eagles Inn complaining about the "Welsh weather" and groups of local fishermen would hurry from the various pubs to make preparations for intercepting the new run of salmon that they hoped the rain would bring.

Some things in Llanrwst have never changed - not one iota!

We will conclude this thumb-nail sketch of Llanrwst and its surrounding countryside with a few of the comments of the early tourists who visited the town during the closing years of the century. They tended to be rather unenterprising and to inspect the same buildings and to visit the same beauty spots. So far as Llanrwst was concerned, it was the shaking bridge, the church and Gwydir Chapel with its memorial brasses, the old Gwydir House and a few nearby waterfalls.

Unfortunately most of them did not find much in the town to admire – probably because they did not consider it picturesque. Thus, the famous Welshman Thomas Pennant, one of the earlier arrivals in the mid 1770s recorded that:

> The town of Llanrwst is small and ill built and has nothing remarkable except the church. . . [37]

or the Reverend Bingley in 1798:

> The town of Llanrwst is finely situated on the eastern bank of the River Conway. In itself it has nothing to recommend it, the streets are narrow and the houses very irregular. . . [38]

The Honourable John Byng, later Viscount Torrington, usually very difficult to please, was feeling in a more tolerant mood when he visited the town in 1793:

> . . . we arrived at Llanrwst, a small market town upon the new Irish road. At first, I thought mine hostess at the Eagles Inn very pert; but I swallowed my bile and after walking round the market place returned like Duke Humphrey -
>
> > "Now Lords, my Choler being overblown,
> > with walking once about the quadrangle,"

but not to dine with him, being well served with salmon, roast fowl, peas and tart: at the fashionable hour of six.

I had been eight hours on horseback: As for poor Flora, she cannot move, and is thinner than a horn Lanthorn.[39] The stables were good; and the hostler active, and intelligent: The harper too, (reckoned a fine one), soon struck up at my door and was admitted: but I begged him not to be fine, or to play with variations, but to dash away good old Welsh tunes. - I now resolved upon a walk, though in truth I had done enough; but then I cannot sit muzzing in an inn: so I took a very pleasant saunter upon the eastern road near the river bank; even until dark; - when, coming in, the harper rejoined me at supper time, and stayed til ten o'clock, at which hour he was obliged to attend a singing party in the town, I went to bed, very tired. [40]

Finally, the *Cambrian Guide*, first published in 1809, and consisting of extracts from the accounts of earlier travellers referred to the river Conwy as follows:

The thick woods and towering hills, which skirt the Conwy on both sides, are enlivened by the busy animation which is presented upon the surface of this river. Vessels are continually passing and re-passing to and from the village of Trefriw, two miles down the river, being the highest point to which the tide flows, and diminutive coracles, used for fishing for salmon and smelts, are frequently plying. [41]

The *Cambrian Guide* also dismisses the Eagles Inn in a pithy sentence of which a modern-day Egon Ronay would be justly proud:

INN. The Eagles is accounted the best inn, yet is an indifferent one, where the owners show much consequential inattention.

In this chapter we have been able to present little more than a thumb-nail sketch of Llanrwst and its district in the late 17th and 18th centuries. It is important, however, to appreciate the nature of the town and the community in which perhaps one of the most successful and prolific of all Welsh clockmaking families flourished. Llanrwst was a rather remote, rural, market town, vital to the very existence of the community it served, busy, rather than prosperous, but in most respects typical of such towns. Certainly, being accessible, relatively properous and serving a large area and population, it was just the sort of town where an 18th century clockmaker could be expected to establish his workshop. In the case of Llanrwst his name was John Owen and he came to the town in about 1745.

NOTES

1. Rev W Bingley, *North Wales including its scenery, Antiquities, Customs and some sketches of its Natural History delineated from two excursions through all the interesting part of that country during the summer of 1798 and 1801*, published in London in 1804. Vol 1, Chapter 23, p449.

2. *Calender of Wynn Papers, 1515 - 1690*, published by the National Library of Wales; No 2462 written in 1666. Most of the original manuscripts are at the National Library of Wales in Aberystwyth; others are in Cardiff and a few elsewhere.

3. See, for instance, *Calender of Wynn Papers* No 335.

4. This long narrow field may still be seen where the road from Gwydir to Betws-y-coed runs close to the river approximately 1/4 mile south of Gwydir. Logs felled high up on the hillside could have been rolled or dragged downhill to the river edge most easily at this point.

5. A small account book now in the Ancaster Papers at the Lincolnshire County Record Office at Lincoln Castle gives details of payments made under these charities throughout the middle years of the 18th century. Ref: 4/ANC/4/7.

6. Some authorities dispute Sir John's claim to be founder of the school.

7. The two houses at Gwydir and one in Brainford or Brentford which the first Sir Richard acquired when he married the daughter of Sir Francis Darcy.

8. A list of these debts in the hand of Watkin Owen of Gwydir is in the National Library of Wales. They totalled more than £10,000.

9. Mary, first Duchess of Ancaster, died in 1689, but provided her husband with an heir, Peregrine, who was to become the 2nd Duke in 1723.

10. Detailed accounts for the early years of this venture in the hand of Watkin Owen have survived. Some of these are in the National Library of Wales, MS 9719E, others in the library of the University College of North Wales at Bangor, Mostyn MS 1440.

11. Estate Management in Dyffryn Conwy, circa 1685, Gareth Haulfryn Williams, *Transactions of the Honourable Society of Cymrodorion*, 1979, pp31 - 70.

12. We know of no finer introduction to the Wynns and their times than the *Calendar of the Wynn Papers*. It contains a short precis of all the documents comprising the Wynn Papers and makes fascinating reading.

13. Inventory of the contents of Upper Gwydir House, 1737, Lincolnshire County Record Office. ANC X/A/16.

14. See Bingley, op cit Vol I, p450 (1804 Edition).

15. Gwydir Estate Rentals, 1780 & 1781, Grimsthorpe Castle Archives.

16. A H Dodd, *A History of Caernarvonshire 1284 - 1900*, published by the Caernarfonshire Historical Society, 1968, pp178 and 180.

17. For the income of a late 18th century clockmaker see 'The Deacon Family of Leicestershire Clockmakers', Part II by P A Hewitt in the *Journal of the Antiquarian Horological Society* No 4, Vol XVI, December 1986.

18. Clwyd County Record Office, Ruthin, PD/69/1/88 et seq.

19. Watkin Owen of Gwydir wrote hints for protecting garden peas from mice and newly planted cabbages from snails in the back of a book on husbandry which survives in the National Library of Wales - MS 10885 c.

20. In the early years of the 20th century an early running strain of salmon from Scotland was introduced into the river. Today the first salmon of the season enter the Conwy in March or April.

21. *Calendar of Wynn Papers* No 600.

22. Rev J Evans, *A tour through part of North Wales in the year 1798, and at other times*; published in London, 1800, p281. Although Evans saw few men in the market, they knitted stockings, just like their womenfolk.

23. National Library of Wales, MS 9719 E.

24. Ibid. Also University College of North Wales, Mostyn MS 1440.

25. Lincolnshire County Record Office, 3 ANC 8/2/20 and 8/ANC/2/9.

26. Lincolnshire County Record Office, 3 ANC 8/2/23.

27. Arthur Aikin, *Journal of a Tour through North Wales and Part of Shropshire*, published in London, 1979, p107.

28. Clwyd County Record Office, Ruthin, Llanrwst Churchwardens Accounts PD/69/1/77 et seq & Vestry Minutes & Accounts, PD/69/1/191 et seq.

29. pishe = parish.

30. *Calendar of Wynn Papers* No 374.

31. Clwyd County Record Office, Ruthin, PD/69/1/191.

32. See *The History of North Wales*, William Cathrall, Vol II, p159.

33. At the other end of the social scale the vestry was much occupied in preventing vagrants from settling in the parish. They were sent back to their own parishes.

34. Lincolnshire County Record Office, 4/ANC/4/5 & 5.

35. Rev J Evans, op cit, p281.

36. Arthur Aikin, op cit p107, reports ". . . we have invariably found the English language understood in the fertile and populous parts".

37. Thomas Pennant Esq, *Tours in Wales*, Vol II, Published in London, 1810, p34.

38. Rev W Bingley, op cit, p452.

39. Flora was his horse.

40. *The Torrington Diaries* 1781 - 1794, published by Eyre and Spottiswoode, London, 1936, Vol III, p270.

41. *The Cambrian Traveller's Guide* published in London in 1813, p799 et seq.

CHAPTER II
The Owens

Hitherto, it has always been taken for granted that clockmaking in Llanrwst dates from the last quarter of the 17th century and that the first maker was Watkin Owen. No less an authority than the late Dr Iorwerth C Peate, the founding curator of the Welsh Folk Museum at St Fagans and author of the invaluable book *Clock and Watch Makers in Wales*, confirms it. Throughout our five year long survey of Llanrwst clocks, copies of the relevant pages of Peate's book were produced for our perusal by clock-owners who knew them by heart and regarded them as completely authoritative.

We are very much aware, therefore, that in arguing that clockmaking in the town did not commence until nearly seventy-five years later, and that the first maker was John, not Watkin, Owen, we need to be most convincing in the case that we put forward. For these reasons it is necessary to relate the results of our research and the reasons for our conclusions in some detail.

Like many another owner of an Owen clock, we began our investigation by looking up the Owens of Llanrwst in *Clock and Watch Makers of Wales*. [1] At the foot of the relevant page in the third edition is printed the small family tree which, on very many occasions, we were to see pinned inside clocks. It is reproduced in full in Figure 6. We now have reasons to suspect that this family tree is the main and, possibly, sole origin of the belief that a Watkin Owen was responsible for making the first Llanrwst clocks at the end of the 17th century.

Its origin is interesting. It appears on a small business card or complimentary slip printed for the firm of Griffith Owen and Son of Llanrwst.

Griffith Owen was the town's most successful retailer of clocks and watches in Victorian times. The earliest record of him trading in Llanrwst is in about 1840 and he was one of the leading members of the town's business community until his death in 1902. [2]

Below the family tree are printed the words "with the compliments of Griffith Owen and Son, Llanrwst." The card measures 4" x 3", is blank on the reverse side and is difficult to date. Certainly it was produced before 1912, at which time a local amateur historian pinned a copy of it into his scrap book, having first, rather primly, snipped off the trade name at its foot. [3] The evidence of silver pocket watches suggests that the firm's style became 'Griffith Owen and Son' sometime in the 1890s which indicates that the card cannot be earlier than this. We can only guess as to who compiled the family tree. Perhaps it was Griffith Owen himself, in response to repeated requests for information from customers who brought him their old Llanrwst clocks to be repaired. The author certainly conducted some research and must have contacted the archivists of Jesus College and Christ Church, Oxford, because the accurate information about the academic careers of Robert Owen and John Owen III could hardly have been obtained otherwise. [4]

Irrespective of who compiled this little family tree, however, the business card must have been in circulation long enough and in sufficient numbers to be the source of much

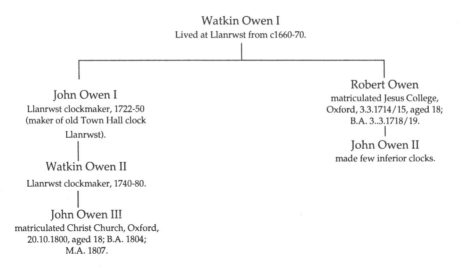

Watkin Owen I
Lived at Llanrwst from c1660-70.

John Owen I
Llanrwst clockmaker, 1722-50
(maker of old Town Hall clock
Llanrwst).

Watkin Owen II
Llanrwst clockmaker, 1740-80.

John Owen III
matriculated Christ Church, Oxford,
20.10.1800, aged 18; B.A. 1804;
M.A. 1807.

Robert Owen
matriculated Jesus College,
Oxford, 3.3.1714/15, aged 18;
B.A. 3..3.1718/19.

John Owen II
made few inferior clocks.

Fig 6: The family tree, probably produced by Griffith Owen

that has come to be accepted as fact about the origins and dates of early Llanrwst clockmakers. [5] Most importantly, Dr Peate reproduced the family tree in his book and, as a result, it has come to be endowed with a credibility that, hitherto, it may have lacked. Dr Peate also included the 17th century Watkin Owen in his list of clockmakers although the family tree does not actually say that he was a maker - merely suggests so, perhaps.

There has always been a tendency for owners and scholars alike to date brass dialled long-case clocks much too early, especially age-worn, be-cobwebbed and smoke blackened specimens. We, for our part, have recorded nearly three hundred clocks signed by Watkin Owen, more than half of them with brass dials. We have concluded that *not one of these* can be dated prior to 1776, when we know that another Watkin Owen of Llanrwst took over his father's clockmaking business. Therefore, we suspect that there has always been a process at work whereby clock owners believe that their clocks are much earlier than 1776 and decide that they must, therefore, have been made by some earlier Watkin Owen. In consequence, many clocks have been ascribed a date that is as much as a hundred years too early.

It would be grossly unjust to ascribe any lack of care to Peate when he included the first Watkin in his list of makers. He conducted an invaluable pioneer survey, excluding only the most glaring anomalies from the contributions that he received. It is the task of ensuing generations of antiquarian horologists to edit and refine his list. We will always owe Dr Peate an immense debt for providing the all important base material.

Certainly the little family tree provided us, too, with a wonderful starting place for our genealogical researches. It will be seen that, from the information given, the date of Robert Owen's birth can be worked out accurately. Sure enough, perusal of the Llanrwst Parish Registers reveals the following entry: [6]

Robertus Filius Watkin Owen de Gwydir, et Maria uxoris ejus baptisatus fuit - die augusti Ao.Dni 1696. [7]

Literally translated this means: 'Robert, son of Watkin Owen of Gwydir and Mary his wife was baptised on the ? day of August in the year of our Lord 1696.' Further examination of the register shows that the couple had three other children, Mary in 1694, Catherine in 1695 and Ann in 1698. So there was a Watkin Owen in Llanrwst at the time indicated by the family tree, and indeed, we have already encountered him several times in the previous chapter; he was His Grace of Ancaster's High Steward at Gwydir.

Not much is known as to how it was that Watkin Owen arrived in Llanrwst. We do know that he was the son of a gentleman land owner in Montgomeryshire, Owen Watkin, who had a small estate called Hydan Issa near Castell Caereinion. [8] The young Watkin probably entered the service of Sir Richard Wynn of Gwydir as his secretary or steward because he was definitely there at the time of Sir Richard's death. It was this Watkin Owen who kept detailed accounts of the expenses incurred at Sir Richard's prestigious funeral in Chester, [9] and it was he who left us a detailed schedule of Sir Richard's quite enormous debts which the baronet's mother, Lady Grace, paid off with his assistance. [10] Later, he was given the task of starting and administering the new timber venture at Gwydir and many pages of quite fascinating accounts for this project in Watkin Owen's own hand have survived. [11] So competent must he have proved himself to be that, finally, he was left in sole charge in the capacity of High Steward.

In 1693 he was married to Mary Wynne by special licence. The marriage bond has survived and duly records that Watkin Owen was from the parish of Llanrwst. [12] It entirely omits to mention, however, the home parish of the bride and our every effort to locate where the marriage was solemnised or the origins of the bride has proved to be unsuccessful. This also means that it has not been possible to identify the branch of the Wynn family of which Mary Wynne was herself a member, but marriage by special licence would be entirely in keeping with the customs of the time and her status as a member of the local gentry. [13]

Watkin Owen of Gwydir was a man of considerable standing in the district, that is certain. He was a respected member of the gentry and in all probability related by marriage to another such family. He held a position of considerable influence and

Fig 7: The Family of Watkin Owen of Gwydir

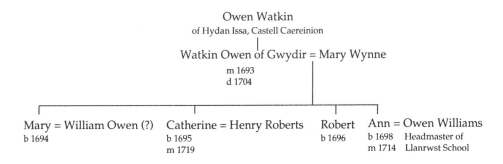

patronage and was heir to a respectable estate in his own right. From the point of view of our story, however, he is found wanting in two respects. Firstly he was not a clockmaker; he would have had scant opportunity to learn the skills and, with all his other duties, no time to practise them. Even more significantly, he did not have a son John as the little family tree would have us believe.

It has been suggested that the couple may have had another son born in some other parish and so far untraced. It is clear, however, that such a son could hardly have been older than Robert as suggested by the family tree. The dates of the births of Mary and Catherine would seem to preclude the possibility. Watkin Owen's will, signed only a few months before his death in 1704 clinches the matter: it quite specifically refers to Robert as his only son.

If John Owen, first clockmaker of Llanrwst, was not the son of Watkin Owen, then who was he? Clearly, the compiler of the family tree believed him to be descended from Watkin Owen of Gwydir: perhaps he was his grandson? John's gravestone in Llanrwst churchyard gives his age as 57 years at the time of his death in 1776, inferring a date of birth of about 1718-19. Was he, perhaps, the son of Robert Owen, the John who is stated by the little family tree to have made few inferior clocks? All efforts to trace Robert Owen after his period at Jesus College, Oxford have also failed. He is likely to have gone on to be ordained in the Church of England but ecclesiastical records for North Wales and the neighbouring English dioceses fail to make mention of him. If John Owen, the clockmaker, was his son then Robert would, of necessity, have had to have been married at a very young age and, moreover, while he was still an under-graduate. This seems very unlikely. It has been suggested that the early anomalous clocks by John Owen discussed in the next chapter could be the inferior output of this other John Owen. This can be disproved by the signatures on their dials which are identical to those that appear on the later output of the great John Owen which are known to have been made by him and are typical of his work. Furthermore, we have found no evidence of any kind to suggest that there were ever two clockmakers of this name in Llanrwst. All this leads us to the conclusion, in the absence of any evidence to the contrary, that if Robert Owen had a son John, then that particular John Owen would not have been one of the Llanrwst clockmakers.

If, then, we persist with the proposition that John Owen, the clockmaker, was a grandson of Watkin Owen, one of Watkin's daughters must have been his mother. Detailed study of all the relevant parish registers has failed to establish that this is indeed the case, the task being made no easier by the poor legibility of these earlier pages.

In 1714, Watkin's third daughter Ann married Owen Williams who had been appointed headmaster of Llanrwst School in 1712. If they had had a son called John, then he could well have been known as John Owen, but, alas, the registers record no such son. Ann's eldest sister Mary appears to have married a William Owen but, once again, there is no sign of them baptising a son John in about 1718-19, as the clockmaker's gravestone requires although they may have done so in 1715. Watkin's third daughter, Catherine, married Henry Roberts in 1719, but again without the desired result. Maybe a son John was born to one of these daughters of Watkin Owen of Gwydir in another parish, but, if so, we have signally failed to establish this happy event. Before leaving the faded and barely legible pages of the Llanrwst Registers we feel bound to mention that in 1717 William Owen of Garthgyffanedd and his wife Mary had a son John, as did Owen Williams of Maethbrod [14] in 1719. Unfortunately there are no grounds for claiming that either of these Johns is our clockmaker other than the year of his birth, and certainly they would appear to have no connection with Watkin Owen of Gwydir.

In the absence of a breakthrough in our genealogical researches therefore, the exact origin of John Owen, first clockmaker of Llanrwst, remains something of a mystery. We still retain a strong conviction that, in some manner, he must have been descended from, or related to, Watkin Owen of Gwydir, but this remains to be substantiated. There are, indeed, many pointers to this connection, albeit mostly circumstantial ones. The name Watkin was given to a son of John Owen, the clockmaker, and later to a grandson and a great-grandson, although, in itself, Watkin was not a common name in Llanrwst. Again, on the quality and appearance of his clocks John must have been apprenticed to a good town clockmaker, probably in Lancashire or Cheshire. This would not have been easy for a young nobody from Wales, for the best clockmakers at that time could pick and choose when taking apprentices. Finally, in the last quarter of the 18th century, John's son Watkin definitely mingled with the local gentry and married into this stratum of society. Let us hope that genealogical researches will eventually be able to establish the nature of the link.

To return to our starting point - the generally accepted belief that the first clocks were made in Llanrwst in the last years of the 17th century by Watkin Owen - our reasons for believing quite otherwise can now be summarised. Firstly, Watkin Owen, the first, was not a clockmaker, he was the High Steward at Gwydir. Secondly, the evidence of more than four hundred clocks signed either by John Owen or Watkin Owen of Llanrwst is that none of them can be dated much before 1750. It would be exciting indeed to be confronted with a genuine 17th century clock carrying the name of Watkin Owen and we would happily and immediately revise our views. Until this happens, however, the overwhelming weight of evidence points to the first Llanrwst clock being made by John Owen in about 1745.

Whoever he was, John Owen had certainly established himself in the town by 1746 because there is conclusive documentary proof of his presence there in that year. It is unlikely, however, that in 1746 he would have been there for more than a year or two. A young man intending to become a clockmaker at that time would normally have been apprenticed at the age of fourteen for seven years. On completing his apprenticeship, he would then have to serve at least two years as a journeyman working for his former master or for some other clockmaker. Only after completion of this stage in his career would he have moved on to establish his own workshop. If John Owen had followed this course, he would not have been free to come to Llanrwst much before 1742 or 1743 at the earliest, assuming that he was born in 1719 as suggested by his gravestone.

In one other important respect the origins of John Owen remain a mystery: no trace has been found of his apprenticeship. If he was apprenticed in Wales, then the most likely place would have been Wrexham, which was probably the only town in the whole of 18th century Wales where clockmakers with the appropriate skills and experience were to be found in the early 1730s. Amongst them were William and Humphrey Maysmor who, at about this time, worked on Town Hill, close to the Parish Church. William had been apprenticed to John Hills in London in 1693 and could be expected to have been a high class clockmaker of the type that must have trained John Owen.

Unfortunately, we have only seen one 8-day clock signed by Maysmor of Wrexham. Its movement exhibited certain similarities to those of John Owen, especially in relation to some of the strike work, but this clock was a lone specimen and had been much altered and distressed over the years, insufficient, in itself, to allow the drawing of too many conclusions. Perhaps more Maysmor clocks will come to light and give a clearer indication as to whether John may have served his apprenticeship in the Maysmor workshop. However, working on the evidence of the clocks alone, it would be easier to conclude that John was apprenticed in Cheshire or Lancashire where, by the 1730s, clockmaking was widespread, well developed and relatively sophisticated. We will discuss John Owen's highly individualistic strike-work in a later chapter. At this stage it is necessary only to point out that his strike-work was of a style and type frequently used in Lancashire and north-west England and very similar to examples that we have seen on some Liverpool clocks, including clocks by John Green of that city. [15]

The arrival of a clockmaker in Llanrwst must have created a stir, even if he was a stranger - and not a Llanrwst native returning to his birthplace. The news must soon have arrived in Conwy town because in May 1746, the Churchwardens of that parish entered into a formal written contract with John Owen of Llanrwst, Clockmaker, for the repair and maintenance of their own church clock. The text of the contract is as follows:

> BE IT REMEMBERED that upon the seventeenth day of May 1746.
> IT IS AGREED BETWEEN John Owen of Llanrwst Clockmaker and Robert Griffith and Robert Hughes of Conway [sic] Churchwardens viz: That the said John Owen is to take the clock belonging to the Conway [sic] Church and to repair it sufficiently, finding all materials himself, and to maintain it sufficiently until the 5th day of May 1747. AND IN CONSIDERATION the said Robert Griffith and Robert Hughes Churchwardens is to pay the said John Owen the sum of One Pound eleven shillings and sixpence in a month's time or when he brings the clock home being finished.
> IN WITNESS whereof we have set our names of the day and year above written
> JOHN OWEN,
> The mark of Robert Griffith R Churchwardens,
> The mark of Robert Hughes R H
> NB When the year 1746 is expired until the 5th May 1747, the said John Owen is to keep and repair the said clock sufficiently, every year and to receive yearly from the Churchwardens of Conway [sic] the sum of ten shillings and sixpence, commencing May 5th, 1748 and that as long as the Corporation of Conway [sic] think proper to employ the said John Owen.
> JOHN OWEN [16]

This is the earliest documentary proof that John Owen was established in Llanrwst as a clockmaker. Since it would have been unlikely that the churchwardens would allow an unknown new-comer to take their clock away, we may assume that he had already been in Llanrwst for a year or two and had earned an established reputation for sound work.

John Owen rented a very small house or shop near the centre of Llanrwst town from Robert Wynn of nearby Berthddu. The house was so small that it was lumped together with other similar properties in the rentals, possible all in a single row or block. In 1750 the rental for the Berthddu Domain, under the heading 'Town tenants Rec'd in June 1750', records a payment of 10 shillings by John Owens, made on 13th June. A year later the entry leaves us in no doubt, it reads 'John Owens, Clockmaker' and the rent had been increased to £1 0s 0d. [17] The location of John's house and workshop seems to have been in what is now Denbigh Street. According to local oral tradition the shop was close to the town square towards the southern end of that street. We also know that the house was first a Berthddu and subsequently a Mostyn holding. A glance at the town map on page 27 shows that the property at the town square end of the street on the eastern side belonged to the Mostyn of the time, Sir Roger. The Mostyn estate also owned property in the town square, Bridge Street and in one or two other places so why is it that the location of the workshop is believed to have been in Denbigh Street? The estate rentals show that John Owen continued to pay rent of £1 0s 0d per annum for what appears to have been the same property, but he also regularly paid a *maes*, or tithe, levied by the vestry meeting of the church. From its exact location in the maes-rolls, and the actual sums paid, it seems that the property later came to be called Tyn-y-pwll. Certainly, John's son Watkin regularly paid tithes for Tyn-y-pwll and we know from 19th century census returns that Tyn-y-pwll was in Denbigh Street. [18] As with so much about John Owen, however, the location of his dwelling and workplace in the town is not entirely certain and there are some unanswered questions. For instance, between the date when John commenced the payment of tithes for the property in the early 1760s and his son Watkin recommencing in the 1780s, two tithe payments for Tyn-y-pwll were made by the Reverend W Lloyd and several others by John Roberts. [19] There is reason to believe that John Roberts may have been a journeyman clockmaker living in the house while John and then Watkin lived elsewhere, but the intervention of the Reverend Lloyd remains a mystery. Nevertheless, it seems reasonably safe to assume that the clockmaker's house and shop was, indeed, in Denbigh Street, somewhere close to the Square.

The registers of Llanrwst church record that a daughter Mary was born to John Owen and his wife Elizabeth on the 18th February 1747. There is no record in the Llanrwst registers of the marriage so Elizabeth must have come from another parish. We have searched the registers for all the neighbouring parishes and some from further afield without being able to identify the marriage with absolute certainty.

Without wishing in any way to make excuses, it must be stated that considerable difficulties attend genealogical research in Wales. The system of using patronyms rather than more individualistic surnames is aggravated by the small number of traditional first names in regular use. This means that positive identification by name alone is usually unsafe, some corroborative additional information being required. John and Owen were just about the most widespread names in use in the Conwy valley and merely to find a reference to John Owen is, in itself, insufficient.

This is by way of a preamble to saying that the most promising entry so far found records the marriage of John Owen and Elizabeth Jones in Eglwysbach on the 21st January 1746. [20] Unfortunately the Eglwysbach register of that period is the most abbreviated that we have encountered. The entry merely records the marriage of John Owen and Elizabeth Jones and nothing more. Certainly situated down river, on the Denbighshire side, some 8 miles distant from Llanrwst, Eglwysbach is just the kind of place where the clockmaker would have found his bride. Eglwysbach folk would have attended Llanrwst market and it would be quite conceivable for John to know the family or to have done business with them. The couple referred to in this entry did not have any children baptised in Eglwysbach and this suggests that the groom came from elsewhere and that he returned to his home parish with his bride.

John and Elizabeth Owen settled down to have a family of eight - six sons and two daughters, the youngest, William, arriving in 1765. It is possible that a seventh son, named Owen, was born in 1762, but since the entry in the register appears to be a later addition some mystery surrounds him.

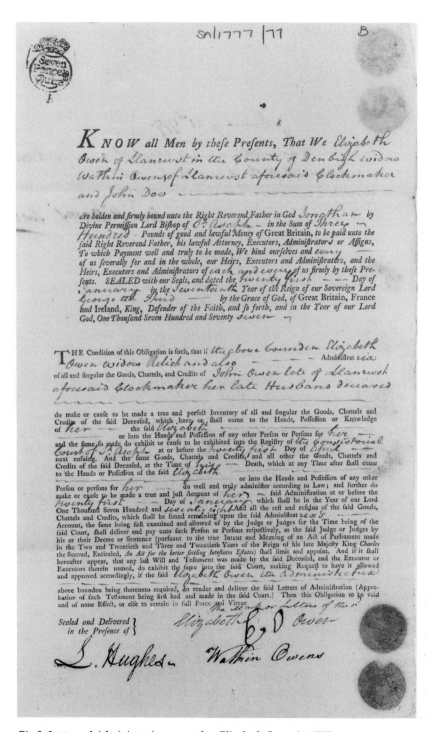

Fig 8: Letters of Administration granted to Elizabeth Owen in 1777.
[National Library of Wales]

John's fourth son Watkin, born in 1755, was to take over the family clockmaking business. This suggests that if his elder brothers John, Samuel and George survived to adulthood, then they must have taken up other occupations. We know, with reasonable certainty, that Samuel eventually became a surgeon. The names of both Samuel and George have been found scratched on clock plates and, in the case of Samuel, two long-case clocks have been found bearing his name on their dials. It seems certain, therefore, that the boys assisted in their father's workshop but subsequently gave up clockmaking in the town. That, apart from the details of his death and all the superb evidence of craftsmanship in his clocks, is all that we been able to discover about John Owen. It seems incredible that so fine and prolific a craftsman worked for nearly thirty years in the town but left so little imprint on its records.

John Owen died in 1776 and was buried in Llanrwst churchyard, close to the east window of the church. The gravestone was thought to have been lost long ago but recently came to light, buried under the turf, and in excellent condition. It reads:

Underneath lieth the,
Body of John Owen late,
Clockmaker in this Town,
who departed this life ye,
tenth day of February,
in the year of 1776,
Aged 57.
Also,
Elizabeth his wife,
Died March 22d 1791,
Aged 69.

John Owen died without making a will, which suggests that his death was sudden and unexpected. Perhaps he fell victim to one of the savage epidemics that, under 18th century conditions, swept so frequently through the town and countryside. A year later, as required by the law, his widow applied to the Consistorial Court at St Asaph for Letters of Administration to allow her to wind up her husband's affairs and to acquire or distribute his worldly possessions. The official document issued to Elizabeth Owen at the time has survived and is reproduced in full on page 40. [21] It is an interesting document because it shows that Elizabeth Owen was supported by Watkin, not by any of her elder sons and that Watkin is described as a clockmaker. Elizabeth could manage to sign with her initials only, but Watkin wrote his name in full. Doubtless he and his brothers would have had excellent schooling at the grammar school in Llanrwst.

Watkin's signature demonstrates another interesting point: the use of Owens instead of Owen. Owens with the appended 's' means 'son of Owen': but today Owen and Owens are used without this specific distinction being implied. There is no doubt, however, that Watkin signed his name that day with the 's' to make the very point that he was the son of John and Elizabeth. Some of his earliest clock dials are signed in this way, the 's' being dropped after a year or two. If confirmation of this deliberate usage is required it can be found in Watkin's own last will and testament. In it his name and, with one exception, the names of his family are written 'Owen'; but in the case of his son Watkin it is written 'Owens'.

The family business is now carried on without a break by Watkin Owen who would

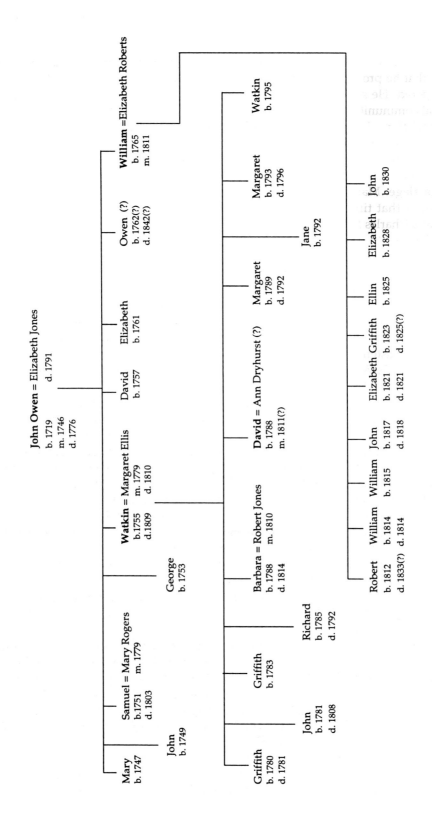

Fig 9: The family tree of John, Watkin, William and David Owen, clockmakers of Llanrwst.

42

have been twenty-one years of age at the time of his father's death. If the large volume of the clocks that he produced and which have survived is anything to go by, then he must have prospered. He seems to have become one of the leading members of the Llanrwst commercial community and, in social standing, there is evidence that he was very much in the upper echelons. Increasingly, he is referred to as 'Mr Watkin Owen' in documents, an indication of his high status in the town.

In 1779, at the age of twenty-four, he married Margaret Ellis of Llanbedr-y-Cennin, a village situated a few miles down the valley on the Caernarfonshire side of the river. It was a good marriage. Margaret was the daughter of Griffith Ellis, a well-to-do gentleman clergyman, at that time curate, later Rector of Llanbedr. One of the witnesses at the wedding was Charles Royle, son of John Royle, the agent at Gwydir and, quite definitely, a member of the gentry and this is a further indication of the circles in which Watkin moved. The couple had ten children but, as we shall see, they were not to be long lived.

Watkin's name now appears regularly in a variety of documents. He witnessed marriages and wills, paid tithes and rents and is mentioned in the church vestry minutes and accounts. [22] All these are tantalizing glimpses but they tell us virtually nothing about the man himself. As with his father, Watkin, the maker of so many fine clocks, remains a shadowy figure, such references to him that have survived doing little more than confirming his existence.

In the mid 1780s Watkin recommenced paying tithes for Tyn-y-pwll. If we are correct in believing that the John Roberts who had previously been doing so was a journeyman clockmaker, then, almost certainly, he left the Owens' employ at this time and set up his own business in Tranwsfynydd. Further research is needed to confirm this, but the circumstantial evidence is strong. It seems unlikely that Watkin moved back into Tyn-y-pwll with his family; instead he probably installed another journeyman there. Certainly, at various times, Watkin leased at least two other properties in the town. He rented for some years a property forming part of the small Plas Isa estate on the north-east outskirts of the town. We do not know the name or exact location of this property, but it does not appear to have been very large or important because it is not mentioned separately by name in legal documents of the time. Towards the end of his life Watkin Owen rented the "House near the Eagles" from the Mostyn estate for an annual rental of £4 0s 0d. [23] This sounds a more substantial property, and the kind of address that would have been favoured by one of the town's leading figures.

In 1803 and 1804 Watkin Owen was churchwarden; [24] his fellow warden was William Williams of Fotty Fawr. He served his allotted tour of duty without any particular distinction.

That is virtually the sum total of our knowledge of the man Watkin Owen until his death on 8th April 1809. He was buried in Llanrwst churchyard a few feet from his father, John Owen. His father had made clocks in Llanrwst for thirty years; Watkin exceeded that by three years. His gravestone may have been erected by Robert Jones, a draper in the town who was married to Watkin's daughter Barbara. [25] Watkin's age at his death is given as 48 years on the stone, but, surely, this is an error because he was born in 1755. Watkin Owen's will is reproduced here in full: [26]

In the name of God Amen I Watkin Owen of Llanrwst in the County of Denbigh
Clockmaker being of sound Mind Memory and Understanding Do make and ordain

this my Last Will and testament as follows - Whereas I have heretofore given to my Eldest Son Griffith Owen several sums of money for his advancement in Life Now I Give and Bequeath to my said Son Griffith Owen the sum of Five Pounds and no More. I Give and Bequeath to my Daughter Barbara Owen the sum of Fifty Pounds. I give and Bequeath unto my son David Owen the Sum of Twenty Pounds, and do recommend it to my Executrix hereinafter named to give or leave him my said Son David the further Sum of Twenty Pounds, in Case his Behaviour will hereafter Merit the same from my Beloved Wife - I give and Bequeath the Sum of Fifty Pounds to my Daughter Jane Owen, and I also Give and Bequeath to my son Watkin Owens the Sum of Fifty Pounds - I Give Devise and Bequeath all that Messuage Tenement, Lands and premises called or known by the Name of Frydd Gleision situated in the said Parish of Llanrwst which I have Contracted for the Purchase, to my Beloved Wife Margaret Owen, her Heirs and Assigns for Ever and to be Disposed of as my said Wife Margaret shall think proper, Subject to the Payment of the Purchase Money due for the same, upon the Vendor's Making and preparing a Satisfactory Title to the same.

As to all the rest residue and remainder of my Personal Estate and Effects of what nature or kind the same consisteth of - I Give and Bequeath the same and every Part thereof unto my said Beloved Wife Margaret, Subject to the Payment of my just debts and funeral Expenses - And I do direct that the said Legacies to my said children be paid to them within Two years after my decease. And I do hereby Nominate Constitute and Appoint my said Wife Margaret Sole Executrix of this my last Will and testament, hereby revoking all other Will and Wills by me heretofore made and do declare this only to be my Will In witness hereof I have hereunto Subscribed my Hand and affixed my Seal this Twelfth day of April One thousand Eight hundred and Nine.

Signed Sealed Published and Declared, by the said Testator Watkin Owen as, and for his last Will and testament in the presence of Us, who in his presence, at his request and in the presence of each other have hereunto Subscribed our names as witnesses the Interlineation of the Bequest of Fifty Pounds to his Daughter Barbara Owen being first made -

Robert Roberts, William Owen, ? Griffith, Atty (all of Llanrwst).

The reference to the eldest son Griffith carries with it, the reader may think, a touch of asperity. Griffith had gone to Liverpool to become first a grocer and later a brewer, and he had obviously required a good deal of financial assistance from his father. Clearly, David Owen was the blacksheep of the family, although there is no specification anywhere of the nature of his shortcomings. Watkin was in the process of buying a property called Frydd Gleision at the time of making his will. Whether this purchase was an investment to earn income or for occupation by his wife or family is not clear, but it is probably the former. We do know that the purchase was completed because Watkin's wife Margaret bequeaths the property in her will. Frydd or Fryddoedd Gleison is a small-holding in the isolated hamlet of Nebo, 4 miles from Llanrwst and a thousand feet above the valley floor. The diminutive farm-house is tucked into the hillside to give it some protection from the great winter gales that roar unimpeded across this barren upland.

Nebo is now isolated and rarely visited, but then, for a brief period, it was on the new turnpike road from Shrewsbury. Ten years later Thomas Telford was to complete the complex and hazardous business of taking his Holyhead road down the side of Dinas Hill and into the village of Betws-y-coed. A few years later the road was turnpiked from Betws to Llanrwst and Nebo would, once again, have faded into obscurity.

Altogether, the will of Watkin Owen is not an illuminating document. No inventory of

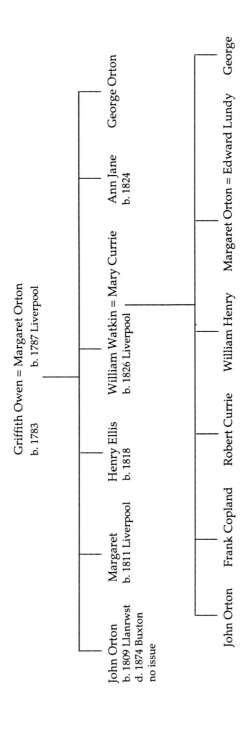

Griffith Owen = Margaret Orton
b. 1783   b. 1787 Liverpool

John Orton
b. 1809 Llanrwst
d. 1874 Buxton
no issue

Margaret
b. 1811 Liverpool

Henry Ellis
b. 1818

William Watkin = Mary Currie
b. 1826 Liverpool

Ann Jane
b. 1824

George Orton

John Orton   Frank Copland   Robert Currie   William Henry   Margaret Orton = Edward Lundy

George

Fig 10: The descendents of Griffith Owen, son of Watkin Owen the clockmaker. [Mr Bob Lundy]
Griffith Owen went to Liverpool where he became first a grocer then a brewer.
He appears to have been the only child of Watkin Owen to have issue.

his possessions accompanies it, or if it did, this has not survived. The will makes no mention whatsoever of the clockmaking business and, after the bequests to his children, the whole of the unspecified residue is left to his widow. It is interesting to note, however, that the business was to be continued without a break by Watkin's younger brother William and his son David; and this must suggest that it was, and probably always had been, a family business. [27] If it was already a partnership with his brothers then there would have been no need to make specific reference to the business in the will, and certainly there is none; the income from Watkin's share would have formed a part of the residue left to his wife. His brothers may have been very much the junior partners or they may have followed different crafts or callings under the business' umbrella. As for Watkin's wife and children, their maternal grandfather, the Reverend Griffith Ellis of Llanbedr, had already made generous provision for them in his will. Certainly, they were well provided for but, sadly, the next few years following Watkin's death, saw a tragic decline in their fortunes. Watkin's son John, who is the last person of that name to feature in the little family tree with which we started this chapter, was already dead. He did, indeed, achieve the academic distinctions at Christ Church, Oxford indicated by the family tree. Next he took Holy Orders and became one of the Chaplains of the College but he died there in 1808. Watkin's widow, Margaret, survived her husband by a mere sixteen months and we reproduce the text of her will in full also. [28]

> This is the last Will and Testament of me Margaret Owen, of Llanrwst in the County of Denbigh Widow. I give Devise and Bequeath, All that Messuage Tenement Lands and Premises commonly called by the name of Frythodd Gleision situate in the Parish of Llanrwst in the County of Denbigh with all my Right and Title therin Equitable and legal unto and equally amongst my Daughters Barbara Owen and Jane Owen, their Heirs and assigns. To have and to hold the same unto and to the Use and Behoof of, my said Daughters Barbara Owen and Jane Owen, (as Tenants in Common) their heirs and Assigns for Ever Share and Share alike. But in case either of my Daughters shall happen to depart this life unmarried or married and without Issue living at the Time of her death, Then I Give and Bequeath the Share of her so dying without Issue to and to the Use and Behoof of the Survivor of my said Daughters her heirs and Assigns for Ever. I Give and Bequeath unto my Daughter Barbara Owen, and my Son Watkin Owen, whom I do hereby nominate and appoint Executrix and Executor of this my Will, All that Messuage or Dwellinghouse and Premises thereunto belonging situate in the Parish of Llanrwst in the County of Denbigh, now in the holding of Mrs Edwards, which I now am possessed of under a lease Granted by Lord Gwydir. Together with all such Sums of money which shall be owing to me at the Time of my Death upon Mortgages Judgements Bonds Notes Agreements Specialities and Simple Contracts (including the sum of £200 and Interest due to me from my son Griffith Owen, and the Money which is due to me from my Son David Owen) And all and Singular other my Personal Estate and Effects whatsoever and wheresoever upon the Trusts following, that is to say Upon Trust that they the said Barbara Owen and Watkin Owen, or the Survivor of them or the Executors Administrators or assigns of such Survivor do and shall with all Convenient Speed after my decease call in and Complete Payment of all such Part of my Personal Estate as shall consist of Money owing upon Securities or otherwise and do and shall Sell and dispose of and Convert into Money such part or parts of my said Personal Estate as shall not consist of Money by Public Auction for the best price or prices that can be had or gotten for the same; and my mind and Will is, that it shall and may be lawful to and for the said Barbara Owen and Watkin Owen and the Survivor of them and the Executors Administrator

and assigns of such Survivor to Compromise or Compound any Sum or Sums of Money owing to me at the time of my decease and to adjust Settle and Compromise all Accounts which at the Time of my decease shall be depending between me and any other Person or Persons whomsoever, and to give or allow such reasonable Time, or Indulgence for the Payment of the same respectively and in the mean time to accept and take such Securities and Assurances for the Payment thereof as they he or she shall in their her or his Discretion think fit. And my Will and Mind is, that the said Barbara Owen and Watkin Owen, and the Survivor of them and the Executors Administrators and Assigns of such Survivor do and shall by and out of the Money so received and raised by the ways and means hereinbefore mentioned Pay and discharge the Purchase Money due to Sir Thos. Mostyn, Baronet his Heirs or Assigns for the said Tenement and Lands called Frythodd Gleision with all Expenses incident to the Purchase Deed, and Conveyance thereof and at the same time take and receive a Bond from the said Sir Thos. Mostyn, his Heirs or Assigns for Peaceable Enjoyment of the said Tenant. and that free from Incumbrances, and my Will and Mind is, That in Case the Freehold of Inheritance of the said Leasehold Dwellinghouse and Premises situate in Llanrwst hereby bequeathed is offered for Sale and my said Executors shall be desirous to Purchase the same and it shall and may be lawful for them so to do and to pay for the same out of the Money to be raised as aforesaid provided they or the Survivors of them do and shall as soon as conveniently afterwards as may be sell and dispose of the same and the Freehold thereof and shall apply the Purchase Monies in the same manner as my other Personal Estate is to be applied; And my Will and meaning further is and I do hereby direct that my said Exectrix and Executor and the Survivor of them and the Executor and Administrators of Such Survivor do and shall by and out of the Money so raised by the ways and means aforesaid, Pay and Discharge the Balance and Balances which shall appear to be due to them and my other Sons and Daughters (if any) under the Wills of my Father the Reverend Griffith Ellis, Clerk deced and my late Husband Watkin Owen deced, after deducting thereout all such moneys as they have respectively received on account thereof. I Give and Bequeath to my Son Watkin Owen, the Sum of Fifty Pounds over and above what he will be entitled to by this My Will. And my Will and meaning is and I do hereby direct that after making the payments aforesaid and Paying all my Just debts, the Expenses of my funeral and of proving this My Will That any said Executrix and Executor and the Survivor of them and the Executors Administrators and Assigns of such Survivor shall and will divide all the residue Money to be raised and made by the ways and means aforesaid (after receiving the Sums of £200 and Interest due from my said Son Griffith Owen, and the debts which shall appear to be due from my said Son David and Daughter Jane) to and equally amongst my Sons and Daughters Griffith Owen, David Owen, Watkin Owen, Barbara Owen and Jane Owen, share and equally share alike. But if any or either of my said Children shall happen to die in the mean time leaving issue such issue respectively to take the part or share or parts or shares the Parent or parents respectively would have done if living. And in Case any or either of my said five Children shall happen to die in the Lifetime of the others or other of them before marriage or attaining the Age of twenty one Years Share or Shares of them him or her so dying (of and in such Personal Estate) shall go to the Survivor or Survivors of them Share and Share alike and be paid when the Original Portion shall become Payable.And I do hereby Nominate and Appoint John Davies of Gwydir Gentleman to be Guardian and Trustee to my said Son Watkin Owen, until he shall attain his Age of Twenty one years.In witness whereof I the said Testatrix Margaret Owen, have hereunto set my hand and Seal this Eleventh day of September in the year of our Lord One thousand eight hundred and ten.

Signed Sealed Published and Declared by the said testatrix Margaret Owen as and

for her last Will and Testament In the presence of us who in her presence, in the presence of each other and at her request have subscribed our names and Witnesses.
Robert Roberts Llanrwst. John Barker Clockmaker, Evan Evans Gwydir Gate.

The property leased from Lord Gwydir had been inherited from her father. One of the men who witnesses her signature was John Barker, clockmaker, whom we believe to have been a journeyman clockmaker in Watkin Owen's workshop and who could well have continued to work there after his death. Once again, it is interesting to note that the guardian appointed for the young Watkin was John Davies of Gwydir, who is described quite specifically as a 'gentleman'. Even before probate was granted on her will, two more of her children, Barbara and Watkin, were dead, and Letters of Administration were issued to Griffith and Jane who with David were now the only survivors of the ten children who had been born to Watkin and Margaret Owen.

At this stage we lose track of the children. But it was a great surprise and pleasure, therefore, when, later in the project, we were contacted by Mr Bob Lundy, who was able to demonstrate that he was a direct descendant of Watkin Owen, clockmaker of Llanrwst. We are entirely indebted to him for the details of Griffith Owen's career after his departure from Llanrwst and for the family tree in Figure 10. It was he who located the burial of young Richard Owen for us in the Llanbedr registers, and painstakingly double checked our own genealogical researches into his family.

There is, perhaps, one other loose end and this concerns the third Watkin Owen that appears in Dr Iorwerth Peate's list of clockmakers for the town: the dates of "about 1740 - 1780" are given for him. We are satisfied that there was no such clockmaker. All the clocks that we have seen bearing the name of Watkin Owen, Llanrwst are clearly the work of one man and his workshop. In our view this third Watkin Owen was 'invented' to provide a maker for clocks that were being ascribed dates that were too early. It would be interesting to know how many other duplicates have crept into the list of clockmakers for this reason.

For the sake of completeness, it should be mentioned that there seems to have been yet another Watkin Owen in Llanrwst - at least there was in the year 1739 when an entry in the Llanrwst registers reads: "Watkin, son of Griffith Owen of Tre Wydyr [29] and Margaret his wife baptised, 7th July 1739".

Apart from this record of his baptism we have no other reference to this particular Watkin Owen. Probably he was related to the original Watkin Owen of Gwydir, and to the clockmakers, but establishing just how is yet another challenge that we must leave to future researchers.

NOTES

1. Iorwerth C Peate, *Clock and Watch Makers in Wales*, published in Cardiff by the Welsh Folk Museum, 3rd edition, 1975, p66.

2. There is a more detailed biography of Griffith Owen in Chapter VI.

3. The scrap-book is in the library of the University College of North Wales, Bangor, MS 5323.

4. The authors are grateful to the archivists of Jesus College and Christ Church Oxford for confirming the accuracy of the information about Robert Owen and John Owen III.

5. We have found a number of the cards pinned inside clock cases, where some of them have obviously been for a very long time.

6. The Llanrwst parish registers are in the care of the Clwyd County Record Office at Ruthin. They also have copies of the bishop's transcripts. These are copies of each year's entries in the registers which were sent to the Bishop at St Asaph. To protect the original registers they have now been copied onto microfilm.

7. The day of the month is illegible.

8. The source of this information is the Will of Watkin Owen of Gwydir. A copy is to be found in the Probate Records of the Prerogative Court of Canterbury in the Public Record Office in London.

9. Accounts, in Watkin Owen's hand, relating to the funeral are in the National Library of Wales, Aberystwyth. They are interesting because they record several payments for mourning clothes which, invariably, were white.

10. The schedule of Sir Richard's debts prepared by Watkin Owen is at the National Library of Wales, Aberystwyth.

11. National Library of Wales, MS 9719 E and Library of the University College of North Wales, Mostyn MS 1440.

12. In the records of the Diocese of St Asaph in the National Library of Wales.

13. John Edwards Griffith in his *Pedigrees of Anglesey and Carnarvonshire Families* records that Colonel Hugh Wynn of Bodysgallen had a daughter Mary who would have been approximately the right age. According to Griffith she never married but he is not always accurate in the information he provides. See *Pedigrees of Anglesey and Carnarvonshire Families* as reprinted in Wrexham by Bridge Books in 1985, p.184.

14. Garthgyffanedd and Maethbrod are townships in the parish of Llanrwst.They lie just outside the town.

15. There is a clock by John Green, with almost identical strikework, in the Museum of Clock and Watch Making, Prescot, Merseyside.

16. The original document, which used to be in the possession of the Porter family of Conwy now appears to be missing. Fortunately it is transcribed in full in *Archaealogica Cambrensis*, 1930, p212.

17. The Library of the University College of North Wales, Bangor, Mostyn MS 5447.

18. The census returns for Llanrwst are in the Clwyd County Record Office, Ruthin.

19. Clwyd County Record Office, Ruthin, PD/69/1/88 et seq.

20. The Eglwysbach registers are in the Clwyd County Record Office, Ruthin.

21. It may be found in the Probate Records of the Diocese of St Asaph at the National Library of Wales, Aberystwyth.

22. For instance, National Library of Wales, Trofarth and Coed Coch deeds, Vol IIIb No 2560, the will of Henry Jones, currier of Llanrwst, witnessed by Peter Titley, apothecary and Watkin Owen, clockmaker in 1790.

23. The Library of the University College of North Wales, Mostyn Papers MS 5462.

24. Clwyd County Record Office, Ruthin. Llanrwst vestry minutes PD/69/1/192 et seq.

25. The inscription reads: "Underneath lies interred the Remains of Margaret the daughter of Watkin Owens Clock and Watch maker of this Town who departed this transitory life on the 28th Day of May in year 1796 aged 3 years. Also the above named Watkin Owens who died on the 8th day of April 1809. Aged 48. Also Margaret his wife who died 12th September 1810, Aged 49. Also Barbara their daughter and wife of Robert Jones of this town, Draper. She died November 2nd 1814 aged 28. Also Anne his second wife who died September 27th 1838 Aged 44. Also Robert their son who died 29th January 1854 aged 29 years. Also the above named Robert Jones, Draper who died August 22 1864, Aged 64".

26. National Library of Wales. Probate records of the Diocese of St Asaph.

27. A clock c1780 signed Watkin Owen & Co. was sold at auction c1986.

28. The National Library of Wales. Probate records of the Diocese of St Asaph.

29. Tre Wydyr = Gwydir.

CHAPTER III
The Clocks of John Owen

John and Watkin Owen lived and worked in Llanrwst for more than sixty years but, as outlined in the preceding chapter, we have only been able to catch the most fleeting glimpse of them as men who lived busy and full lives in the town. Yet, during our field surveys from 1982 to 1987, we found their clocks in abundance, a most remarkable heritage and ample testimony to their commercial prowess and clockmaking skills.

We have located 125 clocks by John Owen, 285 by Watkin and a further 50 by William and David Owen whom we shall consider later. We have every expectation that, in due course, we will attain a total of at least five hundred clocks by the three generations of the Owens and have reason to believe that this may be one of the highest tallies of surviving clocks by any single 18th or 19th clockmaking dynasty so far achieved. We are not, it must be emphasised, interested in claiming some sort of record, but, rather, we wish to highlight the sheer numbers of clocks available to us because they constitute a sufficiently large representation of the workshop's total output to allow meaningful conclusions to be drawn from them.

People frequently ask how many clocks the Owens would have made in total. Unfortunately, they neither dated nor numbered their clocks as did several of their contemporaries. The Hampsons of Wrexham and Samuel Roberts of Llanfair Caereinion were Welsh clockmakers who did so. This system of numbering allows reasonably accurate estimates of both the total production and the rate of production to be made. In the case of Samuel Roberts of Llanfair Caereinion one of his original account books has also survived [1] giving precise details of the clocks that he produced, the rate at which he produced them and the charges that he made for them. For the Llanrwst makers, however, we have no such direct aids and can only attempt to estimate their output based on the number of surviving clocks, contextural evidence and comparison with their contemporaries.

Brian Cave-Browne-Cave, in his study of the Barbers of Winster, a Cumbrian clock-making family that was roughly contemporary with the Owens, calculated that the Barbers could and did exceed forty clocks per annum for quite long periods, but that this was the output of at least two fully qualified clockmakers. [2] The output of the workshop, he argued, was as much affected by the number of clockmakers working and their age and state of health as by external market forces. Indeed, on one occasion, the output fell away to almost nothing, coinciding with the death of one of the clockmakers and the incapacity from illness of the other.

Pryce and Davies in their fascinating study of Samuel Roberts, the Montgomeryshire clockmaker, show that Roberts peaked at a production of twenty-two clocks in a single year, but, again, they also argue that the assistance of a journeyman clockmaker or his son were key factors in the achievement of this output. [3] In addition, it has to be recalled that most of Roberts' output consisted of 30-hour clocks which required significantly less labour input than the 8-day equivalent. The general concensus among these and other researchers is that a well organised 18th century clockmaker's workshop, where the clockmaker himself worked full-time with the assistance, at the very least, of apprentices could produce clocks at the rate of approximately one per fortnight or twenty to twenty five clocks per annum. The output would be somewhat less if 8-day clocks formed a major part of the output. On the other hand production could be greatly increased if two or more qualified clockmakers were at work.

So we can now quote with reasonable accuracy the output figures and rate of production of a number of John Owen's contemporaries:

> Samuel Roberts, Llanfair Caereinion - 600 clocks at a rate of approximately 15 per annum.
> William Snow of Padside in Yorkshire - 836 clocks at a rate of approximately 25 per annum. [5]
> James Wilson, Belfast - 540 clocks at a rate of approximately 12 -15 per annum. [6]
> The Barbers, Winster - 1435 clocks at a rate of approximately 28 per annum.

Therefore, if John Owen had averaged, say, 15 clocks per annum during his thirty year working life in Llanrwst, he would have produced 450 clocks in total. This would seem the upper limit of his likely total output without assistance from a second qualified clockmaker. However, there is some evidence that for the period 1765 to his death in 1776 there may well have been a journeyman working with him, so this total could well have been exceeded. In addition, we know that his sons Samuel, George and, in all probability, Watkin all worked in their father's workshop and must, during the last five years or so, have made a substantial contribution to clock output. Certainly this latter period coincided with a very substantial increase in production if the evidence of the surviving clocks recorded in our survey is anything to go by (see Figure 11).

Since only a few of the clocks carried specific dates, the dates given to individual clocks are, in most cases, our own best estimate based on stylistic and other aspects. [7] It can be argued that there may have been a higher wastage and loss among the earlier clocks, which would tend to distort, somewhat, the production trends indicated in the table. Nevertheless, if we accept that John Owen's total lifetime output was in the region of, say, 500 - 600 clocks, then the clocks we have located represent approximately 25% of the total. If we have over-estimated John's lifetime output, then the numbers recorded in our survey are, correspondingly, a greater proportion of the complete output.

Another question that we have regularly asked ourselves is how many clocks survive

Fig 11: The approximate date distribution of the clocks by John Owen included in our detailed survey [4]

	No	%
1745 - 1754	22	20.8
1755 - 1764	22	20.7
1765 - 1776	62	58.5
Total	106	100.0

Fig 12: Clock number 563, c1750. A fine, early John Owen, moon-phase dial. Note the hatched borders to the plate, the elaborate engraving around the date box, the chequer minutes and the early, slender hands. Cherub and Crown spandrels.

that we have not yet located. Any estimate at this stage can only be an educated guess, but we would suggest that there are at least as many again waiting to be found and recorded. This would represent a survival rate of approaching 50% of John Owen's total production.

How typical were John Owen's clocks and how do they compare with the clocks from contemporary workshops in Wales and further afield? The first and perhaps most surprising fact that emerges is that virtually all John Owen's output consisted of 8-day long-case clocks. Out of the total of more than 100 clocks studied we only came across a single complete 30-hour clock and one other 30-hour dial. Incidentally, no other type of clock by John Owen has been recorded: no bracket clock, no wall-clocks and no watches. However, there exists a single turret-clock attributed to him. Compare this with the output of Samuel Roberts of Llanfair Caereinion, a close contemporary of John Owen, working only 40 miles away in Montgomeryshire. The contrast could not be greater. Pryce and Davies located only three 8-day clocks by Samuel Roberts (rather strangely Roberts himself always referred to them as 9-day clocks) and Roberts' own records refer to two others. The proportions are almost exactly reversed: for John Owen a 30-hour clock was a rare exception; for Samuel Roberts the 8-day clock was made just as infrequently.

If ever there was a town that could claim to be the clockmaking centre of Wales in the 18th century it was Wrexham. Here there existed a number of workshops in production throughout the century. In Wrexham, some 35 miles from Llanrwst, 30-hour clocks were commonplace and, whilst no actual statistics are available, 30-hour clocks appear to have accounted for, perhaps, half the total output in the town. Later in the century clockmakers in Dolgellau, Machynlleth and several other market towns in central Wales produced 30-hour clocks in abundance. However, in Llanrwst there were virtually no 30-hour clocks and there is no record of any made there after John Owen's death. This is in no way unique as 30-hour clocks are very rare in Scotland and apparently unrecorded in Ireland. There are also parts of England where, like Llanrwst, the 30-hour clock never caught on. The same applies for the remainder of north-west Wales: 8-day clocks were made to the total exclusion of 30-hour clocks.

We can only conjecture as to the cause of these striking regional differences in the type of clocks produced. We find it hard to believe that the inhabitants of Llanrwst and its surrounding countryside had some arbitrary reason for demanding 8-day clocks whereas Samuel Roberts rarely sold any at all. Of course, 8-day clocks were significantly more expensive than 30-hour clocks: their cost was from £4 5s 0d to £4 15s 0d compared with an average of £2 15s 0d for 30-hour clocks (excluding the cases), but the relative wealth of the two regions would not appear to have been so significantly different as to influence the selections of clock types so decisively.

We believe that the most likely explanation is that John Owen preferred 8-day clocks and offered them to his clientele to the exclusion of the cheaper variety. Samuel Roberts, on the other hand, regarded the 30-hour as his standard product, and so it became. It must be remembered that John Owen was the first clockmaker to work in the Conwy valley and that by the standards of the time, the nearest existing clockmakers would have been a long way away in Caernarfon or Denbigh. So, John Owen was pioneering a completely undeveloped and unsophisticated market. The only clocks already known in the Conwy valley would have been a few London, Shrewsbury or Chester made examples in the houses of one or two rich families and the turret clock in the tower of Conwy church. The people of the valley may have known that they wanted mechanical clocks - in the prevailing climate sun-dials must have been very inconvenient, but they did not know what type of clocks they wanted. They probably did not even realise there was a choice.

If, in these circumstances, a clockmaker who had learned his trade in a prosperous town workshop in Cheshire or Lancashire where 8-day clocks were the norm - came to the Conwy valley and offered 8-day clocks only, then his clientele would probably have to dig deeper into their pockets and buy the clocks because they had no option or knew no better. If John Owen was a man of bold marketing instincts, and we believe that he must have been, he would have countered requests for 30-hour clocks, if there were any, by marshalling all the arguments in favour of 8-day clocks and, in modern parlance, 'selling up'. In the course of a few years the die would be cast and the people of the district would have become conditioned to 8-day clocks being the norm and because they were reasonably well-to-do, enough of them could afford to buy the clocks to keep John Owen busy. It would, after all, have been the richer households who would have clamoured for John Owen's first clocks, anxious to be able to exhibit this latest and so fashionable status symbol.

It is difficult to believe that this situation would have gone unchallenged. Some clockmaker must, at some time, have recognised the opportunity of selling much cheaper 30-hour clocks in an area where only 8-day clocks were easily available. Locally, the Owens would have been so well established that to try to compete with them with 8-day clocks would have been courting disaster. It is a generally accepted tennet of marketing that to try and compete with an established market leader head on is costly and unlikely to succeed. Rather the newcomer looks for a gap in the market-leader's product range, fills that gap and then begins to compete on a much broader front from a firmly established 'salient'. It is the equally classic response of the market leader to nip the salient in the bud, and to prevent the newcomer from becoming established. Perhaps, that is why there are one or two 30-hour clocks by John Owen. "Of course I can make them," he would say, "here's an example in my shop but I would like to point out the advantages of having an 8-day clock . . ." Any sales or marketing man would recognise the technique.

We make no apologies for employing the parlance of modern marketing and commerce in this context. It seems that there has always been a tendency among antiquarian horologists to over concentrate on the mechanical features of the clocks themselves and the technical prowess of their makers, and to under-estimate or over-look altogether their commercial accumen and skills. Yet, the making of a 30-hour or 8-day long-case clock in the 18th century not only demanded detailed technical knowledge and great manual dexterity, but also the commercial ability to purchase raw materials, hire labour and to sell the finished product. As the century progressed, clockmaking became less a skilled craft practiced by gifted individual craftsmen and more a highly organised specialist and competitive industry. The records of failure and bankruptcy in the archives are as numerous as those of success and prosperity. We shall return to these important commercial aspects in the next chapter.

Before leaving the subject of the relative proportions of 8-day to 30-hour clocks it should be noted that 30-hour clocks were absent in the remainder of north west Wales also. In Caernarfon and Denbigh, where clockmaking started at least a decade earlier than in Llanrwst, 30-hour clocks were rare if they existed at all. Caernarfon is too far away from Llanrwst for it to have influenced the preference for 8-day clocks in so short a time. The dominant maker of the town was Maurice Thomas who seems to have come from a similar background and to have produced similar clocks to John Owen, possibly for much the same reasons; or maybe they got their heads together - clockmakers often did. [8] In Denbigh the clockmakers were not particularly successful or prolific until much later in the century, too late to have much influence elsewhere - certainly not in Llanrwst and the vale of Conwy.

The single 30-hour clock by John Owen that has survived is a nice, well-made example, but conventional in all respects, exhibiting no obvious distinctive features.

Not only were John Owen's clocks nearly all of 8-day duration, they were also relatively sophisticated, urban products and not in any way rural or rustic in appearance, layout and technology. Again, the contrast with Samuel Roberts is very marked. The former, we are told, was a farmer as well as clockmaker, one of a circle of rural clockmakers on the Welsh Marches who produced small 30-hour clocks of relatively primitive and individualistic design. John Owen, on the other hand, produced 8-day clocks that were very much of the same design and style as the output of mainstream English clockmaking which flourished in north-west England. Certainly his clocks would occasion no comment if they bore the name of a maker from Liverpool, Gatley, Bolton, Warrington or Chester: they were mechanically and stylistically similar.

Having examined well over a hundred of his clocks and having dismantled at least 30 of them in the workshop for more detailed study, we are fully convinced that their maker learned his clockmaking in one of the Lancashire or Cheshire clockmaking towns, and we do know that he had his dials engraved there. His movements, with the exception of a few of the earliest, are consistently well made, large and solid, and without much variation in their layout and design. The strike-work apart, his movements are in no way distinctive and rarely do they have any decoration or embellishment. In this respect they are totally unlike those made by makers such as Jonas Barber of Winster, Woolly of Codnor, Gabriel Smith of Barthomley or Samuel Deacon of Barton-in-the-Beans, all fine, individual craftsmen who delighted in refining their own designs and embellishing their work with decorative turning and engraving. John Owen's movements are never boring, they are too solid and well made to be that, but neither is there much excitement in removing the dial from one of his clocks - it is unlikely to reveal anything unusual.

We have been left with the overriding impression that if Montgomeryshire's Samuel Roberts was one of the last of the individual craftsmen doing much of the work with his own hands in his own isolated workshop, then Llanrwst's John Owen was one of the newer breed of semi-industrialised craftsmen - if that is not a contradiction in terms. In 1770 John Wyke of Liverpool issued his catalogue of clockmaking tools [9] that, in its comprehensiveness, is a match for any modern catalogue; he and many others sold clock parts as a wholesaler, and, if required, complete movements - either finished or in the rough. This was the clockmaking scene of which John Owen was to become a part despite his remote location deep in North Wales. By the time his son Watkin took over his workshop, this form of semi-industrialised clockmaking was reaching its height. By then, clockmakers were much more workmasters and businessmen than craftsmen.

If John Owen's movements were to become, in all other respects, very standardised and mainstream, his version of the rack striking mechanism could hardly have been more distinctive. He used a layout for his strike-work which, in horological circles, is sometimes described as incorporating a "two piece locking detent". This, in itself, is not distinctive- it is a layout that, although much rarer elsewhere, was quite common in the north-western

Rack hook

Gathering pallet
with tail

Locking pin

Rack

Rack spring

Lifting piece

Snail

Rack tail

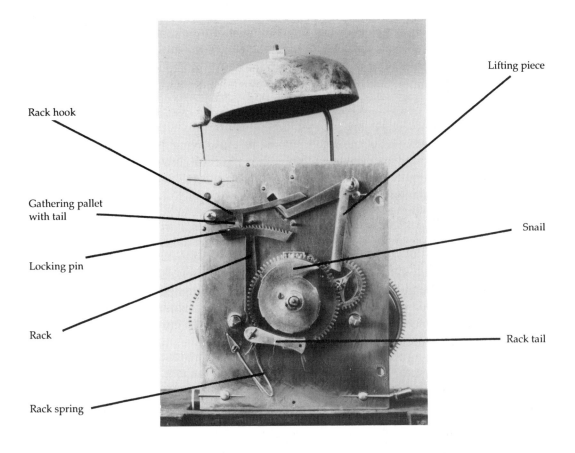

Fig 13: The front of a movement by Moses Evans of Llangernyw, c1795, with the conventional strike-work invariably used by this maker. The mechanism is locked by the tail of the gathering pallet colliding with the pin projecting from the back of the left-wards extension of the rack.

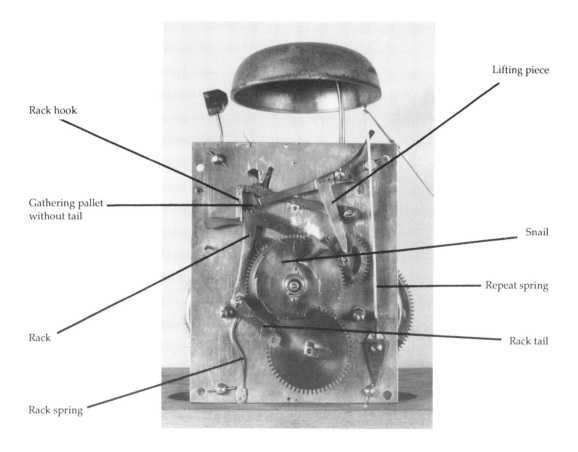

Rack hook

Lifting piece

Gathering pallet
without tail

Snail

Repeat spring

Rack

Rack tail

Rack spring

*Fig 14: Clock number 630. The front of a movement by John Owen of Llanrwst, c1770, showing the
'two-piece locking detent' striking mechanism used by the Owens from 1750 to 1815 approximately.
The mechanism is locked when a pin on the rim of the warn-wheel encounters the detent on the back
of the rack-hook which projects inwards through the vee-shaped aperture.*

counties of England. It is John Owen's stylistic interpretation of the mechanism which is both so elegant and so distinctive.

In Figure 13 (p56) the more conventional version of rack striking is shown, and Figure 14 (p57) shows John Owen's own strike-work. The rack and snail are common to both systems although John Owen and his sons invariably extended the ledge on the rack to the left of the teeth on which the tip of the hook rests to form an upper tail or arm. This does not seem to serve any important, practical purpose although it may act as a counterbalance. The lifting-pieces for both systems are mounted in substantially the same place, but John Owen always provided upward extensions with pins at their extremities. The steel repeat spring or blade rose between these pins to activate the repeat mechanism whether pulled from the left or the right.

It is the rack hook which is entirely different on a two-piece locking detent mechanism. In the conventional lay-out invariably this is mounted towards the top left-hand corner of the front-plate with the downward pointing hook half-way along its length to engage in the rack teeth. In John Owen's versions the mounting stud is in the top right-hand corner, close to the stud carrying the lifting piece. The hook is at the left-hand extremity.

The final element in the strike-work on the frontplate is the gathering pallet. The conventional version has a blade to gather the rack teeth, one by one, and a tail that locks the striking train when it collides with a pin on the rack. In the Owen version the gathering pallet has no tail and is reduced to the appearance of a tiny steel comma very easily lost by restorers in their workshops! Locking is achieved when a pin on the warn wheel encounters a detent attached to the hook and projecting through the frontplate.

The striking sequence of the Owen system is as follows: the pin on the minute wheel encounters the tail of the lifting piece exactly as with the conventional system. The upper arm of the lifting piece rises and the angled detent at its extremity begins to lift the hook. The hook steadily slides up the shoulder of the rack, until it rises sufficiently to allow the rack to fly back until checked by its tail coming to rest on the snail. At about this moment the detent on the hook releases the pin on the warn wheel allowing the train to run momentarily. This is then checked almost instantaneously because the pin on the warn wheel is now intercepted by the long detent at the end of the upper arm of the lifting piece. The lifting piece continues to lift until the pin on the minute wheel clears its tail allowing it to fall back to its resting position. In the process it then releases the warn wheel and the striking train begins to run.

As the gathering pallet gathers each rack tooth, the hook slides up the next tooth and falls down the other side. The number of teeth thus gathered controls the number of blows on the bell struck by the hammer. When the hook has climbed the last tooth, it falls down the steep rack shoulder beyond it, allowing the detent attached to the hook to intercept the pin on the warn wheel thus locking the train.

It would be difficult to argue convincingly that the two-piece locking detent form of rack striking used by John Owen operates significantly better than the conventional layout. It is sometimes suggested that locking high up in the train via a pin on the warn wheel imposes less stress than achieving it by means of the tail of the gathering pallet. Any improvement in this respect, however, is not important because the latter method works perfectly satisfactorily on countless long-case movements. Certainly, John Owen's strike-work is elegant, decisive in operation and, invariably, well executed. The geometry of his layout is always first class and it is rare to get any disturbance of the fly occasioned by the long

Fig 15: Clock number 563, c1750. This movement bears little resemblance to John Owen's later work. Conventional strike-work and horizontal repeat-spring are typical of these early movements, probably bought-in from a workshop elsewhere. The rack-spring is a modern replacement.

travel of the hook up the rack shoulder. One effect of the layout of the lifting piece and hook, is to require a vee-shaped aperture through the front-plate for the two detents. This curved 'vee' in the front plate is highly characteristic of movements from the Owens' workshop, and the scribed radius marks delineating it are almost always to be seen, even when no other wheels are scribed.

Nevertheless, John Owen's strike-work does have one draw-back: it is very demanding when it comes to reassembling the movement in the workshop. The conventional layout is much more tolerant and will usually work first time if sufficient 'run' is allowed when setting up the strike work. The Owen layout is critical to one or two teeth, however, and can be the source of much exasperation in the workshop, especially if time is short. The Owens could have helped a great deal by marking the interlocking teeth as some makers did, but we have never seen a sign of any such consideration for future generations of clockmakers and repairers! We can pass on no fool-proof formula for overcoming the problem because, even after more than fifty Owen movements, we have not yet devised

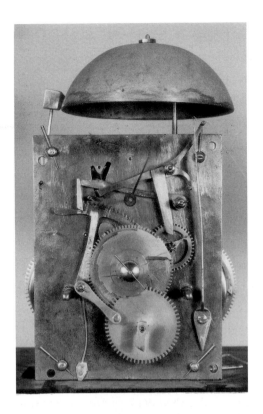

Fig 16: Clock number 28, c1765. This movement is virtually unique in retaining its original rack-spring, date-wheel and repeat-spring intact. The bell, however, is not original.

Fig 17: Clock number 625, c1770-75. By this date the strike-work is all of brass. The date-wheel and repeat-spring are missing. Note the engraving doodle in the bottom right-hand corner of the plate: it is upside-down and reads 'Sam'.

one. We can guarantee, however, that, unless when at rest, the blade of the gathering pallet points towards the centre of the plate and lies so close to the rack teeth that fouling seems inevitable, the mechanism will not run. Equally important is the need to ensure that the hammer tail is virtually touching the next pin which will actuate it.

The presence of this form of strike-work on a clock carrying the name of one or other of the Owens of Llanrwst is a virtual guarantee of the originality of the movement. Fortunately, it is easy to check for the presence of 'Owen' strike-work without removing the dial (which may not be a practical proposition in an antique shop or auction room). Remove the hood and stand at the right side (as you look at it) of the dial and movement. If it is an Owen movement the twin brass arbor bosses of the lifting piece and hook will be visible on the near top corner of the front-plate, usually $1/2"$ to $3/4"$ apart. Sometimes they may be partially obscured by a repeat spring or moon-wheel but they are always there on closer examination.

Go next to the other side and check that there is no arbor boss announcing the presence of a conventionally placed rack-hook. It will not be there on an Owen movement. From the same side it should be possible to discern the rather spatulate end of the hook sitting on the shoulder of the rack - final proof of an Owen movement.

There is one other idiosyncratic detail on John Owen movements (and on all subsequent movements by the family) that helps identification: but checking this usually requires the dial to be removed. The component in question is the small rack-spring that actuates the rack when the hook rises clear of it. On most movements by other makers this is planted approximately in the middle of the lower left hand quarter of the front-plate - its foot secured by a screw. The spring, usually a piece of brass wire, then travels in a south easterly direction until it is under the end of the racktail. It is then bent sharply upwards to engage with the racktail, the spring itself forming a 'vee' (see Figure 13, p56).

Invariably, on Owen movements, this spring is anchored by two small rivets at the bottom edge of the front-plate immediately below the racktail. It thus rises in a straight line, more or less vertically upwards, to engage the racktail. Owen rack springs are usually stiffer and stronger than most, probably because of their straight-line configuration. They are cut out of thin brass plate, the spring itself being integral with the small rectangular or oval foot. The spring is hardened by hammering until it is stiffened and springy. Rack springs are relatively delicate and replacements come in a wide variety of shapes and sizes - some very primitive indeed. The two small rivet holes at the bottom of the front-plate of an Owen movement will always confirm how and where the original spring was attached.

It is often claimed that John Owen always constructed movements with five pillars, but this is not so. Of all the John Owen clocks examined only 16 (or 15%) boasted a fifth pillar and we believe all these to have been constructed in the last ten years of John's working life, which, incidentally, was when his sons were working for him. Five pillars had been quite usual in good quality clock movements made in the provinces during the earlier part of the century but, in spite of any theoretical advantage of the fifth pillar, it was found that a well made four pillar movement performed just as satisfactorily and, moreover, at lower cost. Therefore, the fifth pillar was phased out and it became relatively unusual in ordinary provincial 8-day clocks after about 1750. A few makers retained them, however, and still fewer, including John Owen and his sons, reverted to them. In John Owen's clocks they are by no means confined to his grander or more elaborate examples, but appear apparently at random. Fifth pillars have often been removed by repairers for unknown reasons. Thus, an

Fig 18: Clock number 12, c1771. This is the only Owen movement that we have found which is signed and dated. There is some evidence that one small batch of clocks was engraved in the Owen workshop at this time and that this was one of them. The engraver may have been one of John's sons, Samuel or George. This movement lacks its repeat-spring and date-wheel. The rack-spring is a later improvisation.

Owen movement that appears only to have four pillars should always be checked to see if there is an empty hole or pillar stub at the lower centre of the back-plate.

John Owen movements always have provision for a repeat spring. The layout of his simple repeat mechanism can be clearly seen in Figure 14 (p57). A string is attached to the top of the steel blade spring and hangs down inside the case. Very rarely it may be led off through the side of the hood to hang outside the case - rarely because this practice makes it very difficult to remove and replace the hood. We have only seen two such holes in clock hoods. An old lady who had lived all her life on a farm near Ysbyty Ifan recalled how her father had his Watkin Owen long-case clock next to his bed with the string hanging down within reach so that he could check whether it was milking time in the dark. In this particular clock the original steel repeat spring had disappeared and had been replaced, most ingeniously, by a spring fashioned from the bone handle of a cut-throat razor. It worked perfectly.

The operation of the repeat mechanism is very simple. When the string is pulled - and it works whether the string is pulled from the more usual right or from the left - the spring engages one of the pins on the upper extremities of the lifting piece. This first raises the lifting piece and then releases it to allow the striking train to run. Depending upon how precisely the mechanism has been set up, the clock will usually strike the previous hour until about ten minutes before the next hour, at which time it changes to striking the next hour. It will not operate at all, however, during the warning phase, usually a period of about five minutes or so before the hour itself. Pulling the string at this stage produces no result other than the possibility of a bent repeat-spring.

The exact purpose of the repeat mechanism is much argued about by the experts. We believe that its use by night, as in the case of the farmer from Ysbyty Ifan, was the exception. More normally, we think that the mechanism was used to demonstrate the strike-work of a clock to visitors, just as it is used today. Again, for some reason that is quite lost to us today, virtually all the original repeat springs have long since vanished. The only sign of their presence is the empty, threaded screw hole and associated steady-pin hole in the lower right-hand quarter of the front plate. Brian Loomes has suggested that the fixing holes were invariably inserted in the workshop during manufacture but that the spring itself was an optional extra and only occasionally fitted. On examination in our workshop it appeared that more than half the holes had damaged threads or the shadow of the kite-shaped foot of the spring. This confirms that the spring had been fitted originally and we conclude that they always were, if the fixing holes were present. We can think of no plausible reason for their removal. Repeated or over-strenuous pulling of the string can bend the spring blade, causing permanent interruption of the mechanism. But it is far easier merely to bend the spring back than to remove the blade altogether. To do this, the dial itself first has to be removed. Perhaps the springs were just too bendy, causing recurrent problems, especially if the string was pulled too vigorously during the warning phase, and this resulted in their eventual removal.

Of all the John Owen clocks that we have seen, the majority have been straightforward, square-dialled 8-day examples. All the dials are in brass. There is no record of any painted or enamelled dials by John Owen. A small number have arched dials and a majority of these include a mechanism to indicate phases of the moon. The actual breakdown is as shown in Figure 19 (below).

The arched dials were, of course, more expensive and would have involved a more expensive case as well. Moon-work would have involved further cost both for the dial and for the additional elements in the movement to drive the moon-phase indicator.

On simple arched dials John Owen would use the domed boss in the arch for some enlivening motto - his favourite being 'Time stayeth not'. On the arch round the moonphase indicator he might sign his name but later came to prefer a biblical quotation.

Fig 19: John Owen dial types		
	No	%
Square dials	90	85.0
Arched dials with moonwork	9	8.5
Arched dials without moonwork	7	6.5
	106	100.0

Invariably, he chose 'He appointed the moon for seasons' from the 104th Psalm. This particular quotation also appears on dials by other makers and probably was an 'option' offered by the engraver.

Occasionally, clockmakers produced special clocks for special customers. These involved additional mechanical and stylistic features, designed to impress upon the beholder both the pre-eminence of the owner and the technological prowess of the maker. Two such clocks by John Owen have survived and will be described later.

John Owen's clocks can be divided loosely into three categories which coincide with three clearly defined periods in his working life. These periods are indicated as much by the dials as any other feature of the clocks and we will give a general description of the dials in the context of each of these time periods. In the interests of clarity we will deal with the wooden cases that correspond with the periods in a later chapter.

The Early Period c1745-50

The first group of clocks come from the period immediately following John Owen's arrival in the town, during which time he would have been establishing his workshop and developing his techniques and style. This period is covered by the years 1745-50 approximately.

John Owen clocks of this early period are very distinctive and easily recognised. The dials tend to be rather crudely engraved and to be early in general impression and style. Winding holes are usually ringed and dial centres matted. If engraving is present on the dial centre, it is usually confined to the area around the winding holes and date indicator. The cast brass spandrel ornaments used on the earliest clocks are of the Bird and Urn [10] or,

Fig 20: Clock number 426, c1750. A very early John Owen dial. The centre is matted, without engraved decoration. The seconds disc fits flush with the dial plate. The tapered hands appear to be original. Bird and Urn spandrels.

Fig 21: Clock number 627, c1750-55. This dial demonstrates John Owen's penchant for over-lengthy hands. The minute hand reaches to the outside edge of the chapter-ring. Cherub and Bridge spandrels.

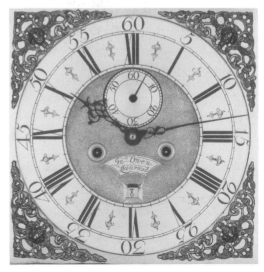

a little later, Four Seasons pattern or one of the versions of the Cherub's Head. Several of these early dials have chequered minute circles in which every other minute division is filled in with black wax. Another early feature is the elaboration of the date indicator aperture or box, the corners, in particular, being given star-like extensions. Seconds dials are usually recessed, this effect being achieved by the use of a separate seconds disc which is riveted behind a large hole cut in the dial plate. On one or two of these very early dials the separate seconds disc is fitted flush with the dial plate, not behind it.

Sometimes, at this period, the maker's name is engraved on the chapter-ring but it is more usual for an applied silvered name-plate to be used. In almost every case the actual signature is rather poorly executed in a spidery and shaky script *eg* Figures 20 & 21 (p64). Clearly these dials are the work of more than one engraver, and we are now satisfied that John Owen did very little, if any, of his own engraving. We will amplify our reasons for arriving at this conclusion when we look at the clocks from his third period. We suspect, however, that John Owen may have applied the signature to his clocks, having first obtained unsigned dials from a specialist engraver. Not only is the engraving of these spidery signatures rather inexpert but, also, this diagnostic feature spans a very long period and dials of widely differing styles - all of which suggests that the signatures, at least, were applied in the maker's own workshop. The use of separate name-plates would have facilitated this process and would have reduced the risk of an engraving error spoiling an expensive chapter-ring.

The movements of these very early clocks are even more obviously the work of several different craftsmen, certainly not less than three. These early clocks tend to be rather rough in their execution and are in marked contrast to John's accomplished later output. Furthermore they exhibit few, if any, of those stylistic and mechanical trade marks that came to distinguish his movements. The strike-work is more usually conventional and it is tempting to suggest that the maker's own, two piece locking detent, system does not appear until after 1750. Repeat springs, when they are fitted, are of an entirely different style and rack springs are located in the conventional position.

Where original minute hands have survived, almost invariably these are far too long, at least by normal London standards, sometimes reaching to the outer edge of the chapter-ring.

Several explanations could be put forward for this rather crude and anomolous early output. It has been suggested that John struggled to produce the earliest clocks with his own hands and that his production only achieved its better known high standard and consistency when he introduced a journeyman clockmaker to his workshop. We do not think that this is a likely explanation, however. The early movements seem to be the work of at least three different clockmakers and it would seem unlikely that a young clockmaker struggling to establish himself in a new town would have gone to the expense and trouble of employing an assistant clockmaker so early in his career. Nor is there any documentary or other evidence that there was a second clockmaker in the town at this period.

A more likely explanation is that John Owen took several years to develop and equip his own workshop, to locate supplies and to train assistants and outworkers, and that during this early period he bought clocks from other makers to supplement his own rather limited output. He might even have made arrangements to do this before leaving his former master's employ. Gradually, until he could dispense with bought-in clocks altogether, his own output would have increased as did the consistency and quality of the design and

Fig 22: Clock number 421, c1750-55. A rare example of Four Seasons spandrels. The hands are modern replacements of inappropriate design. It is quite unusual for the maker's signature to appear on the chapter-ring at this period.

Fig 23: Clock number 29, probably c1755. Not an easy dial to date. The Bird and Urn spandrels, the slender hands and, indeed, the fine early case in which the clock is housed, all suggest an early date. The exquisite half-hour markers and the multiple-ringed minute hand suggest an early example of the Good Engraver's work, some 10 years later. The lunette date opening and applied seconds ring are rare on Llanrwst clocks.

workmanship. We believe that the evidence of the clocks themselves support this explanation.

In summary, therefore, typical features of the clocks from this first period are as follows:

> 12" dials.
> Dial centres matted.
> Any engraving usually around date aperture.
> Ringed winding holes.
> Spandrel types - Bird and Urn or, Four Seasons or Cherub's Head.
> Inconsistent style without distinctive Owen features.
> Amateurish, spidery signatures.
> Recessed or flush seconds dials.
> Over-lengthy minute hands.

The Middle Period c1750-60

Output throughout the 1750s seems to have been relatively low, certainly compared with the sixteen years that followed. The main distinguishing feature of the clocks of the period is that the movements are now the robust, well-made typical John Owen product, exhibiting his special brand of strike-work along with other Owen features such as the vertical rack spring and repeat mechanism described earlier.

The style of the dials changes only slowly. Early features, such as ringed winding holes and the concentration of engraving around the winding holes and date aperture, gradually disappear, as do Bird and Urn and most forms of the Cherub's Head spandrels. A strong note of caution should be sounded, however, both here and at regular intervals throughout the remainder of this book. Unquestioning reliance on a single specific feature or style to give a firm date to an individual clock can be very misleading. The old clockmakers had not read the standard textbooks from which we learn our horology and they were not familiar with the dating criteria that we use today. They followed fashions, it is true; they would want to offer the latest and best and their clocks did evolve but, and it is a very important proviso, they frequently reverted to old fashioned features or styles. Perhaps a customer would ask for a dial, ". . . like Uncle William's", not in the least concerned that the dial in question was of an earlier style. Maybe the clockmaker found several sets of old spandrel ornaments on a shelf in his workshop or he had bought a secondhand clock from an owner who had no further use for it. The clockmaker would want to recycle as much as possible and not to melt down perfectly usable components. The result is that specific and apparently diagnostic criteria given in books such as this should be used with caution and never in isolation. The whole clock should be assessed and a date ascribed, based on the weight of the evidence, not on a single feature. Thus, ringed winding holes or 'Bird and Urn' spandrels may disappear during the middle period but they will, assuredly, reappear in subsequent periods to confound us. Indeed there are, to this day, a small handful of clocks by the Owens which have left us as perplexed after hours of discussion, as they did when we first saw them. Yet to the clockmaker, the explanation for their anomolous features would probably be simple and mundane.

Towards the end of the middle period the engraving of the matted dial centre ceases to emphasise the winding holes and date aperture and, increasingly, occupies the whole of the dial centre. It now becomes what is generally called 'acanthus engraving' a distinctive style that was to dominate Llanrwst dials for the next decade. This period also sees the introduction of a series of rococco spandrels to replace the more classical earlier designs. From now on, Castle Gateway, String of Pearls, Shell and Scrolls, Starfish and a number of other rococco designs are used almost exclusively.

Thus, typical features to be looked for on the dials and movements from the Middle Period are as follows:

> 12" and 13" dials.
> Winding holes no longer ringed.
> Dial centres matted.
> Engraving spread over whole dial centre - usually of acanthus designs.
> Rococco spandrels such as String of Pearls, Castle Gateway and Shells and Scrolls etc.
> Recessed seconds dials.
> Amateurish, spidery signatures.
> Distinctive Owen strikework.
> Vertical rack-spring etc.
> Owen version of repeat-work invariably present though springs usually now missing.
> Minute hands still too long.

The Late Period, c1760-76

Early in the 1760s a number of trends begin to reveal themselves and these culminate in a period of ten years during which the workshop achieves much higher levels of output. It is also during this period that the production takes on a semi-industrialised character – far removed from the individualistic output of a single craftsman.

The most obvious outward signs of these changes can be seen on the dials. On the basis

Fig 24: Clock number 575, c1765. An arched dial by the Good Engraver. The nameplate conceals a second, misplaced date apperture. The bird on the boss in the arch is a pictorial joke by the engraver - i.e. time flies! Large Lady with Fan Headdress spandrels.

Fig 25: Clock number 626, c1770-75. Very similar to the dial in Figure 31 - but with an arch. Once again the jokey 'time flies' bird on the boss. Shells and Scrolls spandrels. Note how the minute circle is delineated by double lines.

of the dials of the early and middle periods it seems very unlikely that they were being engraved in Llanrwst. This conclusion is suggested by the fact that the engraving displayed no idiosyncratic characteristics or design trends that one might expect from an engraver working in remote Llanrwst, far from mainstream influences and fashion. There were no doodles or other engraver's marks on the reverse of the dials nor are there any on the plates of the movements. Such decoration as there was, and this was always scanty, was in the form of simple turned designs produced on a lathe. Unlike the clocks of Samuel Roberts of Llanfair Caereinion there were no signatures, dates or numbers on the movements. If the source of the dials of the early and middle periods is open to some dispute, there can be no doubt about the dials that were to be used during this last period. The dial plates were now entirely anonymous, virtually without any mark on the reverse, of north-west standard design and layout, with the brass of consistent gauge, thickness and quality. Repeatedly, winding holes are cut through the engraved designs which now occupy the dial centres and, on one or two clocks, these holes even impinge on the maker's name. This makes a nonsense of the claims hitherto made by several authorities that winding holes cut through engraved designs are an indication of a changed movement. Changed movements are relatively rare on Llanrwst clocks but, nevertheless, winding holes are cut through the engraving more often than not. Surely this is a clear indication that the dials were being engraved at some distance from the maker's workshop and before the position of the winding squares was known.

The matter is beyond doubt, however, because it is clear that most of John Owen's dials now became the work of a master engraver whose dials are readily recognisable and who must have worked somewhere in the counties of north west England. From the earliest days of our survey we christened this engraver 'The Good Engraver' because the quality of his work was way ahead of anything else hitherto seen on a Llanrwst clock. A perfectionist can find fault with his technique from time to time: he made mistakes in setting out his dials, and on a bad day his engraving tool might slip two or three times on a single dial - whether the product of too much haste, a bad headache or boredom with repetitive clock dials we will never know. It was for his artistic abilities that this engraver was outstanding. He was a true and inventive artist, versed in the fashions and styles of his day: he delighted in stylistic experimentation and giving full rein to his creative imagination. How he must have fretted under the constraints imposed on him by the unimaginative instructions and price limits of his employers.

The first appearance of his dials on John Owen's clocks was unspectacular, sometimes even difficult to identify. Dials with matted centres and acanthus designs superimposed were the order of the day and these allowed him little scope. It is only the signatures on the chapter-rings and, later, the designs in the centres of the seconds discs and half-hour markers that identify his work. He commonly wrote John Owen's name in flowing script (usually abbreviated to Jno. Owen) and the word Llanrwst in stylish capitals, but it was rare for the signatures to be identical. It was the half-hour markers, however, that increasingly revealed his talents for inventiveness, often being very fine indeed and not infrequently echoing the decoration of the centre of the seconds disc.

In the early 1770s a new range of dials by this engraver appears. We have called these dials, somewhat unhelpfully, the 'Exotic Plant Series'. These dials have a plain, non-matted centre that gives the engraver much more scope. These he fills with a rather weird pot-pourri of botanical shapes, sometimes detailed and imaginative acanthus forms, but more

Fig 26: Clock number 28, c1765. Almost certainly an early dial by the Good Engraver - note the decorative borders around the seconds dial and the box around the date aperture, later to become standard features on the Exotic Plant dials. String of Pearls spandrels.

Fig 27: Clock number 13, c1765-70. A typical Acanthus dial of this period by the Good Engraver. Note the attractive scalloped edge to the seconds aperture; also how the design in the centre of the seconds disc echoes that of the half-hour markers. Scroll and Flower spandrels.

Fig 28: Clock number 603, c1765-70. Another Acanthus dial typical of this period. The circular date aperture is unusual; the hands are original. A very early use of the Question-mark spandrels.

Fig 29: Clock number 96, chalk-dated 1773 on its case. A fine example by the Good Engraver from his Exotic Plant series. The beautifully engraved Exotic Plants have no equivalent in nature. West Country spandrels.

Fig 30: Clock number 640, c1770-75. Another typical Exotic Plant series dial. Shells and Scrolls spandrels.

Fig 31: Clock number 625, c1770-75. A slightly different form of the Good Engraver's Exotic Plant series. The weird plant forms are replaced by elaborate acanthus designs. The minute circle is transitional, the double circle is still there, but the radial lines are replaced by dots.

Fig 32: Clock number 14, c1774-76. The minute circle on this lovely Exotic Plant series dial is now merely dots, and the half-hour markers small lozenges. This pattern of cross-over hour-hand was standard at this time. Shells and Scrolls spandrel.

Fig 33: Clock number 60, c1775. The high-water mark of the Good Engraver's art, the high quality of this dial speaks for itself. Sadly it is all that remains of the clock. Castle Gateway spandrels.

usually plant forms that must have come from the artist's imagination rather than from a book of botanical prints. [11]

There are several examples of the Exotic Plant series illustrated in these pages (see Figures 29-32, pp70-71). There are two other design features that typify all the Exotic Plant series dials. Firstly the date aperture and the maker's name are enclosed in a bordered reserve or small box, usually about 2" x 2". Secondly, the aperture behind which the seconds disc is planted is surrounded by a series of elaborate borders reminiscent of the diaper borders to be found in Chinese famille rose porcelain. He also tried one or two other designs but each of these only features on two or three clocks. There also exists a marvellous commissioned dial which will be described later.

About 1775, we see the first examples of the disappearance of the complete minute circle, *ie* formed by two complete circles with radial dividing lines. This is replaced gradually by dots to mark the minutes. There are one or two hybrid dials where the two complete circles remain but dots replace the dividing lines. Our Good Engraver could also be somewhat quixotic as witnessed by the rather dotty bird, a cross between a seagull and a pigeon that he pops onto the bosses of some of the arched dials. At second glance, one realises that he is sharing a little joke with us. The bird is above the motto 'Time stayeth not' but, time flies, the bird tells us.

The work of this engraver is sufficiently individualistic for us to recognise it even when it appears on dials by other makers. Sure enough, it does. At a smart London antique fair we found a fine, arch-dialled moon-phase clock by John Kent of Manchester. The engraving was unmistakably the work of the Good Engraver. A further dial by him is illustrated on page 126 of *Grandfather Clocks and Their Cases* by Brian Loomes, the clock being by John Stancliffe of Halifax. [12] Eric Bruton in *The Longcase Clock* has another example by Joesph Batty of Halifax on page 137. [13] Any of these makers might possibly be the engraver, but a good deal more comparative study is required before this can be proved or disproved. What is certain, however, is that these makers in Lancashire and Yorkshire would hardly be likely to obtain their dials from an obscure market town in North Wales. Therefore, with reasonable certainty, we can conclude that John Owen was obtaining his dials from an engraver, working in all probability in Lancashire, either direct or via a wholesaler or agent.

In the early 1770s, a surprising change seems to have occurred in the movements made in the Owen workshop. There was a significant move away from steel components in favour of brass ones. Hitherto, all the components of the strike-work – rack, lifting-piece and hook - had been made from steel with brass used only for the arbor-bosses. From now on, however, everything was hand made entirely from brass. Even more surprising, so were the seven large mushroom headed screws used to secure the cannon bridge, the crutch, the hammer spring, bell stake and repeat spring. It is not easy to understand the reasons for this change. Steel was significantly cheaper than brass at this period but this may have been offset by the increased ease with which brass could be cut and worked. Alternatively, the workshop may have been using surplus brass to cast these parts. Whatever the reason, the change in raw materials was to be permanent in so far as the strike-work was concerned. The only exception was the using of steel for the screws to which the workshop reverted after a few years - probably on grounds of cost or the fact that steel was the tougher metal for this purpose.

There was one other innovation in the early 1770s and this was to have profound

Fig 34: Clock number 452, chalk-dated 1772 on its case. A fine arched dial with moonphase indication. Note the fishing boat in the centre of the seconds dial. The motto around the arch comes from the 104th Psalm. Large Cherub's Head spandrels.

Fig 35: Clock number 650, c1775. This lovely dial combines all that is best of the Good Engraver's work at this period. Lady with Fan Headdress spandrels.

repercussions for our researches. Someone in Llanrwst at the time began to write the date in chalk inside the clock cases. We shall return to consider the implications of this fascinating subject in Chapter VIII.

The dominating feature of this last period of John Owen's working life however, is the sheer number of clocks produced. Of a total of 106 clocks in our survey, no less than 70 came from this period and we can allocate more than half of these, with reasonable certainty, to the period 1770-76. John Owen must now have had a journeyman in his workshop, possibly John Roberts who paid *maes* for Tyn-y-pwll at this time. By 1770 also, John Owen must have been receiving considerable assistance from his sons. Samuel and George were certainly sufficiently competent to be allowed to scratch their repairers marks on movements, while, presumably, Watkin was a fully qualified clockmaker by the time of his father's death in 1776, the date when he took over the business.

Typical features on clocks from this late period are:

> 13" dials.
> Spidery signatures give way to beautifully engraved ones.
> After c1772 matted dial centres give way to plain engraved centres.
> Beautiful engraving by the Good Engraver
> After c1772 brass strikework becomes standard.
> Rococco spandrels.
> Minute hands now shorter.

These, then, are the three main periods of John Owen's working life and the key stylistic and technical features that typify clocks from each. Obviously there has been a limit to the amount of technical and stylistic detail that we have been able to include. For more detailed information about the dials, movements, hands, spandrels *etc*, the reader should turn to Part Two of this book where we analyse our findings in more detail. John Owen , then, was the first of this dynasty of clockmakers and many will think the most accomplished of them, successful and skilled in his own right, and the father of at least two more clock making sons. When he died in 1776, one of them, Watkin, was just approaching his twenty-first birthday. He was, we presume, newly qualified as a clockmaker and, as we shall show, was ready and willing to assume his father's mantle of horological excellence and commercial competence.

NOTES

1. The original notebook is still in private hands but there are copies in the National Library of Wales in Aberystwyth, and in the Welsh Folk Museum, St Fagans, Cardiff. It is also reprinted in full in *Samuel Roberts Clock Maker* by Pryce & Davies, published by the Welsh Folk Museum, Cardiff, 1985.

2. B W Cave-Brown-Cave, *Jonas Barber Clockmaker*, The Reminder Press, Ulverston, Cumbria, 1979, p108.

3. Pryce & Davies *op cit*.

4. We were unable to carry out a detailed examination of all the clocks we located, hence the discrepancy between the total number of clocks located and the number included in the survey.

5. Brian Loomes, *Yorkshire Clock Makers*, Dalesman Publishing Co, 1972, pp 88 *et seq* and 155 *et seq*.

6. W A Seaby, *James Wilson, Clockmaker of Belfast*, Antiquarian Horology, Vol 14 (1983) p133 *et seq*.

7. Until approximately 1770, when the chalk-dated clocks began to appear in reasonable numbers, a dated clock was a rarity. The dates given to individual clocks, therefore, have to be our best estimate based on stylistic features, the relationship to the few dated clocks, and the limits set by the clockmaker's working years. In this case we are reasonably confident of the split between clocks made pre c1765, and those made in the last ten years or so of John Owen's working life. It is very difficult however to place the clocks made pre 1765 in to five year periods with any great degree of confidence, and we have had to rely on stylistic progressions and intuition!

8. Brian Loomes in *White Dial Clocks*, published by David & Charles, Newton Abbot, 1981, refers to a cartel of Leicester clockmakers who met together to fix prices.

9. This catalogue has been reprinted: *A Catalogue of Tools for Watch and Clock Makers*, by John Wyke of Liverpool, published in 1977 by the University Press of Virginia, Charlottesville.

10. We have decided to use, wherever possible, the descriptions devised by Brian Loomes and used in his various books, rather than to add to the confusion by inventing our own. To suit our own needs, however, we have had to add a few new descriptive names for distinctive spandrel types.

11. We have consulted the Royal Horticultural Society's experts at Wisley, and they confirm that many of the recurring plant forms used by this engraver have no natural prototypes.

12. Brian Loomes, *Grandfather Clocks and Their Cases*, David and Charles, Newton Abbott, 1985.

13. Eric Bruton, *The Longcase Clock*, 2nd Edition, Granada Publishing, London, 1977.

Fig 36: The gravestone of John Owen and his wife Elizabeth, Llanrwst churchyard.

CHAPTER IV
The Clocks of Watkin Owen

The twenty-first birthday of Watkin Owen was still two months away when his father died, leaving him in charge of a flourishing clockmaking business. As usual, we only have the evidence of the clocks themselves to tell us what happened. These show that, if this calamity disrupted the output of the workshop, it was only for a relatively short time.

Watkin, at the age of twenty-one, would have virtually completed his training, assuming he had joined his father in the business as an apprentice at about the age of 14. [1] As he had grown in skill and experience he would have made an increasing contribution to the business and would have participated in the most prolific years of his father's career. Doubtless, in the process, he had developed his own clear ideas as to how the workshop should be run: this is the way of sons when they join their fathers' businesses. Certainly, ensuing events were to show that he was a worthy successor to John Owen.

Watkin Owen's working career of 33 years was amazingly prolific. Our surveys have already located 300 clocks by him, more than double the number that we have recorded for his father and these 300 clocks were produced in a working career which was only three years longer. A direct comparison of the numbers of clocks found in the survey may not be an entirely accurate indicator of the relative outputs of father and son, because wastage of John Owen's clocks is bound to be somewhat higher simply on the basis that, on average, they are 30 years older. This fact alone, however, cannot account for the numerical superiority of Watkin Owen's total output. If we are again correct in assuming that there are at least as many more surviving Watkin Owen clocks as we have already located, then no less than 600 of his clocks are still in existence, or 18 for every year of his working life. This leads to the inescapable conclusion that, in peak periods, he would have been producing and selling a very large number of clocks each year, perhaps equalling the forty per annum achieved by the Barbers of Winster at their peak. [2]

This level of output would seem to confirm the presence of at least a second clockmaker in the workshop on a permanent basis, and that assumes that Watkin himself worked there virtually full time. Yet, one would suspect that selling so many clocks must have consumed much of his time, to say nothing of the time involved in delivering clocks and setting them up, and all the maintenance work and contract clock winding that, inevitably, the business would have attracted. Even assuming that significant elements of the clocks, *eg* the dials, were bought in from outside suppliers, and that much of the repetitive finishing work was done in the town by outworkers, the workshop itself must have been a very busy place. The clocks were all, it must be remembered, designed to go for 8 days and this fact alone required a significantly higher labour input than the production of 30-hour movements. The management and co-ordination aspects alone must have been formidable. All this begins to suggest that there could have been two clockmakers contributing to the output in addition to Watkin Owen himself, to say nothing of apprentices and labourers.

Fig 37: Survey sample of 252 clocks by Watkin Owen

BRASS DIALS	No	%
Square	132	88.0
Arched	5	3.3
Arched with moon indication	5	3.3
Square, one piece	8	5.3
Total	150	100.0
PAINTED DIALS	No	%
Square	85	83.3
Arched	7	6.9
Arched with moon indication	9	8.8
Oval	1	1.0
Total	102	100.0

NB: These dials are usually 13" square plus or minus $^3/8$" but there are a few 14" dials both brass and painted.

Unfortunately, we do not know their names with any degree of certainty. They were not property owners and probably lived in accommodation provided by their employer so that their names were unlikely to appear in rentals or the Llanrwst *maes* rolls. [3] We have already mentioned John Roberts who seems to have been in the workshop between 1772 and 1782 when he moved to Trawsfynydd. In the last year of Watkin's life another clockmaker, John Barker, was working in the workshop. He left after Watkin's death to set up his own business in the town in partnership with a joiner and clock-case maker Edward Jones. [4] We can also assume that John Jones worked for Watkin Owen, leaving after the latter's death. [5] They are the only three clockmakers that we have been able to identify but there must have been others. In addition, the apprentices would have made an increasing contribution before completing their apprenticeships and leaving to establish their own businesses. George Jackson and John Williams were probably two such apprentices.

Although the last quarter of the 18th century saw population growth, increasing freedom of trade aided by the new roads and improved industrial techniques the sales figures achieved by Watkin Owen are nevertheless remarkable. Paradoxically, the economic climate, was not consistently helpful to him and an illuminated address in Grimsthorpe Castle recalls the generosity of the Gwydir Estate in waiving rents due from the tenantry in the Llanrwst valley in hard times occasioned by the American War of Independence and the Napoleonic Wars.

One would suspect that the workshop must have begun to flood the immediate neighbourland of Llanrwst with its clocks and that, already, most of the obvious potential clients would have purchased theirs. In such circumstances, Watkin Owen would have had to make arrangements to sell his clocks further afield via agents or to move downmarket somewhat, possibly with the help of a clock club as Samuel Roberts had done in Llanfair Caereinion. [6] To have built up and maintained so large a clockmaking business in one district and at that time, Watkin Owen must have been, by any standards, an able and successful workmaster and businessman in addition to any skills that he possessed as a clockmaker.

As with his father, Watkin's clockmaking career can be divided into three periods. The first was a very short spell of some two or three years during which Watkin established himself in his father's shoes and made a number of changes in the clocks that the workshop produced. This initial period was to be followed by 20 years of high and uninterrupted output until about 1800. Finally, there followed a period of change and decline culminating in Watkin Owen's death in April 1809. We will deal with each period and their associated clock dials and movements in turn. The clock-cases will be examined in a later chapter.

The Period of Establishment c1776-78

Our clock survey indicates that there was a drop in production following John Owen's death and this is hardly surprising. John's death appears to have been sudden and unexpected because he had made no will and Watkin himself was a very young man to have been taking over such a large and complex business from a much respected father. Furthermore, it is possible that his takeover may not have been immediate or straightforward. After all, his two elder brothers were working for their father in the years leading up to his death: their doodling on the movement plates tells us so. [7] So there may have been a good deal of controversy and discussion before Samuel left, apparently to become one of the town's surgeons, and George left for we know not where. We have found two clocks with the signature of Samuel Owen which could be from the months after John's death when Samuel was still the eldest brother in the clockmaking business. We also received reports from several sources of a clock of about 1780 signed 'Watkin Owen and Co' which may also come from the period before Watkin was left in sole and undisputed charge. It may be that he had to buy his brothers out or go on paying them a share of the profits which could be one of the factors behind Watkin's relentless production of more and more clocks.

It might be expected that the first clocks bearing Watkin Owen's name would be very similar in all respects to the output of the workshop at the time of John's death, but we have found only a very few of this type. Instead, the young Watkin set about making immediate changes, especially to the dials.

We have found only four dials by the Good Engraver which bear Watkin's name. Perhaps he too was near the end of his working life or was worried about the credit worthiness of so young and remote a Welsh clockmaker. We think it is more likely, however, that Watkin Owen was a new broom with his own ideas who wanted to stamp his own authority and identity on the business. In addition, there are strong indications from the clocks themselves that he embarked on a bout of cost engineering. This quite simply involved reducing the cost of his clocks by such methods as reducing the weight of brass in each movement, finding alternative, more competitive suppliers as well as offering features as optional extras that previously had been standard fitments. It should not be inferred for a moment, however, that he reduced the quality of the product in the process: cost engineering need imply no such thing. His clocks tell us that he did all the things we have listed but that the quality of the product remained consistently high.

The dials of the short period 1776-78 give unambiguous evidence that Watkin Owen did

Fig 38: Clock number 324, c1795. A typical 5 pillar movement by Watkin Owen. Note the original rack-spring and the hole in the upward extension of the lifting-piece for the repeat cord.

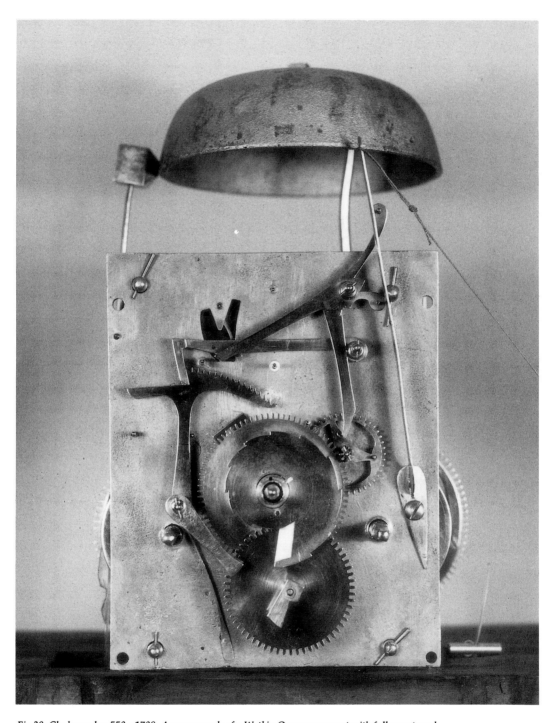

Fig 39: Clock number 558, c1780. A rare example of a Watkin Owen movement with full repeat work.
The repeat-spring is modern.

Fig 40: Clock number 122, c1808. A movement from the last years of Watkin Owen's working life showing the Owen strike-work in a simplified and cruder form.
[Dr W T R Pryce]

not immediately find, what he was looking for. In addition to two Exotic Plant series dials, there is a miscellany of assorted styles, including one or two that may have been the work of the Good Engraver. Others, however, are equally obvious as the work of another engraver. This period sees the last of the full minute circles on the chapter rings: in John Owen's final years they were already being surplanted by dotted minute rings. A number of the dials have seconds circles engraved on the main dial plate, not separate and recessed as had been the more usual Owen practice. This was another innovation tried in John's time. Another style typical of this short exploratory period is the use of diaper decoration for the dial centre, a common feature especially of Liverpool dials at this time. The minute numbers also reached their maximum size during the late 1780s, sometimes almost grotesquely so, so large do they become in relation to the Roman hour numbers. Yet another feature of some of these very early Watkin Owen dials is the use of the word 'Owens' with an 's' in the signature instead of Owen to denote, quite deliberately, that he was Watkin Owen the son of the well known John Owen.

Unfortunately, when the first Owen clocks came into our workshop early in the project we failed to keep specific records of the weight of the components but we are now sure, on the basis of visual examination and comparison, that Watkin reduced the thickness of the brass plates and other components. Certainly, he reduced the size of the plates. John Owen's plates average $6^1/2$" x $5^1/4$" in size whilst Watkin's plates average $6^3/8$" x $5^1/16$". These may seem small reductions but brass was very expensive and was purchased by weight even when converted into clock parts or whole movements in the rough.

All the John Owen movements that we have examined have been fitted with a repeat mechanism as a standard feature but his son dispensed with these. Instead only 1 in 20 of Watkin's movements incorporated the device and none after about 1790. We can be reasonably sure that when Watkin Owen provided a clock with a repeating facility it was an extra paid for by the customer. It has to be stated, however that the spring was not really necessary. Instead, Watkin drilled a hole in the upper extension of the lifting-piece to which a string could then be attached. Pulling this would make the clock repeat the previous hour just as efficiently as his father's more elaborate mechanism, without the problems caused by a bent spring. It is doubtful whether those customers who paid extra for a repeat spring really got value for their money

Decoration of the movements had always been scanty in his father's time but, occasionally, one found simple turned or scribed decoration on pillars, slip washers, strike-work bosses *etc.* This would not do for Watkin, however, and so conspicuous is any form of decoration by its absence that he must have given specific instructions that it was not to feature on his clocks.

All these were steps designed to reduce the cost of his clocks but there was one notable exception where Watkin Owen quite deliberately added cost to his clocks - and for no very obvious reasons. His movements always incorporated five pillars. We have already mentioned that his father used five pillars on about 15% of all his movements and that their use appears to have been entirely random. With Watkin, however, it was obviously deliberate because making and fitting the new pillar would have added cost. We can only speculate as to the reason for this additional pillar. It is possible to argue that the fifth pillar, situated as it is between and slightly above the two winding barrels, adds stiffness and rigidity to the movements at a point where it is subjected to the greatest stress by the drag of the weights. However, this seems to be a theoretical advantage because well-constructed four pillar movements seem to perform just as well. Furthermore, by 1780, most provincial clockmakers had dispensed with the fifth pillar: this makes it all the more remarkable that Watkin should deliberately have decided to go against the general trend. It is our belief that Watkin Owen's fifth pillar was a sales feature rather than an addition to the movement intended to improve timekeeping. In the marketing parlance of today such a feature is called a 'USP' or 'Unique Selling Property'. Briefly, this is a feature of a product that is unique to that particular product or maker and which, because of its uniqueness, is promoted as a strong sales 'plus' by the salesman. The USP does not have to be a feature of great significance although you can be assured that the salesman will promote it as such. A typical modern example would be an international airline that must, of necessity, use just the same aircraft as its competitors and charge comparable fares. Therefore, it chooses to put most or much of its promotional emphasis on a relatively minor feature of the service it offers such as the quality of the meals served in-flight. The USP does not, in itself, have to be a unique feature used to distinguish a product or company from its competitors: it can

Fig 41: Clock number 493, c1777. Very obviously a continuation of the Exotic Plant series by the Good Engraver, but he only executed a handful of dials for the young Watkin Owen. Flowers and Scrolls spandrels.

Fig 42: Clock number 558. One of a batch of at least six clocks produced c1780. All have this effective chequer-pattern dial centre with only the shape of the reserve containing the signature varying. Lady with Fan Headdress spandrels and star half-hour markers.

Fig 43: Clock number 92, c1780. Fine Grass series dial centre with long half-hour markers often associated with this dial-centre design. Question-mark spandrels.

Fig 44: Clock number 75, c1780-85. Acanthus design dial-centre. Question-mark spandrels and the serpentine minute hand which entirely supplanted the straight minute hand in the 1780s.

also be a feature used to justify a higher than average selling price. The important thing to understand is that the USP does not have to be an element or feature of huge significance. What is the relevance of a meal on an aircraft compared with the importance of being transported safely thousands of miles across the world? Sometimes, indeed, USPs are not only of relatively minor significance but may be deliberately added to the product to give the salesman something exclusive to promote.

Our view is that Watkin Owen quite deliberately made the fifth pillar a standard feature of his movements so that he could promote their special quality and superiority. After all, his customers were not in any position to argue that a four pillar movement would have worked just as well and would have cost them less. Watkin's arguments in favour of the pillar would have sounded most convincing. He may also have highlighted other features in this way; for example, the all-brass strikework, demonstrating its superiority over rust-prone steel in the wet climate of the district. [8] We do not believe that this explanation is far fetched. Certainly, he succeeded in preventing any significant competition establishing itself on his territory. Furthermore, it seems certain that Watkin was selling clocks considerably further afield than the immediate environs of Llanrwst and, for example, he may have encountered stiff competition from resident clockmakers in the relatively major towns of Denbigh or Caernarfon. The basic principles of salesmanship, therefore, would have been as important then as they are today.

Whatever the explanation, Watkin Owen's clocks were to have five pillars until his dying day. We have recorded one or two movements with only four: these are either from the first five years or so of his working life or are on movements which have other anomolous features and appear to have been bought in from elsewhere - either to relieve a temporary backlog in supplies or because they became available to Watkin Owen at an advantageous price. We are frequently told by people that they have discovered Watkin Owen movements with only four pillars, but, almost invariably, these are instances where the fifth pillar has been removed.

We can now list the most typical features of the clocks from this short, early period:

> Good quality dials of many designs.
> Occasionally 4, but, more usually, 5 pillars.
> Spandrels: a few earlier patterns and then Lady with Fan Headdress.
> Brass strike-work.
> Repeat-work no longer standard.
> Dials often signed Watkin Owens rather than Watkin Owen.
> Minute hands, where original, straight.

The Middle Period - The Productive Years, c1779-1800

It took Watkin just two or three years to find his feet and to revise the specification of his clocks. This done he seemed to lose interest in any further technical development or experimentation. Instead, he concentrated on selling a virtually standard product in the greatest possible numbers to the widest possible market. Watkin Owen is in no way unique in this. By the late 18th century, 8-day clock movements had reached a stage in their development where, invariably, they were reliable, accurate and did all that was required of them. Their construction and design was to remain virtually unchanged for another hundred years.

Watkin Owen was a businessman who would soon have a large family to feed and a high social status in life to preserve, to say nothing of family shareholders who would look for their share of the profits. He required reliable clocks that represented good value for money and which had the maximum appeal to his customers. Having established such a design, would it not be perfectly logical and sensible to standardise on that design and to concentrate on maximising output and minimising cost? This is what Watkin Owen clearly did, concentrating thereafter on the commercial aspects of his business. We return to this particular subject in a later chapter.

The dials that he finally selected for his clocks were simpler in style and certainly not as fine or as imaginative as those that had been supplied to his father by the Good Engraver. The quality of the engraving continued to be good but the designs were to become repetitive and pedestrian. Once again, most of the dials seem to have been the work of a single engraver; and, we feel sure, one working in Cheshire or Lancashire. They display a highly professional engraving technique with few errors or blemishes but no flair or inventiveness. The dial plates themselves were unchanged in design and without doodle or inscription on their reverse. The designs in the dial centres, now plain and not matted, fall into a number of series or patterns. It seems that they must have been ordered from a pattern book or from a sample with the stipulation that no two dials should be exactly identical. Differences between the various designs are not clear cut because they were executed by a single engraver. Indeed, frequently, they merge one into another so that many 'hybrid' dials exist.

The designs or motifs most usually encountered from this period are:

Cornucopia: Here stylised cornucopias occupy either side of the dial centre. Fine cross-hatching is usually a feature of this design which breaks away into flowers, leaves or formal shapes.

Pimpernel: The engraver favours little pimpernel flowers. These are sometimes the dominant feature, sometimes blended in with other motifs and hybrid designs.

Acanthus Swirl: These swirling designs are now only a faint echo of the full blooded acanthus engraving of the late 1760s. They are now attenuated and formalised; quick and easy to execute but not very interesting.

Little Black Arrows: Creating designs with strings of little black arrows was a particular design feature of this engraver. They are used in swirls, ribbons or swags.

Formal Shapes: Here the designs of the previous series are stiffened into heavy formal shapes, the engraved lines being bunched and linked together. The effect is heavy and stiff.

Fine Grass: In this style the acanthus design has degenerated into swirls of rather grass-like curving lines. This design is often associated with long half-hour markers on the chapter-ring.

Chequer Board: Here the dial centre is divided into a chequer board with only the signatures varying. The execution is rather rough but the overall effect is good. These dials are all dated to about 1780, and may be confined to one 'batch'.

In one respect Watkin Owen was conservative; he liked half-hour markers on his chapter-rings long after so many other clock makers, especially in England, had abandoned them. They finally disappear from his dials in the late 1780s. The markers themselves are frequently rather crude in design and execution, not remotely in the same class as the beautiful half-hour markers produced by the Good Engraver. The commonest form of all is a star crudely executed as seen in Figure 46, clock number 609. but, occasionally, a 'long' half-hour marker is used as seen in Figure 43, clock number 92. These

Fig 45: Clock number 250, c1780-85. Note the four matching corner designs, the half-globes and the square aperture date indication, all signs of an early Llanrwst painted dial. The hands are good modern replacements of the correct pattern.

Fig 46: Clock number 609, c1780-85. This dial centre combines the Cornucopia and Pimpernel designs so popular with this engraver during the early 1780s. Question-mark spandrels and star half-hour markers.

Fig 47: Clock number 622, c1790-95. A typical dial by the Urn Engraver who always engraved the seconds dial on to the dial centre and usually wrote the makers name in flowing script and the word 'Llanrwst' in block capitals with a ligatured double 'L'. Late use of Question-mark spandrels and the serpentine minute hand.

Fig 48: Clock number 478, c1800. A one-piece dial by the Urn Engraver showing all his usual features. Note also the tumbling arabic hour numbers mimicking the painted dials of this period. 'O Jones' was probably the owner. Matching diamond hands.

Fig 49: Clock number 447, c1800. Another one-piece dial by the Urn Engraver with formal designs in the centre and rather curious spandrel features. Note the casting faults on the plate, especially at 5 o'clock.

half-hour markers are not present on all chapter-rings but occur apparently at random. Perhaps they were an optional extra.

Recessed seconds dials became standard on Watkin Owen dials in the 1780s. Initially these had a simple 'compass-rose' decoration in their centre but, later, his seconds dials are devoid of any decoration.

In the first years of Watkin's working life the spandrels in stock in the workshop at the time of John's death were used up. For a while Watkin then used a rather intricate Lady with Fan Headdress pattern. This was soon rejected, however, in favour of the rococco Question Mark spandrel which was to be used, virtually without exception, until well into the 1790s. Early in the 1780s the straight minute hands which had been standard from the earliest days of clockmaking in Llanrwst were superseded by a new, elaborate serpentine pattern which was to become standard for the next ten years.

To summarise, the standard Watkin Owen brass dial clocks for the ten years or so commencing in about 1779 incorporate the following typical features:

> Dials of newer, simpler design.
> Recessed seconds dials.
> Slightly smaller and lighter movements
> Repeat work only occasionally.
> Five pillars always.
> Brass strike-work.
> Owen strike-work and rack-spring exactly as John Owen's clocks.
> No decoration on the movement.
> Minute hands, where original, serpentine.

The quality of workmanship continued to be excellent but the designs predictable and somewhat monotonous: very much a standard product.

However conservative the young Watkin Owen may have been, or perhaps reluctant to alter a product that served him very well, there was one innovation that he could hardly ignore: the advent of white or painted dials.

The first firm evidence of the availability of these white dials is an advertisement offering them for sale inserted in *The Birmingham Gazette* by Osborne & Wilson in September 1772. The new dials were an instant success and were rapidly adopted by clockmakers everywhere. It is important to realise, however, that the new dials were not cheap substitutes for brass ones as we tend to regard them today: indeed, they may have been more expensive. Thus, their rapid acceptance must have been because the clockmakers' customers liked them. Some makers adopted white dials very quickly. Samuel Deacon of Barton-in-the-Beans in Leicestershire was using them by 1774 but he lived close to Birmingham and would have seen the new dials quite soon after their introduction. The Barbers of Winster in Cumbria, almost as remote as Llanrwst, first used them in about 1777. Unfortunately, we have not yet found an early Watkin Owen painted dial clock in a dated case, but all the indications are that he did not try the new dials much before 1780 or 1781. Even then he sold them only sparingly for the next 10 years although whether this was as a result of his own conservatism or his customers' we will never know. Certainly the brass dial dominates his production until about 1790. ꝰ

All the early Llanrwst painted dials have the brass dial type of date mechanism which indicates the day of the month through a square aperture in the lower half of the dial centre; they do not have the more usual small disc displayed through a lunette-shaped opening just below the hands. This must have made the new painted dials even more costly because this date mechanism was both more complicated and beautifully executed. The silvered brass date ring rotated on turned brass rollers as seen on earlier, high quality brass dials but, incidentally, never on those from Llanrwst. This old brass dial system is rarely seen on painted dials and must have been specified deliberately by Watkin. Perhaps, it is the more legible of the two systems and more positive in operation but very much more costly requiring two extra wheels in the movement in addition to the extra cost of the dial. By the end of the 1780s it disappears and the more normal disc and lunette date mechanism becomes standard.

Unfortunately for us, the early painted dials used in Llanrwst were usually fitted direct to the movement without a false-plate and, in the absence of a date disc, they are anonymous as no maker's name is to be seen anywhere. Presumably they would have been by Wilson or Osborne (the two split up and began to trade separately in 1777) and stylistically tend towards the work of the latter although the dials of the two men were always very similar.

Apart from the obvious early date mechanism and the absence of a false-plate, these early dials are also quite easy to identify by their decoration. The beautiful floral or bird designs in the dial corners are either the same in all four corners or the same in opposite corners. In contrast, the dials made by Wilson and used in such numbers by Watkin Owen from the late 1780s until 1800 invariably have one design for the top corners and another for the bottom corners. Moreover, the early dials do not usually have a border around the corner designs whereas the later Wilson designs have raised, gilded borders of commas and dashes. Only in the early 1800s do new designs appear where the design in all four corners is identical, but by this time the square date aperture has long since disappeared so confusion should not arise.

Fig 50: Clock number 255, c1790-95. A Strawberry and Bird dial by Wilson of the type which was so popular from c1785 to 1795 or even later.

Fig 51: Clock number 274, c1800. An unrestored transitional dial by Wilson. Shells were very popular in the designs of 1800-10 and later. The cockerels are a rare design feature as are the hazel-nuts. The hands are original.

Fig 52: Clock number 202. An extremely rare oval dial, apparently signed 'Owen Llanrwst' but this may be an incorrect restoration of the original inscription. Its date is c1785-90, when Watkin Owen was in charge of the workshop. The dial is probably by Osborne. Sadly, the original case has been lost.

In the late 1780s, Watkin Owen adopted the painted dials more generally: maybe his customers were now insisting on them. From now on his dials were to be, with very few exceptions, by Wilson of Birmingham, usually with birds on the dial centre. The corners, as we have already seen, had one floral design in the top corners and another in the bottom corners invariably surrounded by a raised gilt comma and dash border. The flowers in the corners, like the birds in the dial centre, were sometimes a recognisable likeness to real flowers and birds but were just as often rather curious hybrids occurring only in the artist's imagination. In the corners strawberries, moss roses, carnations, honeysuckle and pea flowers were all common, whilst the birds were usually finch-like.

The last decade of the 18th century heralds in a number of major stylistic changes on Watkin Owen's clocks which, with a little practice, are easy to identify, enabling clocks to be dated in the 1790s with considerable confidence. The first was the introduction of matching diamond pattern steel hands which rapidly became standard. Sometimes it is said that diamond pattern hands were associated only with painted and not brass dials, but in Llanrwst this was not the case as they appear on both types of dial from about 1790. This association of this pattern of hand with white dials probably occurs because many makers had already abandoned brass dials by the time the diamond pattern hands were introduced whereas in Llanrwst brass dials were produced for another 15 years.

The other stylistic change was more fundamental: a new engraver was now to work on all Watkin Owen's brass dials for the remainder of his working life. The engraver changed and so did the style, design and layout of the dials. These new dials are easy to recognise as they frequently feature a pair of classical urns in the dial centre. The urns have lids and what is, presumably, water dripping from their rims. The engraver used these urns on most but not all of his dials, although sometimes the urns are integrated into formal scroll designs. Other design features used constantly are wavy grass seed-heads and tight, rather heavy, formal scroll designs consisting of numerous finely engraved lines close together.

Other features enable us to identify these 1790s 'urn-dials' with absolute certainty. The seconds circle is now always engraved on the dial centre and never recessed and the date aperture is circular, never square. Finally, the makers name is almost always in capitals. There is, however, an even more radical feature of these dials. Suddenly the winding holes were no longer cut through the engraved designs as they had continued to do thus far and, increasingly, the winding holes themselves are incorporated in the general design. This is a strong pointer to the fact that, at last, there was an engraver either in Watkin Owen's workshop or at least in the town. Probably Watkin employed a journeyman clockmaker who could also engrave. Whoever the engraver was he was now receiving his dial plates with the winding holes marked or even ready cut so that he could arrange the designs around them. We have only seen one or two of these dials with the design cut by the winding holes whereas previously the practice had been commonplace.

The new engraver was probably Welsh speaking because the double 'L' at the beginning of the word Llanrwst is always meticulously engraved in its joined or ligatured form, something which had happened only occasionally hitherto, or maybe it was Watkin Owen who could at last insist that the double 'L' was written correctly. As for the quality of the engraving, it declined: this engraver was rather slapdash and his engraving tool slipped quite often. Later when he engraved one-piece dials his chapter-ring circles were very shaky and only just circular!

The 1790s were as prolific for Watkin Owen's workshop as the 1780s had been. Brass and painted dials are seen in almost equal numbers; urns or grass seed-heads on the brass ones and birds on the painted ones and both with diamond pattern hands.

Typical features of the clocks from the 1790s are:

> Urns or grass seed-heads on brass dials.
> Initially Question Mark but then Open Oval spandrels.
> Birds on painted dials by Wilson.
> Initially serpentine, but soon diamond hands.
> No repeat work.
> Circular date apertures and engraved seconds circles on brass dials.
> Lunette date apertures on painted dials.

Third Period - Change and Decline c1800-09

As the new century dawned it brought with it a period of change in the Owen workshop and later, in the years leading to Watkin Owen's death, a decline, both in the quality of the clocks themselves and the numbers produced. Much of the initial change was stylistic and reflected design trends that were by no means confined to Llanrwst. There now begins another period of cost cutting and, in due, course even more fundamental changes. The country was now in the grip of the Napoleonic Wars and although production remained high at least until the heady days of Trafalgar, Watkin Owen was once again removing cost from his clocks. He tried new white dial manufacturers, some of whose dials are demonstrably of lower specification - not just in the design but also in the thickness of iron in the plates. The content of brass in the movements is further reduced, as are the average dimensions of the plates and wheels. The shaping of the Owen strike-work components becomes less bold and more simplified and occasionally almost perfunctory. The finishing continues to be reasonably accurate and good, but it was obviously becoming a struggle to maintain standards.

Finally, a few movements made in the period 1805-09, when Watkin died, have a 'foreign' look to them, especially the plates. One movement has the stamp of 'Ainsworth, Warrington' on the back plate, leaving no doubt as to its source. Ainsworth, whose stamp is more usually seen on bells, was an active supplier of clock parts to clockmakers in the period 1800-10. Perhaps his products were so competitively priced as to undercut Watkin's own costs in his Llanrwst workshop?

It should be emphasised, however, that Watkin Owen preserved much of the quality and individuality of his product to his dying day. He never abandoned the fifth pillar, the fitting of the Owen strike work, or the use of brass for the strike work. The fifth pillar, in particular, he obviously regarded as his personal trade mark and perogative. It is very interesting to observe that apprentices or journeymen, for example George Jackson or John Williams, leaving his employ and making their own clocks, often adopted the Owen strike work, or their version of it, but never the fifth pillar.

The period 1800-05 sees the end of the fitting of brass dials to Llanrwst clocks. Those dials made in the old style now had increasingly thin plates and sketchy engraving. The Question Mark spandrels had given way in the mid 1790s to the Open Oval design but in due course this pattern also was superseded and a few much older designs re-appear *eg* the Bird and Urn and the Lady with Fan Headdress. When these earlier designs did re-appear, it was in a somewhat debased form: the castings were smaller and less well finished, rather mean and appearing too small for the dials.

Fig 53: Clock number 171, c1800-05. This dial by Wilson features ruins in the centre and martial symbols in the corners. The hands are good modern replacements.

Fig 54: Clock number 293, c1808. This attractive dial is by Walker and Finnemore; the hands are modern replacements of the correct pattern. Note that the seconds are, by now, only numbered at the quarters.

The final flowering of the brass dial in Llanrwst was in the form of the one-piece dial. This consisted of a single sheet of brass carrying engraved designs only, no separate chapter-ring and no spandrels. We have located seven of these one-piece dials all occurring in the period 1798-1805. They are highly individualistic, almost whimsical in design, and all by the urn-dial engraver. Very obviously these mimic the painted dials that by now reigned supreme everywhere. Brian Loomes suggests that these one-piece dials were the last effort of the engravers to resist the flood of painted dials that was depriving them of a major part of their livelihood. [10] The similarity of the dial shown in Figure 48 (p88) to a white dial of the period is obvious, even to the spandrels in the corners and the use of Arabic instead of Roman numerals for the hour chapters. By now the quality of the dial plates had deteriorated markedly and evidence of casting faults is frequent. Nevertheless, when silvered as they were originally, these one-piece dials are most effective.

This is, perhaps, an appropriate place to say something about the silvering of dials. [11] Today the brass dials in Welsh homes are invariably highly polished, with no sign of any silvering; this is the fashionable way for them to be. From a conservation point of view this regular and vigorous polishing is much to be deplored as it causes serious wear to the engraving. We have had dials in the workshop so worn by over enthusiastic polishing as to make the re-waxing of the chapters and engraving virtually impossible. One thing is certain they were not originally all polished brass. We believe that the chapter-rings and recessed seconds dials were invariably silvered and have seen frequent evidence of this in the workshop in the form of silver residue behind the seconds disc and chapter-ring. Less frequently seen is any residue of old silvering on the dial centres, but it is our belief that they were silvered also. The matted dial centres of John Owen's clocks could not have been silvered but the dial centres with engraving on smooth brass introduced in the 1770s were. In the dimly lit interiors of the 18th century an unsilvered and un-matted dial would be

Fig 55: Clock number 217, c1805. Another rare dial from a clock by Watkin Owen. It is the only example of the peacock feather corner decoration that we have seen. The inscription has been clumsily restored.

very difficult to see and read. They were silvered primarily to improve legibility. The silvered elements and the remaining brass areas and spandrels were lacquered to keep them bright and untarnished. Inevitably, the lacquer would eventually perish and the silvered parts begin to blacken. Someone would then polish or rub the dial and the silvering would soon disappear, leaving the polished brass dials of today. Incidentally, the hands would have been polished, blued by heat-treatment and then lacquered.

The painted dials of the first decade of the 19th century are very varied. The ever popular bird and flower dials persist but their quality declines, especially that of the raised and gilded borders around the corner decoration which rapidly deteriorate and then disappear altogether. Other designs appear, some of them experimental and obviously not finding favour; martial symbols, gothic ruins and even peacock tail feathers all appear at this period and disappear almost as quickly. Other design subjects, especially for corners, are more successful and persist. Among these are sea-shells, geometric fan designs and flowers enclosed in gilded spandrel shaped reserves to instance a few. Generally the quality of both the dial plates and the applied designs deteriorates but only slightly so; the crude decoration of the mid Victorian dial is still a long way off.

Another innovation that first appeared in the last year or so of the 18th century, and which became commonplace in the first decade of the 19th, was the use of Arabic as opposed to Roman numerals to mark the hours. [12] These appear in several forms. If the numerals were arranged in the normal way the numbers 4 to 8 would appear upside down: this was standard practice with Roman numerals. The Arabic numerals do not look so comfortable this way and so were reversed allowing numbers 4, 5, 6, 7 & 8 to be read the right way up. These dials are referred to as having 'tumbling numbers'. Another arrangement was to have all the Arabic hour numbers set vertically and the right way up. Whatever the format these dials with Arabic numerals never look entirely comfortable and were to disappear again in favour of Roman numerals by about 1830.

Also at this time the dial painters changed to a new system whereby the minutes were numbered only at the quarters and not every five minutes; there is usually a stylised star or similar marker at the intervening five minute positions

Not only did the style of the painted dials change but so did their makers. New names to appear on false-plates of the period 1800-09 include Thomas Keeling, (Birmingham 1800-25); Hobson and Todd (Birmingham 1800); Walker and Finnemore (Birmingham 1808-11); Owen and Price (Birmingham 1800-01); Edward Owen (Birmingham 1803-21). [13] These are in addition to the original dial-makers Wilson and Osborne whose dials persist throughout this period. It is hardly likely that Watkin Owen could have dealt directly with so many dial-makers, which suggests that he must have purchased his dials via wholesalers or agents.

Typical features of clocks from this last period of Watkin Owen's life are:

Painted dials of slightly inferior quality, often by new makers.
Numerous new designs on painted dials.
Lunette dates on all painted dials.
A few one-piece brass dials.
Movements smaller and lighter.
Still Owen strike-work and five pillars.
No more brass dials, after about 1805.

In the last few years of his life Watkin Owen's output of long-case clocks declined in number. We can only guess as to the cause but it was likely to have been a combination of factors. The Napoleonic Wars were by then tightening their grip on the economy, disrupting business and trade; pocket watches were becoming the preferred status symbol, most people who could afford a long-case clock having one by now, and perhaps Watkin Owen's own health was deteriorating. He died in April 1809 having produced an abundance of fine clocks for 33 years and in that time establishing a reputation for himself and his handiwork that outlasted his father's and which, even today, lives on as strong as ever in the Vale of Conwy.

NOTES

1. This can only be an assumption, however, because we have never yet seen his name scratched on the movements of a clock, as happened quite frequently in the case of his brothers Samuel and George, nor have we found any other firm evidence of Watkin's presence in his father's workshop.

2. See the previous chapter for a discussion of the output of the Owens and some of their contemporaries.

3. Watkin Owen rented or owned not just Tyn-y-pwll where we believe a journeyman clockmaker was usually installed, but also a small property in the Plas Isa demesne on the north edge of town, and another larger house, near The Eagles, which he himself probably occupied with his family.

4. See Chapter VII, p117.

5. See Chapter VII, p128.

6. See Pryce & Davies, *Samuel Roberts Clock Maker* published by the Welsh Folk Museum, 1985, Chapter IX, p 312.

7. There·is one instance where George has scratched his name just as any repairer might, but more usually it looks as if either Samuel, or George, or both, were practicing their engraving skills. The names are sometimes repeated and are often incomplete.

8. It is very unlikely that the workshop actually used brass for the strike-work for this reason. See Chapter VI p112.

9. For a detailed discussion of the introduction of the white dials see Brian Loomes, *White Dial Clocks*, published by David & Charles, Newton Abbot, 1981.

10. *Ibid.*

11. A chemical silvering process was used. The brass surface was lightly abraded, moistened and rubbed with silver salts.

12. The earliest example of this practice that we can date is the dial signed by Moses Evans, in the dresser now in the Welsh Folk Museum. It is dated 1797. This clock and dresser are described in Chapter X.

13. The dates given are taken from Brian Loomes, *White Dial Clocks*, *op cit*, Chapter IV.

Chapter V
William & David Owen - The Years of Decline

Consternation must have reigned in Llanrwst when Watkin Owen died. For thirty-three years his clockmaking business had provided a livelihood for a small community of workers both in the town and further afield. Journeyman clockmakers and apprentices, labourers and outworkers, foundrymen and engravers, component suppliers and carriers; all had made a living directly or indirectly from the workshop in Llanrwst. What was to happen now? Would the business collapse now that the great man was gone?

In the event business appears to have been very much as usual but now the names on the clock dials were William Owen and David Owen. Superficially, at least, everything else went on much as before.

There is no doubt about the identity of William Owen: he was Watkin's youngest brother and a glazier not a clockmaker, or, at least, it would appear that he had been until his brother's death. Learning more about William Owen presents the all too familiar problem of distinguishing between him and at least four or five of his contemporaries in Llanrwst bearing the same name! There were, amongst others, a William Owen who was an attorney, another William Owen who is described as a gentleman and a landowner and two or three more William Owens in humbler occupations. The index to the account books of the Gwydir Estate lists William Owen as a glazier first and a clockmaker second. [1] He was paid more each year for repairing windows in the Town Hall and at Gwydir than for winding the town clock and the German clock in Lower Gwydir House. [2]

William Owen, youngest son of John Owen, was born in 1765 and was 44 years of age when his brother Watkin died. He had witnessed Watkin's will, signing it in a steady, educated hand. A witness to a will cannot be a beneficiary under that will and, indeed, no mention is made of William among the legatees. There must have been a family conference to decide the future of the family's clockmaking business. The complete absence of any mention of the business in Watkin's will would indicate that he had disposed of his own interest in it by the time of his death, or, perhaps a more probable explanation would be that it was, in reality, already a family business operating under the name of Watkin Owen that would be continued by his brothers on his death.

Fig 56: Of the 42 long-case clocks signed by William and David Owen included in our clock survey the breakdown is as follows:

	c1809-25	c1826-38	Total
David Owen	4	8	12
William Owen	22	8	30
	—	—	—
Total	26	16	42

Fig 57: Clock number 364, c1810-15. A David Owen clock, dial-maker unknown but probably Finnemore.

We have no way of knowing whether William Owen himself possessed any clockmaking skills. It seems likely that he would have assisted in the workshop as soon as he was old enough but whether or not he had received sufficient training to be classed as a clockmaker in his own right we do not know. There was, after all, at least one journeyman clockmaker in the workshop to continue production [3] and it may be that William acquired the title of clockmaker simply by becoming the proprietor or senior partner in the business.

We certainly know that from now on, he is referred to as clockmaker or watchmaker in all official documents although he continued his business as a glazier in parallel with clockmaking. We also know that he continued to lease Tyn-y-pwll and that his landlord was the apothecary and surgeon Peter Titley. [4]

John and Watkin Owen, father and son, had retained a virtual monopoly of clockmaking in Llanrwst and its immediate district. In contrast, William Owen began to encounter competition, not least from the clockmakers or apprentices who had formerly worked in the family workshop and who, after Watkin's death, had left to set up their own independent businesses. John Barker was one of these. Nevertheless, William Owen remained the senior clockmaker in the town and retained the most prestigious clock maintenance contracts. He looked after the town-hall clock supplied by his father in 1761, and the fine dial-clock made by Vulliamy in the parish church, and he also went to Gwydir to wind the German clock in the Lower House. [5]

These regular payments recorded in the church and Gwydir estate accounts continue until about 1836-7 when they cease and other clockmakers take over; nor is there any certain reference to William Owen's presence in the town after that date. His burial is not recorded in the Llanrwst or any neighbouring church register at this date or in the ensuing years, so we can only assume that he sold his business and, in due course, left the town. He would, after all, have been 70 years old and the most likely explanation is that he simply retired. We have been unable to discover where he lived out his retirement.

William's name however, was not the only one to appear on the clocks from the Owen

Fig 58: Clock number 291, c1815. Produced by William Owen, the dial is by Walker and Hughes, but the false-plate is stamped 'Wilson' on the reverse.

workshop after Watkin's death. The other was David Owen and we are less sure who he was. The two most likely candidates are another of John Owen's sons, David, (born in 1757, a year after Watkin himself) and Watkin's blacksheep son David.

The former appears to have been a joiner. In 1800, a joiner of this name was paid by the church for erecting a hovel, or shed, to house the parish hearse. There are a number of other payments recorded for joinery or building works and in 1811 a David Owens was church-warden. If this is our man then he is not the only joiner to have become a clockmaker. Rowland Griffiths appears to have done just the same. With the advent of bought-in movements and dials a joiner, who was used to making clock-cases, could buy the mechanical elements to add to his clock-cases and thus become a 'clockmaker' overnight and there is evidence from Llanrwst and from elsewhere that this actually happened quite frequently.

Our second candidate is the more likely: Watkin Owen's own son David, born in 1788, was twenty-one years old at the time of his father's death and clearly a great disappointment to his family. In his will Watkin leaves a much reduced amount to David requesting his widow to make up the full amount ". . . in case his behaviour will hereafter merit the same". [6] In these circumstances it could well be that the young man, now finding himself the head of the family in Llanrwst, entered the business in partnership with and under the supervision of his uncle William. [7] He may well have trained as a clockmaker with his father, and decided at last to settle down to work in the business, which, in turn, may have been the reason for John Barker leaving it, there being insufficient work in the increasingly difficult times for more than one full-time clockmaker. In the absence of any better evidence, we believe that the David who succeeded Watkin Owen in the business was his son and not his brother.

It is nevertheless strange that we have found so few references to David Owen, clockmaker, when William Owen is mentioned frequently. There is, however, a single reference in an undated schedule of rateable values, indicating that a David Owen owned a house and shop in Denbigh Street and that he rented a further house. [8] The same schedule refers to two houses rented by William Owen and another by Griffith Owen. The profession of the householders are not given so, once again, we are confronted by the near impossibility of being sure as to whether the people mentioned are, indeed, the clockmakers. If they are, and if the Griffith Owen mentioned was also to become a clockmaker, the date of the document cannot be much earlier than 1840. This suggests that David had stayed on in the town at least until this time.

Beyond this we know little or nothing of David Owen, either as a joiner or a clockmaker or as the family's 'black sheep' other than the fact that the name David Owen appeared on the dials of long-case clocks and watches until at least 1838. There is a watch in the collection at the Welsh Folk Museum of this date. Certainly, he, like William Owen, had left the town before the census of 1841. Also at the Welsh Folk Museum at St Fagans, is a watch-case paper proclaiming David Owen as a watch and clock maker, seller of gold rings and other jewellery, and repairer of watches, clocks and timepieces "by the year". This might suggest that David Owen had a shop of his own and separate from William Owen's although the contemporary trade directories make no reference to it. Alternatively, he may have survived William by three or four years in Llanrwst, trading under his own name only after about 1837 but having put his name on part of the output of clocks from the workshop ever since 1809.

David Owen, Watkin's 'blacksheep' son, if, indeed, we have identified him correctly, was the last working member of one of Wales' greatest clockmaking families, which, when he finally left Llanrwst, and there is no reference to him being buried there, had made clocks in the town for no less than 95 years. The end of an era indeed!

Some of the conclusions to be drawn from the simple analysis shown in Figure 56 are obvious. Firstly, the output of the workshop declined sharply throughout the period, and after 1820 was very small indeed, certainly in so far as long-case clocks were concerned. The long-case clock obviously had had its day, because, although there were other clockmakers operating in the town, their output, based on surviving clocks, was even less in aggregate than that from the Owen workshop.

There were several reasons for this decline. The pocket watch was now becoming the status symbol that everyone aspired to, so much so that increasingly clockmakers were referred to as watchmakers and this applied to William and David Owen too. Secondly, the market must have become somewhat saturated with long-case clocks. We know how well they have survived, even to our own times, and how they have been handed on from one generation to the next so that, by 1809, most family homes must have owned at least one. Finally, the Napoleonic Wars were to have a bitter aftermath of disruption of trade, low economic activity and rapidly increasing poverty in towns like Llanrwst. The tenantry was struggling too, and the Gwydir Estate had to waive rents at this period. [9]

There was another factor too: William Owen was not wholly dependent on his clockmaking business; nor were several of his competitors who were involved, also, in joinery and furniture making. They would not therefore, have had the motivation and single mindedness that must have driven John and Watkin Owen throughout the preceding 60 years.

Fig 59: Clock number 138, c1810-15. The movement from an early clock by David Owen. The fifth pillar, which appears to be contemporary with the other four, is quite different in style and may have been added to a bought-in movement in the Owen workshop.

101

Fig 60: The only representation of Llanrwst bridge that we have seen on a clock dial. The clock is by David Owen and dates from the late 1820s or early 1830s.

Figure 56 also shows that David Owen's output of long-case clocks was barely a third of William's, and so very small as to have constituted little more than a side-line. Obviously, both men needed other sources of income and probably concentrated increasingly on jewellery and fancy goods in addition to watches, as was the business trend among watch and clock makers of the period. William presumably continued with his glazing business, although there is no record of it after about 1825.

Of all the clocks produced by William and David Owen none have brass dials and of the white dial clocks only five have arched dials, all with moonphase indicators. One clock by William Owen had a '12 o'clock moon' which is a moonphase indicator below the 12 o'clock position on a square dial, the only example recorded in the whole survey. One interesting feature of the dials on William Owen's clocks is that they were usually signed 'W Owen', and almost never 'William Owen', whereas David's name was always written in full. This must have been deliberate, but whether this was to distinguish William from his renowned elder brother, or to steal some of his thunder we can only guess. Watkin's dials, incidentally, were almost always signed 'Watkin' or 'Wat' and very rarely 'W Owen'.

We have stated already that production from the Owen workshop seems not to have been disrupted by Watkin Owen's death but continued without a break and without any significant stylistic or technical changes. Those trends, however, that had shown themselves during Watkin's last years were to be continued. The reduction in the weight and size of the movements certainly is evident, sometimes to a point where the whole movement or elements of it became positively skimpy; this especially applies to the Owen strike-work which was to continue for a few more years. There is steadily increasing evidence of components and then whole movements being bought in - either complete of in a rough state - to be finished in the workshop. For a few years the five-pillars feature of Watkin Owen was to continue, so much so, indeed, that in two examples that we have seen, there is clear evidence of a bought-in four pillar movement having had a fifth pillar added later - whether this was done by the supplier at the request of the Owens, or whether after arrival in Llanrwst it is impossible to tell. Dials, too, continued to come from the same suppliers, but with new makers appearing from time to time, especially the prolific firm Walker and Hughes of Birmingham.

Sadly, it was not just the production of long-case clocks that declined so inexorably after Watkin Owen's death but also the classic features of the horological craftsmanship of Llanrwst. By 1815 the Owen strike-work, the fifth pillar, the vertical rack spring had all virtually disappeared and certainly do not occur after 1820. On the evidence of the clocks researched, we suspect that finishing of bought-in movements usually replaced the more comprehensive local making of clocks of the former years. The indications are that by 1820 full-scale and continuous manufacturing of long-case clocks had ceased in Llanrwst. Output had declined to such a low level that it would hardly have supported full time workshops. It is more likely that the emphasis was now on the pocket watch and that the long-case clock continued to be available but was no longer a significant source of income for the watch and clock makers. Depending upon the skills retained in their business they would either make or buy in the relatively few long-case clocks that they were now able to sell.

Certainly there continued to be qualified clockmakers in the town whose names were never to appear on clock dials so we must assume that they were employed as journeymen by the more prominent watch and clock makers in the workrooms behind their shops. They would have been employed on the repair and servicing of pocket watches, the repair of long-case clocks and, as required, the 'making' (ie assembling and finishing) of long-case clocks. The evidence of the long-case clocks from the period 1820-50 is difficult to assess. The dials, all of them painted, were, of course, bought in, but the movements which were now very stereotyped and without any noticeable distinguishing features, could have been bought in, either finished or in the rough whilst some at least were probably still made in the town. In 1935 a correspondent to the *North Wales Weekly News* wrote:

> My father was apprenticed to the clockmaking at Llanrwst in 1847 and after completing his seven years apprenticeship, and for some years after, continued making clocks as a journeyman. The castings and forgings for his use were made at the Llanrwst foundry.

So it certainly seems that some clocks were still being made in the town, even if they were now in the minority.

Clockmaking had started in Llanrwst in about 1745; it flourished and grew into a large scale activity, to match, in terms of output at least, any elsewhere in Wales. After 1800, the trade declined ever more rapidly until by 1820 it was of minor importance and by 1850 had virtually ceased. In the third quarter of the 19th century long-case clocks enjoyed something of a renaissance in Llanrwst, but these were mostly imported, case and all, and the number of journeymen clockmakers dwindled to a handful of watch specialists. The rise and fall of an important local industry in Llanrwst had neatly spanned a century.

NOTES

1. The index covers several years from about 1816 onwards. It is in Grimsthorpe Castle.

2. Photographs of the interior of Gwydir prior to the sale of its contents in 1921 show what appears to be an 18th century German wall-clock or *telleruhr* in the Oak Parlour. The catalogue of the sale describes it as "an interesting and very EARLY BRASS DIAL HANGING CLOCK, in Repousse brass work frame". These clocks are usually 30-hour, so if this is indeed the German clock that William Owen was paid to wind, he or one of his employees had to go to Gwydir every day.

3. John Barker seems to have been employed by the Owens at the time of Watkin's death. He was to leave in due course to establish his own business in partnership with the joiner Edward Jones.

4. Clwyd County Record Office, Ruthin - QSD/Land Tax 1825 *et seq*.

5. See Note 2 above.

6. The National Library of Wales, Aberystwyth, Probate Records of Diocese of St Asaph. The will is reproduced in full in Chapter II.

7. Watkin Owen's firstborn son Griffith died in infancy in 1781. John died at Oxford in 1808. At the time of Watkin's death, the second Griffith had already gone to Liverpool to become a grocer and brewer. Richard died aged 7 in 1792.

8. Clwyd County Record Office, Ruthin - PD/69/1/204.

9. There is an illuminated address at Grimsthorpe Castle in which the tenantry express their appreciation of this waiver.

CHAPTER VI
Made in Llanrwst?

From the earliest days of our interest in Llanrwst clocks, we regularly encountered the suggestion from dealers, repairers and clock owners alike that Watkin Owen did not make his own clock movements, but bought them ready-made from somewhere else, probably Birmingham. We took little notice at first but soon realised that this view was widely held, and accepted as established history when, in reality, it might be little more than local folklore. As such, this was clearly an interpretation that needed to be challenged. If it was true that Watkin Owen bought in ready made clock movements, then this would have been quite an early example of such a practice, certainly on such a grand scale. If, on the other hand, it was a myth and without any basis in fact, then it seemed important to set the record straight because, no doubt, most people considered that the suggestion that ready-made movements had been bought in from elsewhere demeaned the clockmaker's reputation.

We have already made numerous references to the increasing specialisation and progressive industrialisation of clockmaking as the 18th century progressed, especially in the north-western counties of England where the process had started at a very early date, initially in connection with watch manufacture but later embracing clockmaking as well. Even in the 'Golden Age' of London clockmaking, spanning the years from the introduction of the pendulum in about 1658 to the end of the 17th century, the famous London makers depended upon a network of skilled specialist outworkers while they themselves concentrated on designing their clocks and finding customers for them. When a clock was commissioned they would place orders with external workshops and craftsmen for the production of the various components, reserving for their own workshops those parts of the manufacturing process in which they had particular skills or interest.

Clock and watch making in London was concentrated in certain well defined areas which meant that such a degree of specialist sub-contracting was easy to organise and to operate. Collection and deliveries could be made in a few minutes, the clockmaker merely sending an apprentice on foot to the workshop concerned. Professor Alan Smith, however, has recently demonstrated that the lines of communication were already very much longer, quite early in the 18th century. He has produced impressive evidence that several leading London watch and clock makers regularly bought watch movements from Richard Wright who operated a small workshop near Rainhill in far-off Lancashire. [1] In those early days, however, the training given to apprentice clockmakers was still comprehensive and thorough and covered all aspects of clockmaking, even down to such highly specialised subjects as calculating wheel counts, engraving dials, casting brass, hardening steel and even making the catgut lines for the weights. This did not necessarily imply that, having completed his apprenticeship, the young clockmaker would be able to carry out all these processes with equal proficiency but it did ensure that he would have a full understanding of every step in the production process.

It was men with this kind of training who, in the last years of the 17th century, began to leave the capital to establish their own workshops in the provinces. Those who settled near to London could still continue to buy specialist components there but, for those living further afield, this would have been at best a slow and laborious process, and for the remotest workshops virtually impossible. Therefore, these early provincial clockmakers had to take full advantage of their thorough training and be highly self-sufficient, doing most if not all of the work themselves in their own workshops. This was slow and not always very efficient, especially if the clockmaker lacked particular aptitudes or skills. In particular, this was true of the need to engrave dials. In consequence, many early dials were lacking in refinement to say the least, and sometimes positively crude in their execution.

It should not be assumed, however, that all provincial clockmaking workshops were started by clockmakers moving out from London late in the 17th and early in the 18th centuries. Clockmakers had operated outside London throughout most of the 17th century, some in isolated workshops, some in centres of clockmaking such as Wrexham in North Wales. There were those, often blacksmiths by training, who made the turret clocks for churches and grand houses, very much the heavy end of the trade. Others specialised in lantern clocks, the only domestic clocks in more or less common use until the advent of the long pendulum and long-case clocks. In due course many of these clockmakers would add new, long pendulum clocks to their output.

It was against this background that, at a very early stage, areas of south Lancashire and north Cheshire began to specialise in the production not just of clocks and watches themselves, but, more significantly, in the manufacture of clock and watch making tools and components and in the provision of specialist skills such as watch finishing, engraving and the like. Metal working skills had existed in the area from the 16th century. Thus, when watch and clock making began to increase in importance, the basic skills and knowledge of metallurgy already existed in the area and the workers turned quite naturally to watch and clock manufacture and allied trades. The emergence in and around Liverpool, Prescot, St Helens and Warrington of specialisation in the manufacture of watch movements, watch and clock components and watch and clock making tools meant that clockmakers within reach of this area could, once again, concentrate on those parts of the manufacturing process that matched their aptitudes, skills and inclinations, buying in where it was more profitable in time or money to do so. There were, of course, still men who continued to do most of the work themselves: these were gifted craftsmen who obviously derived pleasure and, hopefully, profit from doing so. They often embellished their clocks so that the most mundane components became objects of considerable beauty. But such men were the exception: for every Gabriel Smith, Jonas Barber, Woolley of Codnor or Samuel Deacon there were dozens of competent and successful clockmakers producing clocks that satisfied their customers and guaranteed themselves a secure living, even if, today, they fail to occupy much space on the pages of horological books. [2] In short, the gifted country craftsmen, labouring away by the light of a candle, producing, by means of some almost instinctive skill, clocks of prodigious refinement and accuracy was by 1750 virtually extinct if, indeed, he had ever existed. Eighteenth century clockmaking was now much more specialised and fragmented. Increasingly, workshops were interdependent and clockmaking semi-industrialised.

Typical of the men of this period was John Wyke of Prescot and later, Liverpool, who was to go into partnership with Thomas Green. In about 1770, he published a catalogue of clockmaking tools. [3] This was comprehensive indeed, and included virtually everything needed to equip a clockmaker's workshop from the tiniest files for finishing escapements to wheel cutting engines and workbenches. These catalogues were distributed to the wholesalers and agents who supplied the clockmakers themselves and would vie with their best 20th century equivalents in the comprehensiveness of the choice that they offered. Wyke and Green were not just toolmakers, however: their business was very much more diverse. Wyke himself had also carried on a clock and watch making business, and long-case clocks survive signed by John Wyke, Thomas Green and the partnership Wyke & Green. Incidentally and quite possibly significantly, the movements of some of these clocks have marked similarities to the Llanrwst product. [4] The partnership also dealt in watch and clock making components and materials. In particular, they had a flourishing business in pinion wire. So too did another Lancashire toolmaker, Peter Stubbs of Warrington, who died in 1806 but whose business survived to modern times. Stubbs was renowned as a file maker but, like Wyke & Green, he sold a huge range of tools for every purpose. His papers and accounts show that, in addition to tools, Stubbs sold clock parts and clock movements. [5]

Neither Wyke & Green nor Stubbs manufactured more than a small part of their product range on their own premises. Rather they depended upon a host of specialist out-workers who eked out a hard and precarious living making tools, files and clock parts in their own cottages, farms and tiny workshops. It was a cottage industry organised and exploited by the large distributors and wholesalers. Even some of the larger workshops (such as that of Ainsworth of Warrington who specialised in clock parts and movements) sold much of their output to these large wholesalers rather than to the clockmakers themselves.

In the context of this chapter it is important to realise that the Birmingham clock factory is largely a myth. There was no such place in the 18th century and there was not to be until the second half of the 19th century. No matter how large and prosperous a few clockmakers and a few specialist wholesalers were to become, their commercial operations and clockmaking as a whole depended on the use of specialist outworkers concentrated in a few specialised localities which did not, apparently, include Birmingham. [6] In the 18th century Birmingham was an important centre for the production of painted clock dials and brass clock case and furniture fittings, but that seems to have been the extent of Birmingham's contribution to the clockmaking trade before about 1820.

It is to be hoped that the reader will excuse this rather lengthy resume of the structure of clockmaking in the 18th century but it is important to establish the context in which we must examine the proposition that Watkin Owen purchased his clock movements ready made from other makers. We can now dispose of the suggestion that the movements came from a factory in Birmingham, because no such factory existed; during Watkin's lifetime clock factories were perhaps seventy-five years away. In all likelihood this suggestion owes its origins to the word 'Birmingham' found cast into the iron false-plates used to attach the new painted dials to their movements from about 1780 onwards. 'Osbornes Manufactory, Birmingham' or 'Wilson, Birmingham' appears on many false-plates on Watkin Owen clocks. As we have seen, Osborne & Wilson were makers of painted or japanned dials and Birmingham, already a centre of enamelling and japanning, was a natural location at which the manufacture of these dials could be developed. These so-called false-plates came with the dials as a sort of 'universal coupling' that allowed the dials to be fitted easily to any movement: they were not part of the clock movements and were not produced in clockmaking workshops.

It should now also be clear that it would have been exceptional rather than normal for Watkin Owen to have produced every part of his clocks in his own workshop in Llanrwst. We have seen that, in all likelihood, his father had his brass dials engraved in far-off Lancashire and that all the evidence of the clocks themselves suggests that Watkin Owen, like his father before him, was a clockmaker in the new, semi-industrialised and commercial mould rather than an artisan craftsman. Further, it seems clear that the sheer volume of 8-day clocks produced by the Owens in the period 1765-1800 cannot be explained otherwise. Although it was always, apparently, a small workshop in Denbigh Street, it was the base for a business of major proportions. It is inconceivable that all the hours of manual work contained in all those long-case clocks could have been crammed inside its walls. Much of the basic manufacture, perhaps even the major part, must have taken place somewhere else: but where?

Before examining the evidence of the clocks themselves and trying to draw conclusions from them, there is one other subject that needs to be examined: the practicality of transporting components and other materials from Lancashire or Cheshire to Llanrwst.

Clock components were made of brass and steel and were relatively heavy, but they were also small and reasonably compact, easy to package for transport in the pannier of a carrier's pack-horse or on a wagon. The carriers would have been an obvious means of transport available to the Owens. Their pack-horse trains had travelled regular routes throughout North Wales since at least the early part of the 17th century, and, by the time that the Owens had established their workshop, they were running what was virtually a scheduled service. The *Chester Directory* of 1781 reported that the Pwllheli and Llanrwst carriers used the Higher White Bear in Bridge Street as their starting point, and that they came and went at "uncertain times", in contrast to the Denbigh carriers who left weekly. [7]

By 1797, John Owen and David Roberts left fortnightly for Pwllheli and their routes would have been through Llanrwst. Another carrier, R Thomas, left the Falcon Inn in Lower Bridge Street for Llanrwst itself, again at "uncertain times".

Until the new turnpike road from Shrewsbury came to Llanrwst in 1777, the only available wagon route would have been the road from Chester to Holyhead via Conwy, the route taken by the Irish Mail coach from London. If components had been shipped by this route they would have had to be off-loaded at Abergele or Conwy and conveyed by some other means to Llanrwst itself. The distances involved were not great, about 14 miles from Abergele and rather less from Conwy so this would have been feasible too. However, the turnpike from Shrewsbury may not have offered the clockmakers much of an advantage as goods consigned to them would have had to be sent from Chester (or other point of origin in that area) first to Shrewsbury or somewhere else along the route before they could be loaded on a wagon bound for Llanrwst.

There was also another route available, by sea from Chester or Liverpool to Tal-y-cafn. It is, unfortunately, not known how often there were sailings to the Conwy river from Chester or Liverpool in the 18th century, but it seems likely that these would have been irregular and more used for the transport of bulk goods.

Back in the 18th century, however, we are inclined to think that the carriers with their trains of pack-horses would have been favoured by the Owens for delivering their vital clockmaking supplies, not least because, apparently, they came through Llanrwst at least every other week and would deliver their consignments virtually to the door of the workshop without any need for transference from one means of transport to another. No doubt the Llanrwst craftsmen would have built up a close and efficient working arrangement with the individual carriers. The clockmakers could have given their written orders and payments to the carriers who in turn would have delivered them to the specialist wholesaler in Chester or elsewhere and in due course returned with the goods. [8]

The transport of parts and materials from Chester and Lancashire, therefore, would not appear to have been too great a problem for the Owens, even if somewhat slow and cumbersome by modern standards. We can only guess as to how often the Owens themselves went to visit their suppliers; or indeed whether they dealt with middle-men or direct with the workshops themselves. All the evidence, however, suggests that they would have dealt with specialist wholesalers. Many of the earlier records of the Stubbs business have miraculously survived and show that he employed travelling salesmen or 'outriders' as they were called. It seems, however, that these men rarely, if ever, ventured into Wales itself; nor did they usually visit individual clockmakers. Rather, they concentrated on establishing a network of wholesalers who would distribute their goods to the end users. At least one of the wholesalers was in Chester and there would have been others offering a wide choice to visiting country clockmakers. We know from his surviving records that Samuel Deacon, the Leicestershire maker, bought his painted dials from wholesalers or agents rather than direct from the makers themselves and this seems to have been a practice that was widespread at the time. [9]

We have assumed, thus far, that brass clock components would have come from Lancashire and Cheshire. It must be admitted, however, that the manufacture of copper and brass materials and articles was undertaken on a very large scale in Wales itself at this time. In North Wales this industry was centred on Holywell in Flintshire. Various early travellers to North Wales give graphic accounts of copper-smelting and the manufacture of copper and brass goods in the town. Pennant and Aiken provide quite detailed descriptions of the production processes and the products. [10] If these early accounts can be relied on it seems that Holywell specialised in the mass production (by the standards of those days) of raw materials in brass and copper *eg* ingots, sheet, wire, fixings, *etc*, especially those used in shipbuilding. The town also produced a wide range of copper and brass goods specifically for export to overseas markets *eg* pots and pans destined for Africa. We have found no reference to the production in Flintshire of specialist components such as those required for clockmaking. It is perfectly possible that such items were produced, but we believe it more likely that, if the new Welsh copper and brass producing factories did contribute to clockmaking, it was by supplying ingots, sheet and wire to those areas in the adjacent English counties that had specialised in clockmaking for so long.

We now need to return to our starting point, the suggestion that Watkin Owen bought in his clock movements. When we began to question this statement it soon emerged that this idea had probably originated from clock repairers or dealers. They in turn, when pressed, usually gave the main reason for supporting the 'bought-in theory' to be the similarity or standardisation of the movements which, they inferred, implied some form of mass production rather than the movements having been the work of individual craftsmen. One or two went further, claiming to have seen the word Birmingham stamped on the movements. This latter point, as we now know, can be dealt with summarily. The only place that we have ever seen the word Birmingham on Llanrwst clocks is on the false-plates used to attach painted dials - never on the movements themselves. Brian Loomes, in his important and pioneering study of painted dials *White Dial Clocks* , [11] demonstrates very convincingly that the iron false-plates were supplied with painted dials by the dial manufacturers and that they formed no part of the production of individual clockmakers.

The next part of the argument is that because the movements appear to be virtually identical they must have been made in a factory of some sort. Again, as we have seen, there are several counters to this interpretation. First, there were no factories in existence as we know them today. In areas where clock movement or clock part production was concentrated the workers were not in factories but in their own cottages or tiny workshops where they employed exactly the same production techniques and tools as a clockmaker himself would have done in his own workshop, albeit these outworkers tended to be much more specialised and to produce a single type of tool or component. They might produce, or perhaps finish, complete movements but rarely whole clocks. If any further arguments are needed to dispel the factory theory then it needs to be placed on record that, in reality, the movements of Watkin Owen are not identical: similar certainly, standardised to be sure, but not identical with individual components only rarely interchangeable. Detailed measurements of more than 30 Watkin Owen movements in the workshop have demonstrated this.

In any case, once a clockmaker had developed a design for his clocks, and especially the movements, which was both reliable and found favour with his customers why on earth should he change it? Surely he would standardise production around the successful design and layout, to the extent that the manufacturing methods of the day would allow. When the output of the workshop reached the levels attained by the Owens during the last three decades of the 18th century, there would no longer be any alternative but to standardise. How this was achieved we will soon see.

Following this reasoning to its logical conclusion, one might have expected the workshop to have used entirely standard dimensions for all its movements, and to have had master templates for the drilling of all pivot and fixing holes. We have measured all the Owen movements that have passed through our workshop to test this theory, but have discovered that the degree of standardisation achieved falls somewhat short of this. It would be in keeping, however, with a system whereby the workshop used plate and wheel blanks of a nominal standard size, either as specified by it, or which were standard to the supplier. The modest variations in finished size would then occur as the blanks were machined individually or in small batches. We feel that the variations in size of the individual components are in accord with this hypothesis. This would apply equally if Watkin Owen's practice was to buy whole movements 'in the rough' for finishing in his workshop.

At this stage the matter of the scribed marks on the frontplate of the movements is usually introduced into the argument. These marks are circular outlines of all the wheels in the movement scratched onto the front-plate by means of the clockmaker's depthing tool. This ingenious tool was a standard part of every clock and watch maker's equipment and still is so to this day. By this means the wheels can be positioned between the plates so precisely as to ensure that the teeth of the wheels mesh to the exact and critical depth with the leaves of the pinions. Several standard works on long-case clocks cite these scribing marks as proof positive that the movement was hand crafted in the clockmaker's own workshop. Unfortunately, many people then automatically jump to the conclusion that if the scribing marks are not present then the movement was not hand-made by a craftsman and, therefore, by inference, was factory made. This is a non-sequitur; there are a number of ways that a clockmaker might plant his wheel trains without employing a depthing tool to scribe out the wheelwork on the front-plate. The most obvious would be for him to make two movements at once. He would scribe out the wheelwork on the front-plate of the first, pin the front plate to its backplate and drill the pivot holes. He would then use the same frontplate to drill two more plates with which to make the second movement. The result would be two movements, one with a scribed front plate and one with an unmarked front plate. Again, for the record, Owen movements did sometimes have scribed front plates: John's quite often and Watkin's much less frequently.

Having examined more than 50 Owen movements we conclude that they were substantially the products of the Llanrwst workshop. As much as any other factor their similarity and consistency of style and design scarcely allows any other explanation. For a span of nearly 70 years the dimensions, design and constructional details evolve consistently but very slowly. From a design and style point of view there are no sudden changes until the last 5 years in the life of Watkin Owen. It seems inconceivable that this could have been achieved if the movements were coming from elsewhere - not from factories but from a series of outworkers, working in their own workshops, and inevitably exhibiting their work personal idiosyncracies or design preferences, no matter how minor in nature. After long and detailed study of a large number of Owen movements we are satisfied that this type of variability is not present and that all the clocks are the products of one workshop and that they are the product of remarkably consistent and disciplined direction.

We have concluded, therefore, that from an early date the Owens bought in blank and unfinished components in the form of clock plates, wheel blanks and brass rods to be turned into movement pillars. Other blank and unfinished castings may also have been bought such as cannon bridges, cocks, *etc*. We know from inventories of contemporary workshops that clockmakers did frequently have their own furnaces and forges and could cast brass and forge steel components if necessary, but not all of them did, by any means. Owen Evans, clockmaker of Llanerchymedd in Anglesey, who died in 1780, was a contemporary of John Owen. An inventory of his possessions at his death has survived and contains a detailed list of his clockmaking equipment and tools. [12] He was comprehensively equipped to make and to repair clocks and watches and had, amongst other possessions, a wheel cutting engine, lathes, a barrel engine and several other pieces of specialist equipment, but there is no furnace or forge in the list. In Llanrwst town there is no record of a foundry until well into the 19th century and no reference of any sort to the very extensive brass casting and iron forging that would have been required to provide all the components for the Owen workshop. Certainly, it is possible that this was done locally but we believe it to be much more likely that the brass blanks and steel forgings in their unfinished form would have been imported from the St Helens, Prescot and Warrington area where brass and metal working had been long established and where there was cheap fuel in abundance. This view is supported by the remarkably consistent quality and colour of the brass in Owen dials and movements, demonstrating a high level of consistency and proficiency in their production. It seems very doubtful that such consistency and quality could have been maintained by Llanrwst blacksmiths or by a small workshop in the town. Interestingly, casting faults, when they do occur on Owen clocks, are often on the brass strike-work components used from about 1772 onwards and sometimes on the movement pillars. If the workshop was indeed using bought-in brass blanks for plates and wheels, they would, during the ensuing processing of these, have created significant quantities of brass off-cuts, filings and swarf. Rather than waste this or despatch it elsewhere for reprocessing it would seem logical that this should have been melted down and used for the casting of those components that were specific to the workshop and not readily bought in. This would certainly apply to the Owens' brand of strike work. The surplus could then be converted easily into brass rods to be turned into screws and movement pillars, and perhaps this is the most likely explanation for the workshop's switch in the early 1770s from steel to brass for these components and for the sometimes faulty casting of these particular elements.

Other components were certainly bought in from specialist suppliers. The bells are an obvious case in point as are the spandrels which follow the standard English designs and fashions and, almost invariably, are of excellent quality. The brass dials were engraved in Lancashire or Cheshire until about 1790 as we have seen, and, once again, the quality and uniformity of the dial plates and chapter-rings suggests that they originated in Lancashire or Cheshire. In any case it would have been cumbersome to import brass into Llanrwst, cast it into dial plates and then despatch it all the way back to Lancashire for engraving. It is interesting to note in this particular connection that we only see poor quality dial plates on Owen clocks towards the end of the brass dial era when the evidence suggests that the engraving was at last being done in Llanrwst. By then they may have been manufacturing their own dial plates also.

As for the hands that occur on Owen clocks, it is difficult to be sure whether these were bought from specialist suppliers or made in the workshop. We conclude that the earlier clock hands were obtained from both sources, but from about 1780 onwards Watkin Owen's hands are of a consistently fine quality, reflecting the range of standard designs found on clocks throughout the county at this period: and, in consequence, it seems likely that the later hands were bought in. By the time Watkin Owen switched to diamond-pattern hands we have no doubt that he was purchasing them ready-made.

We can be equally sure that the clock weights were made in Llanrwst itself. Nobody in their right mind would import lead weights weighing approximately 12lbs each over considerable distances if the basic raw material, lead, was available locally; and indeed it was. Lead mining in the district had gone on for centuries. Sir John Wynn had opened or re-opened lead workings on his estate and had corresponded with his son Maurice, who had been apprenticed to a merchant in Hamburg, about finding the best markets for his ore. [13] In the middle of the 18th century the Gwydir Estate had decided to re-open the workings once again and detailed accounts in the hand of the Gwydir agent of the time, John Williams, have survived. [14] From then on lead-working seems to have been reasonably continuous in a series of mines in the hills behind Gwydir. It would not have been difficult for the workshop to have obtained supplies of lead to be cast into clock weights. Their local origin is confirmed by the unusual shape of Llanrwst weights used on most Owen clocks from the earliest times through to the final demise of the workshop. They have a conical top, which is rarely seen on clocks by other makers and which makes their identification easy. [15]

It has to be said, however, that we have found no specific references to the smelting of lead in Llanrwst. Instead, the ore was usually sent to Flintshire for smelting. In this case pig lead would have to be sent back to the town for the casting of the clock-weights. We remain convinced that the weights were, indeed, made in the town because their distinctive shape is not found elsewhere, but there is no evidence to confirm just how this was done. Perhaps they melted down scrap roofing-lead and the like; this would be in keeping with our discovery of scrap cast-iron inside Llanrwst lead clock weights.

What more do the Owen clocks tell us about the methods used to manufacture them? The most interesting fact to emerge is that the clocks were not so much mass produced as batch produced. As we progressed with our clock survey, we began to notice clocks that bore consistent similarities and, furthermore, they often shared not just one but several identifying characteristics. For instance, for a few years we ourselves owned a John Owen clock of the 1765-70 period with a matted dial with acanthus engraving in the central zone. The dial was unusual, however, because the hole cut in the dial centre to accommodate the seconds disc had a deeply scalloped edge. The movement itself was somewhat taller than usual and the dial plates had two fine, scribed lines around their perimeter, a form of decoration that, previously, we had not seen. Finally, the movement had five pillars. A few months later we saw another similar dial with a scalloped second circle; closer examination showed that the movement also exhibited the other unusual features. Some time later we found a third.

Yet another group soon emerged, this time early in John's working life about 1750-55, and finally the most striking one of all, this time by Watkin Owen and bearing the date 1780 on one of the cases. In this particular group we have now found no less than five clocks bearing remarkable similarities to each other. In all we believe that at least a dozen distinctive groups have now emerged and we would expect the number to increase as we find more clocks and thus enlarge the proportion of the total output that we have available to study.

Originally it was assumed that we were seeing either batches of dials or dials ordered from a single pattern or sample and, in so far as it went, this was perfectly true. The Owen dials were clearly ordered from pattern books or samples and not singly but by the half dozen or so at a time. For most dial designs we have found a counterpart, and in many cases several similar, though never identical examples. Clearly it was stipulated that no two dials should ever be exactly the same; if this were not so engravers would have repeated designs more closely and more often. Sometimes the differences were very slight; the chequer board dials of about 1780 only differed in the form of the signature or the shape of the reserve containing it.

We soon began to realise, however, that clocks with similar dials usually shared other features in common; hands are a case in point and sometimes, but not always, the spandrels. Increasingly, indications that the movements were virtually identical also began to emerge and finally, to our astonishment, the cases too. We now believe that there is very persuasive artefactual evidence that the clocks were produced in batches in the workshop and not singly, and, furthermore, that the production of a batch of clocks sometimes included their cases.

Batch production obviously makes sense, reducing labour and supervisory costs and increasing the rate of output. We suggest that John or Watkin Owen might decide to manufacture a batch of from three to ten or more clocks simultaneously depending on the current rate of demand. Orders would be placed for the dials, bells, spandrels, weights and all the other bought-in components. Brass blanks for the movement plates, wheels, cocks and bridges *etc* would also be purchased or prepared in the workshop. They would all be machined or hand-worked so that they were virtually identical in size. All the pillars would be turned to a single pattern and exact matching sets of wheels cut and finished. When all the components were assembled the first two plates would be pinned together and the wheel trains carefully scribed on the first plate. The pivot holes could then be drilled. One by one all the other plates would be drilled using an already prepared front plate as a pattern. This would avoid the tedious business of scribing all the front plates individually and would result in only one of the movement exhibiting scribing marks. Assembly could then continue, movement by movement, until all were complete. This method allows the critical business of finally sizing the pivot holes with the broach and setting up the escapement to be done individually by a skilled clockmaker to ensure good performance of each clock.

In the meantime the cases were being manufactured to the order of the clockmaker and again in a batch with all the similar cost savings and speeding up of the process that this would allow. This is surprising because, hitherto, most authors have assumed that the customer would go first to the clockmaker to order the clock and then separately to the casemaker to bespeake the case in which to house it. This may, indeed, have happened in the case of individual clocks although, even then, it is sensible to assume that the clockmaker and the casemaker would subsequently liaise to ensure that their individual handiwork matched and fitted when they were finally delivered to the customer. When the Owens were manufacturing a batch of clocks, however, this method of ordering clock and case separately would hardly seem feasible. Presumably the individual purchasers were given minor and superficial options from which to choose, of the kind that could be incorporated at the last moment without interfering with the smooth flow of production. A choice of spandrels, and whether to have plain or reeded hood pillars and quarter columns on the case would be the kind of thing; in no way different from the factory-fitted options offered to the modern car buyer. Using this basic method of production one could envisage that if the workshop already had orders for a number of clocks, they would manufacture a batch of six or eight to ensure availability to meet orders obtained subsequently and before a new batch could be initiated.

We now believe that this is how production was organised in the Llanrwst workshop especially during periods of strong demand. In slacker times the batches would be small, or give way altogether to the manufacture of individual clocks as they were ordered, to reduce the amount of money tied up in the workshop at any one time.

We have been challenged in this theory by people arguing that we are not so much seeing clocks manufactured at one time in a single batch as clocks that were ordered and manufactured individually to an established pattern or "just like Mr Williams' clock". We no longer believe that this can be the case, although it may well have occurred from time to time. Those date indications on clocks and their cases available to us suggest that the time span covered by a single batch of clocks is very short and not spread over a number of years which could be the case if they were ordered from a pattern. Furthermore, it would present very great practical difficulties in the workshop to reproduce minor design details to match those on a clock manufactured two or three years earlier, and, in any case, why bother to try? No one, after all, ever sees decorative fine line turnings on the movement once the clock is assembled.

The evidence for this highly organised and systematic batch production is still circumstantial, but increasingly, as more and more clocks come to light and fall into their group or batch, we feel they leave little room for any other explanation of their method of manufacture. Hopefully, at some future date, the matter may be resolved once and for all. This could be done by collecting four or five clocks from an obvious batch, taking them into the workshop and establishing to what extent the movement parts and wheels are interchangeable. We expect that the movements would be virtually identical and hope that we may, one day, have the opportunity of conducting this trial.

We conclude then that Watkin Owen did not buy in his movements ready made, but neither did he produce every component in his Llanrwst workshop. Rather, he followed what was, increasingly, the custom among provincial clockmakers of that period and operated as a specialised and skilled workmaster and businessman to whose outstanding success many hundreds of his clocks still bear witness. As workmaster he would have placed much of the repetitive, semi-skilled finishing work with out-workers living in the town. Finishing clock-teeth, crossing-out wheels, fettling spandrel castings and many of the other finishing processes all required time and practice rather than skill. There would have been no shortage of men, women and children only too willing to supplement their meagre family income in this way. Doubtless Watkin Owen would have ensured that his most reliable outworkers would earn a little more by working for him, than by resorting to their only local alternative - knitting interminable woollen stockings.

Throughout this chapter we have discussed production trends in the context of Watkin Owen. The evidence of the clocks, however, suggests that our conclusions are equally applicable to John Owen, certainly from about 1765 onwards and there is at least one batch that goes back as far as the early 1750s.

There is an interesting footnote to this chapter. If Watkin Owen did not buy in complete clocks it seems that several of his contemporaries in North Wales may have done so. During our clock survey we came across clocks which were not by Llanrwst makers. Some homes that we visited contained as many as four or five and we usually photographed them all. Again, as with the batches, we began to realise that a number of clocks by several North Wales makers had dials by a single engraver. In due course we began to suspect that the movements, too, had come with the dials, not just because the winding holes were incorporated in the engraved designs, but also because the movements bore a marked if superficial similarity to each other. There is now strong prima facie evidence that brass dialled clocks, that is the dials and movements, were supplied during the 1780s to the following makers from a single source: Minshul of Denbigh, John Roberts of Trawsfynydd, John Thomas of Pentrefoelas, Henry Jones of Dolwen, Evans and Roberts, Amlwch and Thomas Griffiths of Beddgelert. There is also an unsigned dial in this series that we found in Llanrwst. None of these 'makers' appears to have been particularly prolific, but there is one other clockmaking family some of whose brass dials come from this single source and they are the Evanses of Llanddoged and Llangernyw who will be discussed in the next chapter. They are of significance because, by the standards of the district, they produced a large number of clocks, and did so for at least 50 years.

NOTES

1. Alan Smith 'An early 18th century watchmaking notebook ', *AHS Journal* Vol XV, NoVI, p605.

2. Gabriel Smith made clocks in and around Chester in the first quarter of the 18th century. Jonas Barber came from Winster in Cumbria and was more or less contemporary with Gabriel Smith. James Woolley was a very eccentric mid 18th century maker from Derbyshire and Samuel Deacon made clocks in Barton-in-the-Beans in Leicestershire in the last quarter of the century. All were innovative clockmakers whose clocks and movements were often finely decorated; very much above average amongst their contemporaries.

3. The catalogue has been reprinted by the University Press of Virginia for the Henry Francis du Pont Winterthur Museum, 1978.

4. Several clocks by Wyke and Green have been seen with strike-work which is very similar to John Owen's. There is one in the Prescot Museum.

5. The Stubbs Papers are in the Manchester City Record Office.

6. We are indebted to Alan Treherne of the University of Keele who has done much work on the clockmakers of the west Midlands. He has shown that in the late 18th and early 19th centuries, there were large concentrations of jobbing clockmakers in parts of Staffordshire, especially the Newcastle-under-Lyme area.

7. *The Chester Directory* for 1781 can be seen in the Chester City Record office.

8. The carriers did not only deliver components for clockmakers; they also brought the time with them. We were told that in Bala, up until the end of the last century, the arrival of the carrier was important because he brought with him the correct time, by which the townsfolk regulated their clocks and watches.

9. See Brian Loomes, *White Dial Clocks*, published by David & Charles, Newton Abbot, 2nd Edition, 1981. Chapter 5.

10. Thomas Pennant, *The History of the Parishes of Whiteford and Holywell*, published by B & J White, London, 1796, p206 et seq. Arthur Aikin. *Journal of a Tour through North Wales and part of Shropshire*, London, 1797, Chapter XVI.

11. See Brian Loomes, *White Dial Clocks*, published by David & Charles, Newton Abbot, 2nd Edition, 1981. Chapter 5.

12. Welsh Folk Museum Archives; Will and probate Inventory of Owen Evans, Llanerch-y-medd, Anglesey.

13. For instance *The Calendar of Wynn Papers*, No 922.

14. They are mostly at Grimsthorpe Castle.

15. See Figure 111, p177.

CHAPTER VII
The Lesser Makers and Retailers

This chapter is devoted to short biographies of the other makers and retailers who lived and worked in and around Llanrwst in the 18th and 19th centuries. They are divided loosely, into two categories: (1) the makers and (2) the retailers. It should be made clear at the outset, however, that the distinction is not clear-cut. It will be seen that even during the brass-dial period several so-called makers were buying clocks from other makers and having their own names engraved on the dials. Equally we have already discussed the decline of clockmaking in the town making the point that, whilst after about 1820 the clock and watch makers increasingly operated as retailers, some clocks would have continued to be made in Llanrwst at least until 1850. We feel, however, that it will be helpful to distinguish between the earlier 18th and early 19th century men who were predominantly makers and the many watch and clock makers who, in the last three quarters of the 19th century, operated mainly as retailers.

The Makers

BARKER, John
    See BARKER AND JONES

BARKER AND JONES, Llanrwst.
    Seven long-case clocks were located during the clock survey signed 'Barker and Jones, Llanrwst'. One or two of the dials had been incorrectly restored to read 'Barker and Sons'. All the clocks were from the period 1810-20. There are very few records of John Barker, clockmaker, in the town. In 1809 he married Mary Jones, and William Owen, Watkin Owen's brother, was one of the witnesses to their marriage. A church *maes* or mize was levied in 1812 and "John Barker, Clockmaker", paid 10d. He also witnesses the will of Margaret Owen, Watkin's widow. There can be little doubt that John Barker was a journeyman in the Owen workshop, not least because most of the Barker & Jones clocks have movements with Owen strike-work. He must have left the Owens' workshop some time after Watkin Owen's death to set up as a clockmaker on his own account in partnership with Edward Jones. Edward Jones was a joiner who had produced clock cases for Llanrwst clockmakers since 1800 or earlier. His cases are invariably of good quality and distinctive design. We describe them more fully in the chapter on cases. About the man, however, we know nothing. The partnership produced clocks of noticeably good quality, including a fine, arch-dial example with moon-phase indication. John Barker's name does not appear in the *maes* roll of 1820 and it must be presumed that by that date he had left town or died; neither do we see any more of the handiwork of Edward Jones after this date.

Fig 61: Clock number 271. This Wilson dial on a Watkin Owen clock, enables us to identify the case-maker Edward Jones who was later to go into partnership with John Barker.

EVANS, Moses, Llandogged and Llangernyw. [1]

Only one other clockmaker of any significance ever established himself in or near Llanrwst during the second half of the 18th century; his name was Moses Evans. Unlike several other contemporary clockmakers there is nothing to indicate that he was ever closely connected with the Owens of Llanrwst. Nothing in his clocks suggest that he had been apprenticed to John Owen or had served as a journeyman in his workshop. Yet, apparently, he was able to produce good quality clocks for nearly 40 years in spite of the proximity of the Owens. Moses Evans was not the only member of his family to be involved in clockmaking; we found three fine clocks signed by Owen Evans, presumably his father, and another by Thomas Evans, a clockmaker from Bontuchel who, on the evidence of his clocks, may have been related to him. Moses Evans' name appears on the dials of some 40 clocks located during our survey, 15 with brass dials, 25 with painted dials. Most of his brass-dial clocks come from the common source mentioned in the last chapter which supplied at least half a dozen contemporary North Wales clockmakers.

More research will be required if it is to be established whether the Evans family may have been that source or merely drew many of their clocks from it. Until then it must remain only a possibility, on the evidence of the clocks, that the Evans family supplemented their own sales by providing clocks, or, at the very least, dials to other so called clockmakers for many miles around.

Researching the family history of Moses Evans was, as usual, a frustrating exercise; not only was there a multiplicity of Evans in both Llanddoged and Llangernyw but in the latter village there were two men named Moses Evans, apparently unrelated. Owen Evans, Moses' father, rented a small farm called Ty Gwyn from the Gwydir Estate for an annual rent of £7 1s 0d. Ty Gwyn is in the parish of Llanddoged, a village barely two miles from Llanrwst as the crow flies, but five hundred feet above it and commanding wonderful

Fig 62: Clock number 355, c1815. A Moses Evans clock. The false-plate has a scalloped edge and is signed Walker & Hughes.

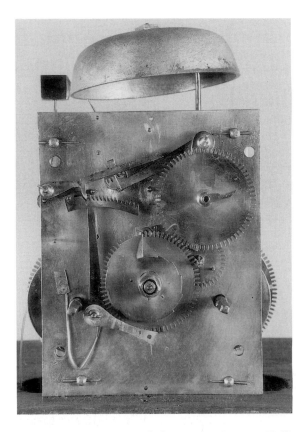

Fig 63: Clock number 355, c1815. Moses Evans' conventional strikework layout is quite different from the Owen system. The large wheel, top right, drives the moon disc.

views of the town and the upper Conwy Valley. The farm itself is small and isolated, a mile or more beyond the village towards Maenan. Today, the buildings that Owen and Moses Evans would have known have been replaced by 19th century ones but some earlier outbuildings seem to have survived. The present occupants have never seen anything to suggest that clockmaking was once carried out there.

In 1734, Owen Evans married Jane Lewis and the record shows that both the bride and groom came originally from Llanrwst. Moses seems to have been the couple's only child. He was baptised on the 25 May 1744. Moses himself married Jane Jones of Llangernyw in 1779 when he was 35. Owen Evans continued to pay rent for Ty Gwyn at least until 1770 but he must then have died or moved away because by 1775 the rent was being paid by Moses and Jane Evans. Moses was not to marry his Jane until 1779 so presumably it was he and his mother who were now the tenants of Ty Gwyn. Unfortunately, for the tidiness of this record there is a fine arched-dial moon-phase clock signed Owen Evans Llanddoget which appears to be dated 1777 so maybe Owen was still alive but had left Ty Gwyn. In due course Moses and his wife Jane left Ty Gwyn in Llanddoget and moved to Llangernyw, Jane's home village, where the records show them to have lived at Pentrewern. Again we are not sure of the exact date of the move but the evidence of both the records and the clocks puts it at about 1785.

Llangernyw lies close to the banks of the River Elwy some 7 miles from Llanrwst on the road to Abergele. The big house of the village was Hafodunos, the ancestral home of the Lloyd family, and nearby was Melai the ancient seat of another distinguished branch of the

Fig 64: Clocks signed by Moses Evans, c1775-1819

	Brass		Painted
Square Dials	11	Square Dials	19
Arched with Moon	1	Arched	1
Arched with Moon			2
Dresser Clock			1
	—		—
	12		23

NB : Five of the clocks are chalk-dated.

Wynn family. Cathrall gives the population of the village as 593 in 1801. [2] There is a farm by the name of Pentrewern on the east bank of the River Elwy close to the bridge that carries the road from the village to Llansannan and Denbigh. Tradition has it that Moses Evans spent the remainder of his life in this farm until his death in 1809 but we have not found any evidence to corroborate this. Pentrewern is also a township of the parish of Llangernyw: so, in describing Moses Evans as coming from Pentrewern the records do not definitely locate him in the farm that carries that name today, but there is every possibility that he did live there.

For the sake of completeness we record that Moses Evans had a son Thomas by his concubine Margaret Jones in 1801, but we have found no record of any other children. To add to the confusion, there was also another Moses Evans, a carpenter, in Llangernyw. He and his wife Catherine had two children baptised in the village, Griffith in 1815 and Robert

Fig 65: Clock number 105. A Moses Evans clock with a dial by Osborne. The case is dated in chalk 1798.

in 1823. Moses Evans II died in 1831 aged 49. There is nothing to connect him with Moses Evans the clockmaker other than his first name, and the fact that he too lived in Pentrewern. Moses Evans our clockmaker died in April 1819 aged 75.

We have studied 35 clocks signed by Moses Evans spanning the period circa 1775-1819. A simple analysis of these is shown in Figure 64 (p121). We found no painted-dial clocks by Moses Evans signed by him in Llanddoged so that all painted dials by him post-date his move to Llangernyw. Of his brass dials all but five are signed in Llanddoget. One brass dial clock of about 1780-85 is signed Moses Evans, Llanrwst. In addition to the clocks by Moses Evans, we found three clocks, all arched-dial moon-phase examples signed Owen Evans, Llanddoged. They give every indication of having come from the same workshop as did another fine clock signed 'Thos Evans, Bontuchel'. Bontuchel is a village on the river Clywedog about 4 miles from Ruthin.

We can safely draw two main conclusions from our examination of the clocks. Firstly, they neither stylistically nor mechanically bear any resemblance to the clocks from the Owen workshop in Llanrwst. We have not had the good fortune to work on as many Moses Evans clocks in our own workshop so any distinguishing features that we can cite are based on superficial examination of clocks in situ in their owners' homes. Generally, however, the movement plates are much thinner than the equivalent Owen plates, as usually are the pillars of which there are invariably four. The slightly tapered pillars with narrow knops appear in the mid 1790s as they did on the Owen clocks, but whether this was merely the fashion of the day, or denoted a common source of bought-in pillars we do not know. One feature of many Moses Evans movements is that the top right-hand pillar (as viewed from the front) is moved downwards and inwards away from the corner of the plates. This was a sensible and not infrequent variation to the standard four pillar movement; there are no wheels to prevent the move and the effect would have been to increase the stiffness of the movement when assembled.

Also, invariably, the Evans strikework is conventional and in no way similar to the Owen system. If Moses Evans had learned his clockmaking in the Owen workshop then he adopted none of the Owen design features and we think it more likely that he was apprenticed elsewhere.

The second conclusion that we can draw from the Evans clocks is that Moses Evans came from exactly the same mould as did the Owens: he produced sophisticated main-stream clocks, bearing no resemblance to the highly individualistic output of a rural craftsman such as Samuel Roberts of Llanfair Caereinion. This is important because Moses Evans, like Samuel Roberts, is sometimes referred to as a farmer clockmaker but there the similarity ends. We have no doubt at all that Moses Evans dealt with exactly the same suppliers, wholesalers and carriers as did the Owens and was exposed to all the same stylistic and commercial influences as they. Whether he depended wholly on clockmaking for his income is a different matter. The number of surviving clocks suggests that he may not have done so and he must therefore have relied on the farm to supplement his income. However, it would be unwise to draw too firm a conclusion in this respect from the number of his clocks that we have found. Our publicity was always directed towards locating Llanrwst clocks and only in the later stages of the survey did we begin to look for clocks by Moses Evans also, so the number of his clocks that we found may not be in the same ratio to the clocks he made as in the case of the Owens. Several of Moses Evans' brass dials were engraved by one hand, the same hand that engraved the dials for Minshul of

Denbigh, Roberts of Trawsfynydd, Jones of Dolwen, Griffith of Beddgelert and, of course, Owen Evans of Llanddoged and Thomas Evans of Bontuchel. Furthermore, almost invariably, the winding holes are incorporated in the intricate engraved designs, which suggests that the engraver worked in or near the workshop where the movements were made. At this stage of our researches we have no alternative but to leave it to the reader to decide whether an Evans workshop could have originated these dials and movements or whether Moses Evans bought them like the others. If it is the latter, then there is a challenging test of detection to be undertaken to locate where that workshop was.

Two factors may have some bearing on the final conclusion. A few (three to be precise) of Moses Evans' dials were not engraved by the same engraver; they were executed by the Owen engraver. The reader may make of this what he will. On the other hand a workshop in Llanddoged or Llangernyw would have been very centrally placed to supply dials and movements to clockmakers in Denbigh, Trawsfynydd, Bontuchel, Pentrefoelas, Dolwen and Beddgelert. Maybe, eventually, a clock or a document will be found that will reveal the truth about the maker of all these similar clocks; until then we can only surmise, but it would be satisfying to establish that it was Moses Evans or one of his family.

In most other respects Moses Evans followed the styles of the times. His painted dials come from the same dial makers and were decorated with the same designs as were those used by the Owens. As we shall see in a later chapter, his clock-case styles were also the same and he obviously shared several case-makers in common with the Owens. All his clocks were 8-day and it is interesting that he made no effort to cut into the Owens' hold on the market by introducing the significantly cheaper 30-hour clock. In one respect, however, he broke ground that, as far as we know, had not been covered either by John or Watkin Owen. He made at least one clock to be incorporated into a grand piece of domestic furniture. The splendid dresser clock made for John Lloyd in 1797 is described in detail in the chapter on special clocks. Other clocks in dressers and cupboards are recorded by Moses Evans, but sadly the examples that we have seen proved to be much later marriages of Moses Evans dials and movements with pieces of furniture. No turret clocks, wall clocks or bracket clocks by Moses Evans have been recorded. A pocket watch by him passed through the London sale-rooms in 1990.

There is one final point requiring comment before leaving the Evans family. We have already referred to Owen Evans whose signature appears on three fine arched-dial moon-phase clocks and whom we assume to have been Moses Evans' father. The late Dr Peate lists another contemporary Owen Evans as working in Llanerchymedd in Anglesey. He is of particular interest to antiquarian horologists because, as we have seen, his will and inventory of goods have survived. The latter document is full of interest. Is it possible that the two Owen Evanses could be one and the same person? This would at least explain the disappearance of the Llanddoged Owen Evans in the early 1770s. The obvious way to answer the question was to find a comparable arch-dial clock signed Owen Evans, Llanerchymedd and compare it with the three Owen Evans, Llanddoged clocks already located. The task was not to prove easy; clocks of any kind by the Anglesey maker were conspicuous by their absence. Then, one day, an antique dealer from a large Midlands city mentioned that he had a dial and movement by ". . . someone called Evans from an unpronounceable Welsh town". We happened to be in the city in question a few days later and called on the dealer. There in a dark corner was a fine brass, arched, dial and movement by Owen Evans, Llanerchymedd! There are two clear recollections of the next

Fig 66: Clock number 31, dated 1790. By Rowland Griffith of Llanrwst. Since Rowland Griffith had been, until this date, a joiner, it seems safe to assume that he made this case.

Fig 67: Clock number 31, dated 1790. By Rowland Griffith, Llanrwst. The most unusual movement of this clock has 'No 1' indistinctly engraved at the foot of the steel front-plate.

ten minutes. First the disappointment of realising that there was no similarity whatsoever between the Llanerchymedd and Llanddoged clocks, and, secondly, the hazards of photographing the dial under the feet of the passers-by on the pavement outside; our flash-gun had broken but it was sunny outside.

GRIFFITH, Rowland, Llanrwst.

The census enumerators' books for the 1841 census gives the age of Rowland Griffith, clockmaker, as 80, which infers that he was born about 1761 but not in Llanrwst or Denbighshire. However, the Llanrwst Burial Register records his death in 1842 aged 84 years, so there is a slight discrepancy. [3]

He appears to have started his working life as a joiner but confusion exists because there may have been more than one joiner called Rowland Griffith. The Gwydir Estate rental records a payment of £32 17s 6d to "Rowland Griffith and Partners" for railings in 1766, [4] when our man would have been only 5 years old! He would still have been only 19 in 1780 when the estate paid Rowland Griffith, joiner, a total of £42 3s 6d for repair work at Gwydir. [5] Payments to Rowland Griffith, joiner appear in the Llanrwst church accounts for 1789 and 1793. The *maes* rolls record payments by Rowland Griffith in 1784 and 1786, by Rowland Griffith, joiner, on a number of occasions between 1788 and 1805 and by Rowland Griffith, clockmaker, in 1812 and 1820. In the case of these *maes* payments there seems no doubt that they were all made by the same man. In 1780, Benedicta, daughter of Rowland Griffith and his wife was baptised in Llanrwst. In 1813, Rowland Griffith, now a widower, married Margaret Hughes. The 1841 census records him as living in Denbigh Street where he was a widower again; the only other people living in the house being William Owen, a clockmaker, and Jane and Elizabeth Owen, both servants. In addition we found three other references to Rowland Griffith. John Jones of Hafod-y-porth, Beddgelert, whose will was proved in 1782, left to his son, inter alia, "A Press Cupboard, lately made by Rowland Griffith". [6] Iolo Morganwg refers to "Rowland Griffith the harp-maker, also a cabinet-maker, a joiner, carpenter, architect, in short a man of *genius* and industry. In his several professions, he has built a great many decent houses in the town in modern style, and has been a very great improver of the town...." [7]

Finally, the *Dictionary of Welsh Biography* has the following entry:

GRIFFITH, ROWLAND - Harpist and harp-maker, a native of Llanrwst. In his old age he lived in one of the almshouses in Llanrwst called the 'Bowls'. Here he made several harps, being the last of the Llanrwst harp-makers.

Clearly, here is fertile ground for future researches. In the meantime we must leave it to the reader to decide how many men called Rowland Griffith lived in the town, or whether one single individual possessed such many and varied accomplishments.

In 1790, Rowland Griffith, the joiner, now nearly 30 years old, produced a most astonishing clock. It is housed in a smart oak case typical of the period and, undoubtedly, is of Llanrwst origin. The very fine 13" painted dial by Wilson displays the maker's name in a particularly intricate cartouche en grisaille; the dial corners have raised, gilded, formal designs. It is the movement, however, which must have a good claim to being unique. The front-plate is of steel with the wheel pivots mounted in large brass bushes that appear to be original. Furthermore, the steel front-plate is significantly larger than the brass back-plate, so that the latter has to sit on a wooden rail mounted on the seat-board.

Fig 68: Clock number 166. A George Jackson clock. There are signs that this clock was Jackson's masterwork. The dial was by Osborne and the case almost certainly by Edward Jones. The similarities in this movement to an Owen front plate are obvious.

Fig 69: Clock 198. A movement by W Owen of Edern on the Lleyn peninsula. The front-plate is stamped 'Ainsworth, Warrington' but, in all other respects this is an Owen of Llanrwst movement.

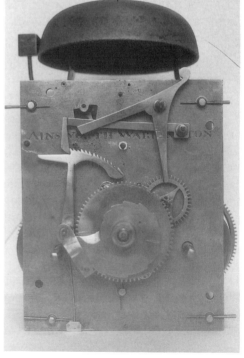

There is no false-plate and the front-plate appears to have been made larger than the back-plate to accommodate the dial feet in its far corners, outside the area that would otherwise have been covered by the plate. The bosses of the conventional steel strikework are elaborately turned. At the foot of the front-plate is the engraved inscription "No 1 1790". This very eccentric movement is generally of very good quality but has no features in common with the Owen movements of the period. The clock, in slightly different circumstances, could well have been an apprentice's master-piece. Whether Rowland Griffith served a full clockmaking apprenticeship in his 20s, and, if so, with whom, we will probably never know.

Having witnessed No1, we waited for No 2 and No 3. Alas, this was not to be. As a clockmaker, Rowland Griffith appears to have been something of a damp squib. Although he apparently worked as a clockmaker until his death in 1842, we were only ever to locate four more clocks by him, all rather mundane examples, conventional in all respects. One imagines that he may, as one of the town's joiners and furniture makers, have been called on regularly to make clock-cases, and that this had given him the idea of learning clockmaking too; clockmaking was, after all, a much more prestigious craft. Thereafter, he may have discovered that competing with Watkin Owen was not so easy after all, and so he reverted to joinery and furniture making, to say nothing of harp making and architecture, at least until after the death of Watkin Owen. It remains a mystery, however, how a man who, for at least 25 years, is listed in trade directories as a clockmaker, and who, for a time, employed a journeyman clockmaker, should have left us a mere handful of clocks and no pocket watches whatsoever. Perhaps, after all, there was only one Rowland Griffith, and his busy life as a joiner, carpenter, harp-maker and architect left too little time for much clockmaking.

JACKSON, George, Llanrwst.

Four clocks signed by George Jackson, Llanrwst, were found during the clock survey. None was dated, but stylistically they suggest a date of 1800 plus or minus 5 years. One of the four is a brass-dial clock of rather homespun appearance. The dial engraving is very much in the style of the Owen engraver of the period, but is probably not by him and may well have been executed by Jackson himself. Of the three painted-dial clocks examined, one is a rather grand 14", arch-dialled, moon-phase clock which has the look of an apprentice's master-piece; the other two are conventional, square, painted dial clocks of the period.

Clearly, all the movements are the work of Jackson, being rather crude and unpractised, but, nevertheless, retaining a good deal of character. The movement plates of one of the clocks are stamped 'Ainsworth, Warrington'. In every case the maker employs his version of Owen strike-work, which suggests strongly that he was a journeyman or apprentice in Watkin Owen's workshop - perhaps a man who made a few clocks in Llanrwst on his own account before leaving the town to work elsewhere.

Dr Peate suggests that Jackson moved to Dolgellau where there are records of a clockmaker of this name from about 1805 onwards. The Dolgellau parish registers record the baptism of "Anne, daughter of George Jackson, Watchmaker and Catherine his wife". However, the Llanrwst registers record the marriage of George Jackson to Ellen Roberts in 1797. The register does not give the profession of the groom, but, presumably, he is the clockmaker. The couple had a daughter, Jane, in 1799 and a son, George, in 1802. If the

Dolgellau and Llanrwst clockmakers are one and the same man, he must have married again. The matter could be settled if a long-case clock of the period, signed by George Jackson, Dolgellau could be found; the presence of Owen strikework would confirm, beyond any doubt, that the Llanrwst clockmaker had moved to Dolgellau.

JONES, Henry, Dolwen, a small village close to the modern town of Colwyn Bay.

Dr Peate records that this maker was also a silversmith and mentions a clock signed by him and dated 1766. The two examples we inspected are from the period 1780-85. The dial and movement of one of these clocks was from the unknown workshop that supplied various clockmakers in North Wales with their clocks at this time.

JONES, John, Llanrwst.

Dr Peate in *Clock & Watch Makers of Wales* mentions at least one clock by this maker with a brass dial which suggests that he was making clocks under his own name by 1805 or earlier. We, for our part, could only find one mention of a John Jones in the Llanrwst records: in April 1816 William, his son by Elizabeth, his wife, was baptized. We did, however, find five long-case clocks, all with painted dials, as well as watches by John Jones. Two of the long-case clock movements had Owen-type strikework albeit with stylistic variations based on the mechanisms normally produced in the Owen workshop. As with George Jackson, John Williams and John Barker, this indicates that John Jones had worked in the Owen workshop in some capacity. The case of one of the watches is hall-marked for the year 1814-15 and the long-case clocks are of the type and style produced in the period 1805-20.

This would be the extent of our knowledge of this maker if it were not for a letter written to Dr Peate in 1951 by William Jones, jeweller and silversmith of Colwyn Bay. The following extract is interesting:

> Your book makes several references to members of my family, and I thought the following brief notes may be of interest to you should an addendum or revised edition of your book be published at any future time.
>
> Of the first generation, I can only offer you what is family tradition, and we have no papers or letters of any kind to confirm it. He was JOHN JONES who lived at Llanfair-Talhaiarn about the year 1820-1825. My mother recalls her father saying that she had married into the family of old John Jones, the *Amseriadurwr* of Llanfair TH. My maternal grandfather died aged 81 in the year 1905. My uncle, William Humphreys Jones, of the fourth generation, still lives at Prestatyn, and tells me that he remembers his father saying that he was the third generation of watchmakers in the family. I can recall my own father's pleasure when I said I would be a watchmaker and he said I would be the fifth generation of watchmakers in the family.

The word *Amseriadurwr* literally means timekeeper or chronologist, but could perhaps be better translated as master clockmaker. There are no documentary records that we have been able to find concerning a clockmaker called John Jones working in Llanfair-Talhaiarn, a village between Llangernyw and Abergele, in the 1820s. It is possible, therefore, that John Jones of Llanrwst moved to Llanfair TH about 1820. [8] Certainly, none of the clocks signed by him in Llanrwst are much later than 1820. For John Jones of Llanfair TH to have merited the title *Amseriadurwr* one would certainly expect clocks to still exist that carry his signature: yet there is no record of any. All this suggests that the *Amseriadurwr* of Llanfair TH and John Jones, Llanrwst may have been the same man. Our efforts to trace John Jones in the Llanfair TH registers were by no means untypical. Between 1817 and 1836 seven men by the name of John Jones were buried in the village churchyard, any of whom may have been the clockmaker - or none.

OWEN, George, Llanrwst.

The third son of John Owen, George was born in 1753. He worked in his father's workshop in the 1770s. His engraved doodles are as frequent as those of his brother, Samuel. He also scratched his name on one or two movements just like any other repairer. Like Samuel he appears to have given up clockmaking after his father's death. No clock signed by George Owen has been recorded.

OWEN, John, Conwy.

A clockmaker of this name was buried in the town in April 1790, but nothing more is known of him, nor have any of his clocks been recorded.

OWEN, Samuel.

Born in 1751, Samuel Owen was the second son of John Owen, clockmaker of Llanrwst, and elder brother of George and Watkin Owen. Samuel Owen worked in his father's workshop in the 1770s and the frequent engraved doodles on the clock movements is evidence of his existence there. On his father's death in 1776 he soon gave up clockmaking and became a surgeon in Llanrwst. In 1779, he married Mary Rogers and died in 1803.

Two clocks with square, brass dials signed by Samuel Owen have been found. Both have engraved seconds circles and a distinctive engraving style. The movements are typical of the output of the Owen workshop in the 1770s. It is suggested that these two clocks were produced after his father's death, but before Samuel left clockmaking, leaving the way clear for his younger brother Watkin.

OWEN, W, Edeyrn, (Edern). Edern is a small village on the Lleyn perninsula.

We include this maker here on the evidence of a single clock so signed that has passed through our workshop. It had a painted dial of about 1805-10 and a movement made either in Watkin Owen's workshop, or perhaps was the work of someone who had worked there. The case in which it is housed is a typical Llanrwst design for that period.

ROBERTS, John, Trawsfynnydd, in north Merionethshire.

During our clock survey, we found two clocks with brass dials and three with painted dials carrying the name of this maker. These all appear to date from the mid 1780s. One of the brass-dial clocks came from the unknown workshop that was producing clocks for several clockmakers in North Wales at this time.

It is only our conjecture that this was, in reality, the same John Roberts that occupied Tyn-y-pwll in Llanrwst for a number of years, leaving in about 1784. He may, therefore, have been a journeyman clockmaker working for the Owens. The cases housing these Trawsfynnydd clocks are interesting and distinctive. At first glance they appear to be standard Llanrwst cases for the period, but on closer examination it will be seen that the frieze in the hood above the dial is very shallow, sometimes being little more than 1" in depth much less than on the equivalent Llanrwst case. On the evidence of these five examples this is a reliable indicator of a Trawsfynnydd case of the 1780s.

THOMAS, John, Pentrefoelas.

We found one clock signed by this maker. We cannot be sure whether this is the same clock mentioned by Peate who refers to a clock with a silvered chapter-ring whereas the clock we inspected had a dial all of polished brass, although the silvering may have disappeared in the intervening years. The dial and movement of the clock that we inspected were by the workshop that provided so many makers in North Wales with their clocks in the 1780s. The movement originally had repeat work. The date indicator is a disc behind a lunette opening in the dial. The case is a typical example of Llanrwst cases of about 1785. No personal details are known of John Thomas.

UNIDENTIFIED WORKSHOP.

This is the name we have given to a single workshop which appears to have supplied brass dials and movements to at least nine makers in North Wales during the period 1770-88.

That the dials are the work of a single engraver there can be little doubt. In many examples, too, the winding holes in the dial are incorporated in the engraved designs and the movements themselves bear a strong superficial similarity to each other. All this evidence suggests that the movements came with the dials. Admittedly these preliminary conclusions are based on examinations of the clocks in situ in private homes; a more detailed examination of several of these clocks in the workshop could put the matter beyond doubt. So far we have found clocks from the Unidentified Workshop bearing the names of the following makers:

> Owen Evans, Llanddoged
> Moses Evans, Llanddoged
> Thomas Evans, Bontuchel
> Evans & Roberts, Amlwch
> Minshul, Denbigh
> Henry Jones, Dolwen
> John Roberts, Trawsfynnydd
> Thomas Griffith, Beddgelert
> John Thomas, Pentrefoelas

We have also come across an unsigned dial and movement from the Unidentified Workshop and a splendid arched-dial clock also from the workshop signed "Griffith Owen, Mill Wright". Whether this means that private individuals could purchase clocks from the workshop with their names on the dial, or whether this particular mill-wright was branching out, we leave the reader to decide.

The identity of this workshop remains a mystery and represents a challenge to future horological researchers. Two of the clocks have a date hand concentric with the hour and minute hands indicating the date by numbers engraved on the inside of the chapter-ring. This is a method of date indication most commonly found in Cheshire and may, therefore, be taken as a clue to the whereabouts of this workshop.

It may or may not be significant that various members of the Evans family feature so significantly amongst the clockmakers obtaining clocks from this workshop. Before jumping to the conclusion that one of the Evans' might be the clockmaker in question, it is important to remember that not all their brass dials appear to have come from this single source. Until the matter is finally resolved the identity of this workshop remains, perhaps, the most fascinating mystery in Welsh horological history. Certainly, it calls into question the status of some so-called 'clockmakers' in North Wales and whether they should continue to be ranked as such. Perhaps some of them were, in fact, agents, retailers or repairers who, from time to time, merely bought and sold clocks actually made elsewhere.

WILLIAMS, John, Llansantffraid.

The only evidence we have for the existence of this maker is a single brass-dial clock signed 'John Williams, Llansantffraid'. Llansantffraid is, today, much better known as Glan Conwy. As with the single example by Robert Jackson, the dial is highly reminiscent of the brass dials engraved in Watkin Owen's workshop about 1790-95. This clock is of good quality. The spandrels are the standard Question-Mark pattern and the engraving good, if uninspired. The strike-work is a rather clumsy version of the Owen mechanism, executed in brass. The long-case in which the movement is housed is a standard Llanrwst pattern for this period. On the evidence of the clock, John Williams must have had connections with the Owen workshop: possibly he had been an apprentice there.

The Retailers

BERRY, R, Llanrwst.

At least three generations of this family have traded as watchmakers and jewellers in Llanrwst. R Berry apparently established himself at Coventry House in the last quarter of the 19th century. A direct descendant of his was still in the same business in the mid 1980s.

DANIEL, Robert, Pentrefoelas.

There is a watch-case paper in the Welsh Folk Museum, bearing Robert Daniel's name and the date 1872. Apparently, Robert Daniel was a tailor who dealt in clocks and watches as a sideline.

DAVIES, David, Llanrwst.

The Llanrwst registers for 1855 refer to this otherwise unknown clockmaker.

DAVIES, E and Sons, Llanrwst.

Peate records a watch-case paper dated about 1900.

DAVIES, Pierce, Llanrwst.

The 1861 census returns record a clockmaker of this name living with his father, William Davies, a nail maker, in Scotland Street. Peate lists a Pierce Davies as a clockmaker in Market Street, Abergele for the period 1868-87. They are probably one and the same.

DAVIES, Samuel, Llanrwst.

Slater's Directory for 1850 lists Samuel Davies under clockmakers and gives his address as Scotland Street. The 1851 census enumerators' books describe him as a watchmaker, give his age as 26 and record that he was living with his mother, Elizabeth, a pauper. No surviving clock or watch by Samuel Davies has been recorded.

DAVIES, Theophilus, Llanrwst.

The first reference to the presence of Theophilus Davies in Llanrwst is in the 1851 census returns where his age is given as 30 and his place of birth as Barmouth; his wife Hannah came from Llanrwst. They had three daughters, Mary, Matilda and Hannah. In 1851, the family address is given as Talybont. Seven years later they had moved to Little Bridge Street, and by 1871 they were in Watling Street. In 1876 Theophilus Davies was back in

Fig 70: A clock by Theophilus Davies, c1860. The corners contain a rendition of the Four Seasons. The falseplate has no maker's name.

Bridge Street.

The name of Theophilus Davies appeared on more than a dozen long-case clocks located in our survey. Without exception, they are the large, wide, florid, so called Yorkshire clocks of the third quarter of the 19th century. In at least two of the cases were address labels, evidence that the cases had been consigned to Davies by rail via Bangor and Conwy. These cases are thought to have originated from Anglesey.

Theophilus Davies and his family seem to have left the town about 1880.

EDWARDS, Cornelius, Llanrwst.

The 1881 census enumerators' returns list a 20-year-old clockmaker of this name in Watling Street. He was born in St Asaph.

EVANS, George Gray, Penmachno.

We found two long-case clocks of about 1870 signed by George Gray Evans.

GRIFFITH, R, Penmachno.

Peate records the existence of a long-case clock signed by him, but gives no further details.

HUGHES, Richard Pritchard, Llanrwst.

About 1883, Richard Hughes acquired the business of Robert Williams in Denbigh Street.

By 1890, he had moved to a shop in Willow Street, which is today occupied by an estate-agent, at the top of Station Road. His advertisements state that he was a watchmaker, jeweller and optician. He later moved to Caernarfon.

JONES, David, Llanrwst.

A leading watchmaker in the town during the first half of the 20th century. Still remembered as 'Dafydd Wats' by surviving contemporaries, his shop was at Berlin House.

JONES, Edward, Llanrwst.

We have never seen a watch or clock signed Edward Jones, Llanrwst, but there is a watch-case paper in the collection of the Welsh Folk Museum at St Fagans, dated 1838. The 1841 census returns give his age as 45 and confirm that he was born in Denbighshire. This Edward Jones would be far too young to have been the same Edward Jones who was a joiner and a clock-case maker. Edward Jones had a wife Jane, and five children, Anne, Mary, Margaret, Edward and Ellen. Edward Jones and his wife were Wesleyan Methodists and their children were baptised in the town's Wesleyan Methodist Chapel. According to *Robson's Directory* for 1840, which lists him as a watch and clock maker, Edward Jones lived in Denby [*sic*] Street. The family must have left Llanrwst shortly afterwards as there are no further references to them.

JONES, H, Conwy.

Various trade directories record H Jones as working in Uppergate Street about 1868-74.

JONES, John, Conwy.

A directory for 1868 records him as working in Castle Street with his brother Thomas (*qv*). There is a watch-case paper in the Welsh Folk Museum issued by John and Thomas Jones.

JONES, Robert, Conwy.

Directories record his working in High Street and Castle Street about 1835-44. We found one long-case clock of similar date. It is tempting to look for a relationship with Thomas Jones (*qv*) but further research will be necessary.

JONES, Thomas, Conwy.

The trade directories record him working in Castle Street about 1874-87. Thomas Jones was working in Castle Street in 1868 with his brother John. See also Robert Jones.

JONES, William, Llanrwst.

We found three long-case clocks of the period 1830-50 signed by this maker. In 1816 William, son of John Jones, watchmaker, and Elizabeth his wife was baptised and this is probably this clockmaker. He may also have been a joiner as there are records of a joiner of this name in Llanrwst at the time.

McGILL, William A, Llanrwst.

Slaters Directory for 1880 lists a watch and clockmaker of this name living in George Street.

OWEN, Elizabeth, Llanrwst.

See William Owen.

OWEN, Griffith, Llanrwst.

Griffith Owen was Llanrwst's leading watch and clockmaker for 60 years. He started in business there about 1840-42 and lived and worked at Greenwich House, Denbigh Street, until his death in 1902. Griffith's father, himself called Griffith, lived at Bodesi, a small, isolated farm high up in the Ogwen Valley near Capel Curig. In 1807 he married Jane Williams of Llanrychwyn and their third son, Griffith, was born at Bodesi in 1818. Shortly afterwards, the family moved to Penyrallt in Llanrychwyn parish. The Griffith Owens were in no way related to Watkin Owen's family. [9]

The first mention of Griffith Owen in Llanrwst is in *Pigot's Directory* for 1840, where he is listed as a watch and clock maker working in Denbigh Street. In spite of this, he is more generally thought to have started in business in 1842. This is the year that old Rowland Griffith died, and it seems likely that the young Griffith Owen acquired his business. Certainly, this would account for the claim made frequently in Griffith Owen's trade advertisements that his business was established in 1791, the year after Rowland Griffith made his clock 'No 1'.

On the departure of Humphrey Owen from the town in 1845 or 1846, Griffith Owen took over the clock winding and maintenance contracts for the church, the Gwydir Estate and the Town Hall. From the very earliest days he seems to have prospered and his position as the town's leading watch and clock maker was never to be seriously challenged for the remainder of the century. Many more long-case clocks and watches carrying the name of Griffith Owen have survived than the output of all of his contemporaries counted together. He did not confine his activities to watch and clock making and retailing, however. As was the widespread practice of watch and clock-makers of that period, he also conducted business as a jeweller. In addition, he practiced as an optician and specialised in fishing tackle: he sold the fishing licences issued by the Gwydir Estate. His advertisements also proclaimed him to be a general ironmonger. He did not, however, double up as a public-house keeper as a number of the other tradesmen in the town were to do. This was hardly likely because, for many years until his death, Griffith Owen was a much respected elder of the great Seion chapel in Station Road. His chapel connections seem to have stood him in good stead because he provided clocks for most of the many chapels in the valley. Contemporary photographs show him to have been a handsome man with more than a passing resemblance to prime minister Gladstone.

About 1844 he married Grace Roberts and the couple had a very large family, no less than 14 children being born in the years between 1845 and 1869. Their eldest son, Hugh, became a watch and clock maker, first in Llanidloes, and then in Bangor. Another son, Edward G Owen, also trained as a watchmaker but died at the early age of 19 years. All the children were given a good education, one becoming a doctor, another taking a university degree in engineering. In the 1890s, the name of the business was changed to Griffith Owen and Son, when Griffith took his son Robert Griffith Owen into partnership.

Griffith Owen died on 30 March 1902, aged 84; his widow died four years later, aged 80. They were buried in the graveyard at the Seion chapel in Llanrwst where their gravestone is still to be seen. The business continued in the town until it was wound up shortly after the Second World War.

More than 30 long-case clocks by Griffith Owen are recorded in our survey, covering the period 1840-80. It is noticeable that the clocks are, usually, of good quality and certainly, on average, they were of better quality than those sold by his contemporaries. More than a dozen watches by him have been recorded as well as numerous dial-clocks in the chapels.

Fig 71: Victorian Llanrwst's leading watch and clockmaker, Griffith Owen with his wife and family.
The photograph was probably taken in the early 1870s. [R Idloes Owen]

We are greatly indebted to Mr R Idloes Owen for much information about his great-grandfather, Griffith Owen.

OWEN, Humphrey, Llanrwst.
Humphrey Owen was not, apparently, related to the Watkin Owen family. He appears to have come to Llanrwst in about 1840 and the 1841 census gives his age as 25 and records that he lived on the north side of Denbigh Street. Significantly, he took over the more prestigious clock winding contracts previously held by William Owen, and this may suggest that he had bought the latter's business. If so, he may have acquired Tyn-y-pwll also. It is interesting to note that the census reference places it on the north side of Denbigh Street. Certainly, for the next few years the account books show that Humphrey Owen wound and maintained the German clock at Gwydir, and the dial-clock in the church.
In 1842 a son, William, was born to Humphrey Owen, watchmaker, and Elizabeth his wife. The trade directories for 1844 list him as working in Denbigh Street but, he was not to stay in the town for long and, after a few years, he moved to Caernarfon where Peate lists him as working in Bangor Street from 1856 to 1874 and in Eastgate, as late as 1890. In 1846, Griffith Owen took over the clock winding contracts for the Gwydir Estate and Llanrwst church, and this may coincide with the departure of Humphrey Owen. During our survey we located a few long-case clocks signed 'H Owen', all typical of the 1840s. We have neither heard of nor seen any watches carrying his name.

OWEN, Robert Griffith, Llanrwst.
Robert Griffith Owen was born in 1864, the eleventh child of Griffith and Grace Owen.

He was taken into partnership by his father in the early 1890s and he ran the business for some years after the latter's death. However, by 1920 he was practicing as an optician in Llandudno and living at Brooklands, Lloyd Street in that town. He died in 1926.

OWEN, Thomas, Llanrwst.

Dr Peate records a single long-case clock by this maker but we have found no clocks carrying his name nor any other references to him.

OWEN, William, Llanrwst.

The 1841 census records that a William Owen, clockmaker, aged 25, was living in the house of Rowland Griffith in Denbigh Street, Llanrwst, and that he had been born in Denbighshire. Ten years later he was described as a "watchmaker" and was living in the house of a miner, William Davies, in Scotland Street, Llanrwst where he is listed as a "visitor". Presumably, in reality, William Owen was a journeyman clockmaker.

William Owen, the younger brother of Watkin Owen had a son William born in 1815 and this may be the same person. The William Davies, with whom he was living, may be the same William Davies that is described as a "nail-maker" in the 1861 census.

OWEN, William, Llanrwst.

The 1841 census lists a William Owen, aged 40, as a watchmaker. He lived in Little Bridge Street, Llanrwst, with Elizabeth Owen, aged 15, and Henry Parry, aged 20, both also listed as watchmakers: presumably, all three of them were actually employed by one of the town's clock or watch makers.

PARRY, Henry, Llanrwst.

See William Owen above.

PARRY, Robert, Llanrwst.

In the collections at the Welsh Folk Museum there is a silver hunter watch signed "Robert Parry, Llanrwst" with the hall-mark for 1863. We have seen no other reference to him.

PARRY-JONES, J, Llanrwst.

We have seen a single watch signed "J Parry-Jones, Berlin House, Llanrwst.'" The hallmarks were not recorded but we would give a tentative date of about 1870-90. Peate lists a John Parry-Jones in Aberystwyth in the period 1868-87. Berlin House was later the shop of David Jones, watchmaker and jeweller of Llanrwst.

PETCH, Alfred, Conwy.

Directories record him working in Castle Street about 1887-90.

ROBERTS, C, Llanrwst.

Peate lists a clockmaker of this name. He is recorded as a subscriber to the volume of poems *Grawn Awen* by W Williams, 1826. We have found no other reference to him.

ROBERTS, Edward, Llanrwst.

The Denbighshire Postal Directory for 1885 lists a watch and clock maker, Edward Roberts, in Denbigh Street, Llanrwst.

ROBERTS, John, Llanrwst.
Directories for the period 1887-90 list a watch and clock maker of this name in Denbigh Street.

ROBERTS, Robert, Llanrwst.
Peate records a single long-case clock by this maker.

THOMAS, Moses, Conwy.
The directories record him working in Castle Street, Conwy town, about 1874.

TURNER, Thomas, Llanrwst.
The Llanrwst parish church registers for 1836 record the birth of a daughter, Elizabeth, to Thomas Turner, clockmaker, and his wife Mary. This is the only reference to him that we have found. Presumably he was a journeyman.

WILLIAMS, Ann, Penmachno.
The directories record her in Penmachno in about 1880. In reality she was, presumably, the widow of Matthew Williams [qv].

WILLIAMS, Matthew, Penmachno.
The directories record Matthew Williams as working in 1874. We have found a single long-case clock carrying his name which appears to have been made at least ten years earlier than this solitary reference.

WILLIAMS, Owen, Llanrwst.
Owen Williams was apprenticed to Richard Pritchard Hughes (qv) in Station Road, Llanrwst. He then spent some time in Holyhead as an improver before returning to establish his own clock and watch making business in Llanrwst. He built a new shop in the town at the top of Station Road on the corner opposite R P Hughes' old shop. The shop replaced part of the old Crown Inn and, in consequence, was known as the Crown Buildings. On his death, his son, W Scriven Williams, to whom we are greatly indebted for much of this information, presented the numerous watches left by customers in his father's workshop for repair but never reclaimed, to the Welsh Folk Museum at St Fagans. The name of Owen Williams is found on many dial-clocks from the early years of the 20th century, and on watches.

WILLIAMS I, Robert, Llanrwst.
The first clockmaker of this name came to Llanrwst in the early 1840s and is recorded by the trade directories as working in Denbigh Street. He was born at Llangernyw, in about 1815. The Llangernyw registers for that year show that two Robert Williams were born: one was the son of Peter and Elizabeth Williams of Cefn Isa; the other of Robert and Elizabeth Williams of Hafodty.
His wife, Margaret, came from Llanrwst and, by 1845, the couple had a son Robert Thomas, daughter Margaret, and two more sons, John and Evan. Robert Williams died in 1861, aged 41 followed by his wife a year later. They were buried in the churchyard of the new St Mary's church, Llanrwst, where their stone still survives.
We found ten clocks by him during our clock survey and there is a watch in the collection of the Welsh Folk Museum with the hall-mark for 1860. Inside the case of an arch-dial moon-phase clock by Robert Williams we found the following receipt:

Llanrwst, 17th September 1860
Mr. Robt. Roberts Bought of Robt. Williams

	£	s	d
A Arch Moon Clock	6	0	0

Warranted for Seven Years
Received the above sum.
[Signed across a stamp] Robert Williams

It is unlikely that the £6 would have included the handsome oak case. A similar clock would have cost much the same a hundred years earlier. See also ROBERT WILLIAMS II.

WILLIAMS II, Robert, Llanrwst.

At the time of his father's death, in 1861, Robert Williams II would have been only 15 years old but, somehow, he managed to continue the business despite the fact that his mother was to die in 1862. Ten years later, in 1871, the census shows that he had married, and that Robert's sister Margaret and brother Evan, who were still at school, were living in his house. We have located two clocks signed "Robert Williams" which, in all probability, were made by Robert Williams II. *Slater's Directory* of 1883 lists his wife Ellen Williams and not Robert himself. This suggests that, by this date, Robert had died and that his widow was continuing the business. The business was eventually sold and was continued by R P Hughes.

Fig 72: A clock by Robert Williams, Llanrwst from the middle years of the 19th century. Dialmaker unknown.

Fig 73: The shop of Owen Williams, at Crown Buildings, Station Road (Stryd y Moch), Llanrwst, c1900. Owen Williams is standing on the left.

NOTES

1. Llangernyw was often spelt Llangerniew in the 18th and early 19th century.

2. *The History of North Wales*, written and compiled by William Cathrall, printed in Manchester by J Gleave and Son, 1928, Vol II, p165.

3. The census enumerators stated ages to the nearest 5 years, hence the apparent discrepancy. See E Higgs, *Making Sense of the Census*. London HMSO, 1989 (Public Record Office Handbook, No 23) p68.

4. This rental is in the Ancaster Papers at the Lincolnshire County Record Office - 2 ANC 6/134-141.

5. The rental for 1780 is in Grimsthorpe Castle.

6. Quoted by L Twiston-Davies and H J Lloyd-Johnes in *Welsh Furniture, An Introduction*, published by the University of Wales Press, Cardiff, 1950, p3.

7. *Transactions*, Denbighshire Historical Society, 16, 1967, 'Iolo Morganwg in Denbighshire' extracts from his itinerary in 1799. Transcribed by Mr Elizabeth Williams, p98.

8. Llanfair TH is the commonly used abbreviation for Llanfair Talhaiarn.

9. The family tree of Griffith Owen can be seen in Appendix IV.

CHAPTER VIII
Llanrwst Clock Cases

When John Owen arrived in Llanrwst in about 1745, his craft, clockmaking, was new to the town. Young though he was, he had to start entirely from scratch and there was no one in the town who could have been of much assistance to him. The blacksmiths were workers in metal and to that extent may have been able to contribute something but most of them were very much at the heavy end of the trade and would have had to be taught new techniques before they could make any significant contribution to clockmaking. Indeed, as we have seen in an earlier chapter, John Owen's earliest clocks indicate that it was several years before the young clockmaker had fully established his workshop and had developed his own distinctive style as a craftsman.

When it came to the timber cases to house the clocks that he made, there would have been no such problem. There was already a well established tradition of furniture making in the town and the surrounding villages. John Owen would have had to do little more than demonstrate his requirements; the materials and the craftsmanship were readily and abundantly available.

The origins of furniture making in Llanrwst are unknown, but we do know that it had developed beyond the making of simple domestic items perhaps two hundred years before the advent of clockmaking. When, in 1921, the entire contents of the Lower Gwydir house were sold, some of the finest and most richly embellished manorial furniture ever made in Wales came under the hammer. The introduction to the sale catalogue [1] sums up the importance of the lots on offer as follows:

> It may be safely said that it is very rarely that collectors have the offer of so many items, at one time, of such antiquity and of such undoubted authenticity as those now catalogued. It is an established fact that the majority of the English [sic] furniture of antique interest now offered was made expressly for the Wynn family, for the Castle, at the period of which the several pieces are typical, the majority of the oak work having been made on the estate. . .

There is more in this vein and, although the modern scholar might wish to know more of the evidence for some of the claims, the illustrations in the catalogue leave little doubt that they were substantially justified.

Sadly, the Gwydir furniture is now scattered, and the present whereabouts of very few of the items is known: even the sumptuous oak panelling was stripped from the rooms of the house. [2] Fortunately, the sale catalogue and other printed sources have left us with a good record of the appearance of the house and its furniture. Studies of the illustrations and descriptions leave no reason to doubt that many of the finest oak pieces were made by local craftsmen.

Most of the Gwydir furniture was so grand as to be princely rather than manorial, and, certainly, it demonstrated the standard of craftsmanship to which the Wynn family had access. Whilst they might purchase their plate, furnishing fabrics and other smaller

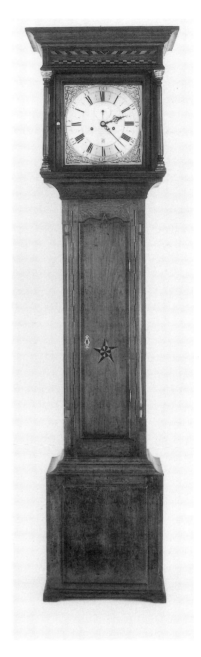

Fig 74: Clock number 627, c1750-55. An early John Owen case in which oak is used throughout, including the solid caddy-top. The otherwise simple design is lifted by the cock-beading on the door, the inlay on the door and the pencil-rounds on the front corners of the trunk. Note also the cresting to the hood.

Fig 75: Clock number 28, c1760-65. A very fine case housing a John Owen clock. This elaborately cross-banded and inlaid oak case was the work of the same joiner who made the case for the Musical Clock (see Chapter X). The original pale green glass in the hood door is retained by small oak wedges driven into slots, a rare feature.

Fig 76: Clock number 575. A fine oak case, cross-banded in oak stained dark, for a John Owen clock. The gilt-wood finials are modern replacements of the correct pattern. The skirting is also modern. Compare this case with the solid mahogany case of the Titley clock in Chapter X.

Fig 77: Clock number 642, c1770-75. A typical case of the 1770s. Note how thin the door and plinth panel have become resulting in both splitting. The feet are probably replacements.

Fig 78: Clock number 14 by John Owen. A good example of a Llanrwst 'architectural' case from the early 1770s. The case feet and the brass finials are modern. Note how the profile of the top of the trunk door is repeated on the plinth panel - a common feature.

Fig 79: A very rare mahogany case from Llanrwst, c1772-76. Its original brass-dialled clock by John Owen was, sadly, vandalised so the case now houses a painted dial and movement by Watkin Owen.

Fig 80: Clock number 75. This typical Llanrwst oak case from the late 1770s is chalk-dated 1777. Note the architectural pediment and the very prominent medullary rays in the applied plinth panel. Similar thin 'slapped-on' panels were also a feature of the Llanrwst dressers of this period.

Fig 81: Clock number 493, c1778. Another case from the late 1770s, housing a Watkin Owen clock. Note the typical ogee bracket feet which have so often been lost and incorrectly replaced.

luxuries in far-off London, [3] it would have been impractical for them to obtain much of their furniture from suppliers so far from home.

Today, the items of furniture for which the Llanrwst district is best known are the *cwpwrdd tridarn* and the dresser which have survived in great number. The court-cupboard or *cwpwrdd deuddarn* of the 16th and 17th centuries gave way in parts of North Wales to the grander three tier version, known as the *cwpwrdd tridarn*. Llanrwst seems to have been at the centre of their production and many of the finest came from this district. The *tridarn* was part ceremonial, part utilitarian, the kind of item presented to a couple on their marriage, or to mark some other special occasion. Frequently, they are dated and bear the initials of the recipients. It is thought that the *tridarn* then evolved into the familiar dresser form in the second quarter of the 18th century, dressers of this early period deriving many features from the *tridarn* such as the wide canopy and the turned droppers.

As the 18th century progressed the dresser lost its ceremonial connotation and increasingly became a work-a-day and domestic item, but, nevertheless, remained one of the most important items of furniture in any house. Inventories of the period show that the more well-to-do houses would have had a dresser, a linen-press (often en suite with the dresser) and a bureau in addition to tables, chairs and all the more essential but mundane items; and, of course, a long-case, weight-driven clock.

This is not the place for a detailed discussion of Welsh domestic furniture of that period. Suffice it to say that much of the finest and most distinctive was produced in and around Llanrwst by men who, whilst producing vernacular furniture of character and quality, never quite emulated the sophistication and exotic materials of the fashionable cabinet makers in some English towns. And so it was that they were to prove willing and able to apply their distinctive skills and style to the countless clock cases that John Owen, his successors and their various customers needed to house their clock movements.

Country furniture at that time, whether manorial or work-a-day, was made by joiners. [4] Most, if not all joiners, would have made furniture, many of them specialising in particular items. We know the names of many of these joiners from the registers, rentals and *maes* rolls, but, as with the clockmakers, we know very little about their personalities, and it is only on rare occasions that we are able to ascribe a particular piece to a specific joiner by name. However, as with the clockmakers, we have many fine examples of their work to study and to record, and, as a result, we can draw a number of conclusions with reasonable degrees of confidence.

It is clear, for instance, that a hierarchy existed amongst the joiners, the most skilled and fashionable being entrusted with the production of the better, more expensive pieces whilst the work of others was much more mundane and sometimes, even primitive in nature. We know this because it soon becomes possible to recognise the work of the individual craftsmen, not just by the style of the individual pieces but also by the individual quirks and characteristics that they developed.

We know, too, that the clock cases were made by these very same men. So similar, indeed, are the construction techniques and design features, that, sometimes, it appears that the clock cases were made as a part of a set comprising clock, dresser and linen press. This fact should, incidentally, be of considerable significance when, eventually, scholars come to study vernacular Welsh furniture in more detail, because clock cases can quite often be dated whereas the furniture usually cannot and this should help in building up a framework of dates for the furniture.

Finally, it is of considerable significance that there are signs that the long-cases, like the clock movements themselves, were constructed in batches, at least from about 1770 onwards.

We do know the names of one or two joiners who also made clock cases. Rowland Griffith was a joiner who became a clockmaker. Presumably, the making of clock cases gave him the opportunity to observe at first hand the prestigious craft of clockmaking and tempted him to diversify, and, thus, to be in the position to provide the fully completed clock, not just the case. He operated as a clockmaker in Llanrwst for nearly fifty years, but it seems that his experience did not accord with this theory because only a handful of his clocks have been found. Probably, he continued to derive most of his income from joinery even if he did find it more prestigious to call himself a clockmaker.

There was another clock-case maker whose work became familiar long before we knew his name. We came to recognise his craftsmanship by its quality and by his own distinctive preferences for the use of dentil mouldings and brass case ornaments. Finally, we discovered a remarkable clock that is signed on its painted dial not just "Watkin Owen", but also "Edward Jones, Joiner". Whether this clock was made for a customer who wanted the name of the case maker to be recorded in addition to that of the clockmaker or whether the clock belonged to Edward Jones, himself, we shall never know. We do know, however, that the case exhibits all those characteristics that had become so familiar and that, at last, we had identified their maker. Later, Edward Jones went into partnership with John Barker the clockmaker. [5]

We think other joiners gained access to the ranks of the clockmakers not by being qualified as such, but by buying dials and movements and selling them in cases of their own manufacture. Samuel Roberts of Llanfair Caereinion, on the evidence of his account book, sold a number of clocks to individual joiners and casemakers who, presumably, inserted them in cases of their own making before selling them. [6] If it was reasonable for joiners to diversify by selling clock cases, equally it would be an obvious move for the clockmakers to diversify into case making. We cannot adduce positive proof that the Owens made cases for their own clocks, but there is some convincing, circumstantial evidence that they did so. Furthermore, it is just the sort of thing that one would expect Watkin Owen, in particular, to do. Watkin Owen's brother, David, was a joiner often employed by both the parish church and by the Gwydir estate: hence the necessary skills existed within the family. We know, also, that from about 1770 onwards, clock cases were often produced in batches and increasingly that their production became concentrated into two or three workshops. Perhaps the most intriguing piece of evidence, however, is the fact that in 1794 the church paid Watkin Owen 5s 6d for a deal plank. [7] It was, furthermore, a plank imported from Riga in the Baltic. [8] From about 1780 onwards the oak back-boards in the clock cases had begun to be replaced by very wide deal boards, undoubtedly imported. In so small a place as Llanrwst the churchwardens, in acquiring a piece of timber, would have had no need of a middle man. This suggests that they bought timber from Watkin Owen because deal planks were part of his stock-in-trade. Until firm evidence of the making of clock cases by the Owens is found, our interpretation must remain conjectural and based on circumstantial evidence. Certainly it seems likely that they made clock cases as well as clock dials and movements.

Just as there was no shortage of craftsmen to build the cases, equally, there was a ready supply of the basic raw materials. In particular, oak grew in abundance, especially on the

Fig 82: Clock number 530. A Watkin Owen case from the early or mid 1780s, badly in need of restoration. The clock has lost its architectural pediment, its ogee bracket feet and is decidedly lop-sided. The chequer-board frieze and door and plinth panel mouldings indicate that this was once a high quality case.

Fig 83: Clock number 324. A late Llanrwst architectural case from the mid 1790s, housing a Watkin Owen clock. Note how in this style of case the architectural pediment is no longer superimposed on a continuous cornice but is integral with the now broken cornice. The skirting replaces ogee bracket feet.

Fig 84: Clock number 478, c1800. A fine example of a late Llanrwst architectural case housing a Watkin Owen clock. The fretted frieze, mouldings to the door and plinth and original ogee bracket feet are all quality features. The gilt wood flambeaux finials are original.

Fig 85: Clock number 325. A fine and rare case from Watkin Owen's last five years, now in need of expert restoration. Fruit-wood is used throughout, the only such case we ever found.

Fig 86: Clock number 569. This Llanrwst case from the mid-1780s houses a clock by Moses Evans. The embossed paper frieze is the only example so far found.

Fig 87: Clock number 283, c1810-15. A late Llanrwst swan-necked case of excellent quality, probably made by Edward Jones. Note the short door and simulated panel beneath it. The brass case ornaments and dentil mouldings are typical of Edward Jones. The clock is by William Owen.

Fig 88: Clock number 355, c1815. Another Edward Jones case, this time housing a clock by Moses Evans.

Fig 89: A much later case, probably c1850, but still very much a product of Llanrwst in the late Llanrwst swan-necked style. The clock is by Robert Williams of Llanrwst.

hillsides behind Gwydir. Indeed, in the times before conifer plantations gradually took over, oak was the dominant tree in the district and harvesting it provided a livelihood for many of its inhabitants. Not only was oak universally used for building and for furniture making, but there was a steady demand for large oak timbers, throughout the 18th century, for ship building. In 1747 the Gwydir Estate sold more than £4,000 worth of oak, elm and ash to timber merchants from Liverpool. [9] Thus, by the time oak was needed for clock cases it was still readily available locally, but, as the century progressed, it became less plentiful and was of inferior quality. From the surviving clock cases it is clear that, by 1800, imported oak from the Baltic began to be used. In John Owen's time, however, locally grown oak was still the staple material for furniture making in Llanrwst, and, naturally, this included clock cases.

The use of other timbers for clock cases was very much rarer. We have located approximately 500 Llanrwst clocks in their original cases and, of these, one was in a case of yew-tree, one in a fruit-wood case, three in pine cases and three in mahogany. [10] This does not include the later Victorian cases which were not made in Llanrwst and which, usually, consisted of softwood carcasses finished with various exotic veneers. All the remainder were in solid oak, occasionally with cross-banding and inlays but, more usually, plain.

The soils of the area are predominantly acid which does not suit the yew tree, and, consequently, relatively few yew trees grow wild. In the volcanic hotch-potch which constitutes the geology of the area however, basic rocks are occasionally thrown up and the overlying soils are suddenly much less acid, so there would always have been a few yew trees available to joiners. Occasionally, therefore, dressers and other items of 18th century domestic furniture are found made from yew and these are much prized today. We found one clock case in solid yew housing an early John Owen clock. This had a rather crude, caddy top on its hood. The caddy itself was also made in solid yew which made the hood exceedingly heavy and hazardous to remove.

The local soils do not suit walnut either; it is a tree that prefers deeper, more fertile ground. As a result, locally-made walnut furniture is rarely seen. Occasionally, walnut veneers are used, but on clock cases only for cross-banding on some of the early, grander examples, and again on early 19th century cases.

Our survey also revealed a single clock case in solid fruitwood, probably pear, housing a Watkin Owen clock of the 1800-10 period. With fruitwood, however, it is the timber's susceptibility to attack by woodworm that has led to its rarity. Fruitwood timber would have been readily available in the Conwy Valley in the 17th and 18th centuries. Apple and pear orchards were a common feature of the district and the word *perllan* (orchard) appears frequently in place names. Watkin Owen of Gwydir records in his accounts a purchase in Chester of a gross of good corks "to bottle ye sider". [11]

Good quality deal or pine boards would not have been plentiful in the valley. The native Scots pine was never very common and the systematic planting of softwood trees did not start before the third quarter of the 18th century. However, in the 1780s, imported deal from the Baltic seems to have arrived at Llanrwst, presumably via Liverpool. Certainly, we have only found three clocks in deal cases, one stained and polished to simulate oak, one painted an indeterminate wood colour, and one case that has been stripped. Originally, cases made from pine would have been stained, polished or painted - never left 'natural' as is fashionable today. Probably, there would have been more deal or pine cases than the relatively small number of clock cases located by us suggests, but wastage, as a result of woodworm and decay, will have reduced the number of surviving cases drastically.

Mahogany was used just as infrequently. This exotic timber would have been readily available via Liverpool, but, clearly, this was regarded as a luxury timber by Llanrwst joiners and clock case makers. The result was that they used it only for special orders: we have located a mere three mahogany Llanrwst cases, housing clocks by John Owen. Caernarfon clocks, on the other hand, are, not infrequently, seen in fine mahogany 'brick work' cases, which give every appearance of having been bought ready-made from Liverpool. But all three examples of mahogany clock cases from Llanrwst were obviously locally made. They were all well made, too, but the joiners made no concessions to this fashionable and expensive timber: they still used standard oak designs.

Other timbers may have been used for the manufacture of clock cases in Llanrwst. Occasionally, dressers and linen presses are seen in elm, the upland variety or wych-elm, which grew abundantly and well in the valley. Elm is, however, notoriously vulnerable to attacks from woodworm and we have never seen a clock case in this timber. Sweet or Spanish chestnut, although much less common, also grew to a large size at Gwydir. Clock cases may exist in this timber, but they are easily mistaken for oak and we cannot claim to have identified one.

The only other timbers used in clock case manufacture appear in cross bandings and parquetry inlays. Usually, on earlier clocks, cross-banding is in walnut, but sometimes in oak, stained a darker colour than the rest of the case. In the 19th century, when cross-banding becomes very common, a wide variety of timbers are used. The traditional timbers for inlays are bog-oak and holly. Bog oak is oak which has been pickled over the centuries in peat bogs and becomes, as a result, black, hard and almost glass-like. It was available in small quantities and we have seem a complete door on a Welsh clock case made from bog oak. Close examination suggests, however, that the Llanrwst joiners more usually used holly or sycamore veneers, stained black, for the parquetry inlays. Holly and sycamore were abundantly available throughout the district.

To demonstrate the evolution of Llanrwst clock cases it is helpful to categorise them by time period and by style, and, where applicable, to make comparisons with contemporary dressers and furniture. Before doing so, however, it is appropriate to sound a warning, yet again, against the slavish following of dating criteria and stylistic progressions. It is possible to demonstrate how the cases do, indeed, evolve over time and to offer general criteria for assigning dates to them, but not all cases, or their makers, followed these distinctive styles all the time. There are numerous reversions to old-fashioned and outmooded styles, and whilst there is little doubt that they are genuine, many cases display few, if any, of the features exhibited by a majority of the cases of any given period. It is essential to take an overall, synoptic view of all the features of both clock and case before arriving at a date: placing too much emphasis on specific features results, often, in confusion and very inaccurate dating.

Fortunately, all Llanrwst makers sent their customers to the same casemakers, which enables Llanrwst clock cases to be assessed over all and not in relation to particular clockmakers. Whilst reference may be made to individual clockmakers in the following pages, therefore, it is safe to assume that cases by a particular joiner could be found housing clocks by any clockmaker working in Llanrwst at the time.

JOHN OWEN - THE EARLY PERIOD, c1745-60

For the first twenty years or so following the beginning of clockmaking in the town, the clock cases were to be very variable in style, giving the impression of having been the work of numerous casemakers. This variability applied to the style of the cases, the construction techniques and to the overall quality of the finished product. Some of the cases are of excellent quality, with successful styling and felicitous proportions. Others are made roughly and, to put it kindly, look decidedly experimental. This is hardly surprising. In a community where there were many joiners making domestic and manorial furniture, who may never have seen a clock case, there would have been many different approaches to the production of the first cases. Many joiners would have been anxious to get in on the act and to demonstrate their ability to produce good cases. Some would have succeeded and have gained for themselves a reputation and a regular flow of clients. Others would flirt with the new fangled clock cases but having been less successful, would have moved on to work more suited to their craftsmanship and inclinations. Inevitably, too, the clockmakers had their own preferred case makers whom they would have recommended to customers. The designs used for the first cases were varied, too. Some cases, especially those housing the more expensive arch-dialled clocks, bore a remarkable resemblance to cases being produced in Lancashire and Cheshire; one or two to the rather idiosyncratic cases of the Wrexham makers. Obviously, joiners would have asked for drawings and patterns, and, doubtless, John Owen was able to produce sketches and dimensions. Any clocks already in the district and imported from outside the area must have attracted a lot of attention and would have been the subject of much measuring and sketching. Perhaps, a few cases were commissioned from experienced makers at Wrexham, Chester or in Lancashire and deliberately imported into Llanrwst as patterns. The early Llanrwst clock cases suggest all these things and, from the surviving examples, it is clear that most are derivations of styles already commonplace elsewhere.

So many stylistic variations exist that it is difficult to list the typical styles of this early period. Some, however, do recur and, clearly, these were amongst the more popular because, eventually, their makers received repeat orders. Where styles do recur they are, at this period, usually the work of the same craftsman as the construction techniques frequently demonstrate. Later, a Llanrwst style was to emerge that was followed by most, if not all, the local case makers. In the early period, however, a stereotyped style usually suggests the work of a single joiner.

There are, however, a number of indicators of early Llanrwst cases which are common to most makers and to most case styles.

The oak boards used in this period are always thick and heavy. Cases are made from boards often $1/2$" thick and, occasionally, even thicker: they are exceedingly heavy. The timber itself is of very fine colour and figuring. For the door and front plinth panel straight grained planks were selected, but, usually, the side panels are much more interesting, full of curly grain and rich figuring. Some of these very early cases are very dark, almost black, but, more often, they are rich chestnut or deep, lustrous red. This colour is only, in part, derived from the nature of the wood and the effects of ageing. Most new cases were stained and polished by the maker, and in Llanrwst it is clear that makers preferred warm and rich, middle-of-the-range colours. Many cases today are darker at the top and bottom than in their middle section; smoke having deepened the colour of the hoods and splashes from passing feet the bases.

The back boards in these early cases are always very interesting, although, sadly, many have had to be replaced. Frequently, when original, they have been fashioned from a single

THE CLOCKMAKERS OF LLANRWST

Fig 90: Clock number 76. An early case with an arched hood, the only example we found of this style although it is quite common elsewhere in the north-west, especially Lancashire. The narrow door is a reliable indicator of an early Llanrwst case. Clock by John Owen, dated on the case, 1755.

Fig 91: Clock number 54, c1750-55. An early example of a swan-necked hood housing a John Owen clock., although the outline of the hood differs only slightly from the previous example. This case is cross-banded in walnut.

heavy plank of oak and, because the back board is rarely seen, the timber was left rough, either coarsely sawn, or trimmed by the case-maker's adze.

Flat topped hoods were most common during this period, with a tendency for the hood cornice to be rather wide, except in the case of the very simple coffin-like cases which were decidedly 'up and down', with hoods and plinths little wider than the trunk. The caddy-top is quite common, too, the caddies invariably fashioned from solid pieces of timber. Sometimes, these caddies are surrounded at the front and sides by carved crestings. However, both caddies and cresting have not always survived leaving hoods that now are flat topped. For arched dials either the hoods are of the arched style or with a broken-arch. Contemporary with these are some of the earliest swan-necked hoods which, clearly, have developed from the broken-arched form; the swan-necks are still very flat and convex, giving the top of the hood an outline little different from a broken-arch hood. The architectural pediment, soon to become the dominant hood style in Llanrwst, makes its first appearance at the very end of this period.

Hood pillars either have separate, turned, wooden bases and capitals or these are turned integrally with the pillars themselves. When the bases and capitals are separate they have been turned from holly, sycamore or pine, coated with gesso and gilded. The water gilding technique was invariably used which, together with a thorough burnishing, left a very shiny and brilliant finish. Not often has this survived, but, sometimes, it may be found, more or less intact, below two centuries of grime, polish and varnish. Just occasionally, silver leaf was used in place of gold leaf, presumably to save a penny or two; the silver leaf was then coated with a gold-coloured lacquer to give a finish virtually indistinguishable from the real thing. When, however, bases and capitals are integral with the oak hood pillars themselves, for some reason they are not gilded.

The glass in the hood doors from this early period is always very thin, full of flaws and usually greenish, sometimes markedly so, giving the silvered chapter-ring and polished dial plate a very odd appearance. Sometimes the hood has side windows too, through which the movement can be admired. Unfortunately, over the centuries, this old glass has become very brittle and often it has not survived. The glass is usually held in place by a combination of putty and small headless nails or sprigs. On some cases, however, the glass is held in position by small oak wedges driven into slots in the door frame.

Chequerboard inlays of various forms are commonly found on hoods of this period, whilst, occasionally, the friezes incorporate pierced frets to allow the sound of the bell to be heard more effectively.

Case trunks in this early period are relatively slender but deeper than usual from front to back, resulting in a cross section which is virtually square. Quarter columns on the trunk are usually confined to the grander cases at this time; on the more standard cases either they are very small or absent altogether. It is interesting to observe that some of the cases have right-angled corners with no pillars at all, others have their corners modified to a 'pencil round' and in others this feature is further evolved to become a corner dowel rather than a column. It is only between 1760 and 1765 that quarter columns, up to 4" in diameter, become virtually standard. Their capitals are never gilded at this period, nor are they replaced by brass castings.

The trunk doors in the early period tend to be narrow, sometimes as small as 6" in width. A narrow door is, perhaps, the most reliable indicator of a very early Llanrwst clock case. Cross banding, usually in walnut, appears on some of these earlier cases, although it is

Fig 92: Clock number 554 by John Owen. This case from the early 1750s is the only example of the use of yew-tree wood that we have found. The caddy-top appears occasionally in this period and is invariably fashioned from solid timber. The square, reeded hood pillars are of doubtful originality.

Fig 93: Clock number 450, c1765-70. The swan-necked hood has fully evolved in this example of a clock by John Owen. This case is also exceptional in that it is constructed throughout in mahogany, one of only three that we found.

never a common feature and becomes very rare indeed after 1780, before becoming common again in the 19th century.

The case plinths are vertically boarded, sometimes without superimposed or applied panels, sometimes with. If applied panels are present, these are usually square or rectangular, with a moulded edge. Shaped tops on plinth panels are a later development.

As for the feet, only rarely have these survived from this early period, so it is difficult to know their original form. Some shaped skirtings on the cases today could well be original as may be some ogee bracket feet. Clock case feet often have fallen victim to damp earth or slate floors and, in consequence, original ones have usually not survived and are the exception.

Distinguishing features of cases from this first period may be summarised as follows:

A miscellany of styles and construction techniques by numerous makers.
Dark and lustrous colours.
Cross-banding relatively common.
Cases narrow in width, but relatively deep, front to back.
Timber thick and cases very heavy.
Trunk doors very narrow.
Quarter columns either absent or very small.
Plinths either without a panel, or if a panel is present, its top straight not shaped.
Back-boards, if original, from a single rough-hewn oak plank.
Caddy-tops from a solid piece of timber.
Hood pillars often integral with the door.

JOHN OWEN - THE LATER PERIOD, c1760-76

We have seen how, in the early period, cases were made in a wide variety of forms and styles. Obviously, the purchaser of a clock went to his local joiner to commission him to make the case. In the period that followed - which ended with John Owen's death in 1776 - we can observe significant changes taking place. Firstly, a distinctively Llanrwst style of clock case emerged, typified by the architectural pediment on the hood and, increasingly, this is adhered to by most of the local joiners still making clock cases. Secondly, there are clear signs that the manufacture of the cases began to be concentrated in fewer workshops and that specialist makers of cases were emerging. Finally, the timber itself began to change: wood was used more sparingly and the favoured colour becomes a mid brown and not the more usual dark or red colour of the earlier cases. Invariably, very much thinner boards were used.

Most people's idea of a typical Llanrwst clock case is one that is rather wide in the trunk for its height, has a broken architectural pediment on the hood, and a thin applied panel on the plinth which, invariably, is split. The impression of width is strengthened by the large quarter columns and the relative lack of height caused by the absence of the original feet. This may be an over-simplification, or even a caricature, but there are a large number of Llanrwst cases today that come uncomfortably close to this description. They are more typical of the 1780s however: in the period 1760-76, when John Owen was enjoying his heyday, this Llanrwst style was still emerging and developing.

How the people of Llanrwst came to acquire their predilicition for the very distinctive architectural pediment is obscure. This particular hood style was not new: it had featured on some of the earliest London long-case clocks. Nor was it confined to North Wales: it was to be used from time to time in many parts of England especially in some of the counties of the East Midlands. Nowhere, however, was it to enjoy such protracted popularity as it did in Llanrwst.

The stylistic principles of the design, based as they are on classical architecture, are simple. So is its construction. Almost invariably, in Llanrwst, the method used was to prepare a small additional length of the moulding used for the cornice of the hood and to construct the pediment with this, having first extended the frieze board upwards on which to plant the pediment mouldings. Thus far the construction of these pediments is standard, but the actual detailing of the design is almost infinitely variable. The pediment is sometimes unbroken

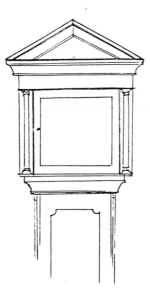

but much more usually broken and shaped at the centre (see Figure 77, p142).

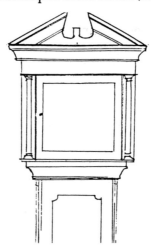

The pediment may commence from the ends of the hood cornice (see Figure 86, p149)

or be inset (see Figure 80, p144)

It can be extravagant (see Figure 96, p163)

or meagre (Figure 105, p169)

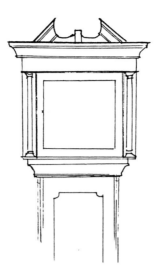

The first architectural pediments began to appear about 1760 and, thereafter, they increased in popularity very quickly. By the time of John Owen's death, architectural pediments appeared on at least half of all cases. Incidentally, over the years, many of these pediments have been removed, presumably when the clock was moved to a room with too low a ceiling. There are usually clear signs of the amputation, however: often the pediment has been crudely sawn off without any effort to make good the scars. This is fortunate for the restorer who can judge the section and angle of the original pediment from the stumps.

In addition to the pediment itself, the hood was usually completed by the addition of one or three finials mounted on small blocks, or, in the case of the central one, on an extension of the frieze board.

Invariably, in the 18th century, these finials were of wood and very large, either ball or flambeau shaped. They, like the capitals of the hood pillars, were water-gilded. All surviving original finials that we have found, and they are relatively few, are of this type. We have seen nothing to suggest that brass finials were ever used in the 18th century in Llanrwst. Incidentally, hood pillar capitals and bases made of brass, if original, are always of a plain and simple design, but most, if not all, are later replacements too.

In the early period, some hood pillars are integral with the hood doors, but by the later period they are always separate and free standing. Integral turned bases and capitals become much less common, giving way to separately turned soft-wood and gilded capitals.

Just as the hoods of the cases begin to sprout architectural pediments, so, too, do their waistlines begin to broaden. This follows, closely, the contemporary design trends in Cheshire and Lancashire. Indeed, with the pediment removed, a Llanrwst case of about 1780 resembles a Cheshire case very closely, although the latter is usually finer in execution. Broadening of the case trunk was to be further accentuated by the increasing diameter of the quarter columns which, sometimes, now exceeded 4". The columns are now either plain or fluted: there seems to have been no particular preference in Llanrwst. Later quarter columns, however, are more usually fluted.

By 1765, almost all plinths incorporated an applied panel with a moulded edge, this

160

Plate 1: Llanroost (sic) Bridge, c1797. Aquatint by Laporte . [Gwynedd Archives Service]

Plate 2: Llanrwst Bridge today.

Plate 3: Clock number 324, c1795. A typical Wilson dial in un-restored condition. The matching diamond hands are also original. Note the fineness of the original seconds hand.

Plate 4: Clock number 283 by William Owen, c1810-15. This dial by Hobson and Hodgkins has survived in remarkably good condition. The main hands are original.

Plate 5: The dial of the Owen Hughes clock. The owner's name is painted on the arch in red. The pretty swag of flowers was added to conceal the unevenly placed winding squares. The hands all appear to be original. For some strange reason the man o'war on the moon-disc is either on fire or exploding. See also Plate 6.

Plate 6: Clock number 283 by Watkin Owen, c1780. See also Plate 5.

Plate 7: Clock number 356 by Barker & Jones, c1812-15. See also Plate 8.

Plate 8: Clock number 356 by Barker & Jones, c1812-15. A fine moon-phase dial by Finnemore. The movement in this clock has typical Owen strike-work. See also Plate 7.

Plate 9: A fine early case of clock number 29 by John Owen, c1750-55. The narrow door is an early feature. This case is in oak, cross-banded with walnut and inlaid with bog-oak and holly. Over the years, this clock has taken on a decided lean.

Plate 10: The very fine case of clock number 558 by Watkin Owen, c1780. The timber which is honey-coloured has a lovely patina. The simple moulding to the door and plinth panel are a rare but high-quality feature. Only the brass finials are modern.

Plate 11: A long-case clock signed by Robert Williams, Llanrwst (probably the younger) from the 1860s. The large and wide 'Yorkshire' case was probably made in Anglesey.

moulding being exactly similar to that on the door. The top of the plinth panel is now shaped, and, with increasing frequency, repeats the profile of the top of the trunk door. Moreover, these profiles become highly variable, almost as if the case maker was trying to provide each clock with a unique and matching door and plinth panel top.

Until about 1770, both the plinth panels and the trunk doors have a moulded edge but, thereafter, there is a tendency for the panels to be made out of very much thinner oak boards, no longer with a moulded edge. Plinth panels are sometimes as little as $1/8$" in thickness. The doors are made from a somewhat thicker plank, but the rebate around the edge is cut so deeply as to leave a bare $1/8$" lying over the frame to match the plinth panel. Such thin and wide panels, and they are usually a single board, inevitably shrink and split, usually down the centre from top to bottom. So too, quite often, do the doors.

At this period, too, the waist mouldings under the hood and on top of the plinth became very elaborate and they remained so until the 1790s. There are some indications that comparison of the profiles of these mouldings may give a clue to which cases came from which workshop, but more detailed work is required to test this theory.

Finally, the feet of the cases were now, nearly always, of ogee bracket construction. The ogee moulding was continuous down each side of the case but was broken at the front, the mouldings extending approximately one quarter of the width and having shaped ends (see Figure 112, p177).

All too often the original bracket feet have been lost, and the case now stands on a replacement skirting or merely on the downward extensions of the main frame to which the ogee mouldings were originally fixed.

In the early John Owen period the points of similarity between the clock cases and locally made dressers and cupboards are not so obvious, being confined, in the main, to the colour and nature of the timber used. Dressers featured fielded rather than flat panels, but these could not easily be used on clock cases for practical reasons. As the 1750s progressed, however, plain applied panels with moulded edges began to appear more and more often, on the clock cases as well as on the contemporary dressers. The change to thinner applied panels without mouldings (sometimes called 'slapped-on panels' by dealers), which occurred about 1770 on clock cases, was again mirrored on contemporary dressers. But now the similarities increase in frequency. Ogee bracket feet were used on dressers as, indeed, were quarter columns. Even the chequer-board inlays, which became such a popular decorative feature on the hoods of clock cases, were used as embellishments on the friezes of contemporary dressers.

More obviously, this period saw the beginning of a decline, both in the quality and colouration of the timber used in the Llanrwst area. This general trend applied equally to dressers and clock cases. Boards are now less thick, not just in the interests of economy but probably, also, because the sawyers' equipment and techniques were improving. The colour of the oak from this period is less interesting too. The dark lustrous reds of the earlier period give way to mid and light browns. Indeed some clock cases and dressers are so light in colour as to suggest that no original colour stains were applied.

From now onwards the same features in the timbers used, construction techniques and decorative features occur on both clock cases and dressers.

Distinguishing features of cases from the later John Owen period may be summarised as follows:

Fig 94: Clock number 604 by John Owen. An early flat-topped hood from the 1750s. This example is decorated with an amusing fret in the frieze and a chequer board immediately below the hood. The earliest examples of this style are usually without decoration.

Fig 95: Clock number 487 by John Owen, 1765. We found a few clocks from the 1760s with 'frizzy' cornices such as this one. This particular example is exceptional in that it is dated in the frieze and has no seconds indication although it has an 8-day movement.

Fig 96: Clock number 565 by John Owen. An early example of an architectural pediment which is difficult to date but is probably c1760. The pediment is decidedly exaggerated. This is also a rare example of the survival of the original giltwood finials.

Fig 97: Clock number 505 by John Owen. A much more conventional example of the architectural pediment dating from the early 1770s. The finials, although of the correct type, are of doubtful originality.

163

Cases now from fewer workshops.
A Llanrwst style emerges, especially the architectural pediment.
Trunks broaden and are less deep, front to back.
The oak lighter in colour.
The timber thinner and the cases less heavy.
Back-boards now sawn oak planks.
Case ornaments wooden, water-gilded.
Plinth panels have shaped tops, usually matching the top of the trunk-door.
Quarter columns much larger, either plain or reeded.
Chequer-board hood friezes.
Hood pillars stand clear of the hood-door.
Ogee bracket feet.
Thin, 'slapped-on' panels at end of period.
Chalk-dates appear at end of period.

WATKIN OWEN - THE ARCHITECTURAL PERIOD, c1776-1800

The first two decades of Watkin Owen's working life were his most prolific years. This period also saw the full flowering of the Llanrwst clock case with its distinctive architectural pediment. Other styles were used, but it seems that these could not compete with the architectural form in popularity. In Watkin's first few years there were a number of cases made in experimental styles - not least a series of hoods with swan-necked pediments even though the cases housed standard 13" square dials. These swan-necked cases for square dials are sometimes quite successful, in stylistic terms, especially if the case is otherwise reasonably tall and slender. The results are less happy, however, when the case is rather short and wide. The swan necks themselves are of two forms: the more usual provides the cornice to the hood, but, occasionally, swan necks have been planted, rather like an afterthought, on top of a normal flat-topped hood with straight cornice. The swan necks on these cases are inclined to be exaggerated in length and angle, giving a very odd, horned appearance to the clock. Not surprisingly, the casemakers concerned did not persist with this style, although it appeared again in the early years of the 19th century.

The late 1770s and early 1780s also saw an increase in the use of fretwork in the hood frieze. This development had begun earlier in John Owen's time but became very popular again during Watkin's most prolific years. Sometimes the earlier frets were genuine sound frets, backed with flannel or similar material. This permitted the striking of the clock to be heard more clearly, but, later, the frets were to become 'blind' with a board behind them.

In the late 1780s a very distinctive form of hood fret became very popular and, undoubtedly, this was characteristic of a single very prolific workshop. It consisted of horizontally extended geometric shapes in a variety of forms.

A typical case featuring this form of fret has a relatively small pediment set well in. This particular style was most popular in the period 1788-98. The cases involved are, often, very light in colour.

Until the early 1790s the architectural pediment was constructed just as it had been in John's day and was just as variable. In the 1790s, however, the late form of the architectural pediment came into being. Here, the cornice is no longer continuous across the full width of the hood. Instead, it has become 'broken' and incorporated into the pediment.

This final form of the architectural pediment appeared occasionally in the late 1770s but was then discarded for ten years or so. After about 1792 it began to reappear, superseding the earlier form. Its presence on a Llanrwst clock case is a very strong dating indicator for the period 1792-1800 (see Figure 106, p172).

Many of the cases having this late form of the architectural pediment seem to have been the work of one particular casemaker. His craftsmanship is invariably of good quality and may be distinguished by the fact that he returns to the earlier fashion of having a simple moulding on the edges of doors and plinth panels. Another casemaker, whose work first becomes identifiable in the late 1790s, is Edward Jones, already mentioned in this chapter. Dentil and reeded mouldings and friezes are his trade marks, and, later, he adopts brass case fittings, the first Llanrwst maker to do so.

Another innovation of the period 1780-1800 is the introduction of wide, deal planks in place of oak for the back-boards of the cases. These first appeared about 1780 or, perhaps, a little earlier, but by the end of the century, they were virtually standard on all cases. There are some indications that these wide deal boards were imported from the Baltic.

Throughout this period a few grander clocks were produced with arched dials, both brass and painted. For these, invariably, the case hoods had swan-necked pediments. In the early examples these pediments are rather flat (see Fig 98, p166) but later, like eyebrows, they became more raised (see Fig 101, p167).

Throughout the period, plinth panel tops usually follow the door tops exactly.

The height of the typical Llanrwst case is approximately 7' 0" (or 6' 8" or 6' 9" if an architectural pediment has been removed). Unfortunately, exact height is often difficult to measure because the original feet are missing or have been replaced.

Distinguishing features of the cases from the period 1776-1800 may be summarised as follows:

> Architectural pediment reigns supreme.
> Trunks wider still, and quarter columns larger.
> Quarter columns reeded, more often than plain.
> Frets in the hood-frieze.
> Ogee bracket feet.
> Shaped top to plinth panel matching the top of the trunk door.
> Hood pillars stand clear of the hood door.
> Case ornaments wooden, water-gilded.
> The later form of the architectural pediment takes over in the 1790s.
> Very elaborate mouldings under the hood and on top of plinth.
> Imported deal back-boards.
> Oak frequently very light in colour.
> Chalk-dates quite common.

THE LATE WATKIN OWEN PERIOD - THE YEARS OF DECLINE, c1800-09

When we examined Watkin Owen's dials and clocks, we described the last ten years of his life as a period of change and, sadly, decline. It was a period when he appeared to be struggling to reduce the costs of clockmaking in the context of deteriorating economic conditions, a decline in the demand for long case clocks and even some local competition. This was a time when the old methods of clock movement and clock dial making began to change and innovations were tried. These same trends were also reflected in the making of

165

Fig 98: Clock number 600 by Watkin Owen. A swan-necked case housing a brass, arched-dial movement from the 1780s. The paterae on the swan-necks have lost their radial parquetry decoration.

Fig 99: Clock number 461 by Watkin Owen. Another example from the mid 1780s. The brass hood pillar capitals are probably later 'improvements'. The finials are also relatively modern, the outer eagles having lost their orbs.

Fig 100: Clock number 130 by Watkin Owen. A good quality swan-necked case from the early 1790s. Note the elaborate fretwork in the frieze.

Fig 101: Clock number 165 by Watkin Owen. This swan-necked case dates from c1800-05. The signature on the dial is the exception that proves the rule that Watkin Owen clocks were never signed 'W Owen'. Note the very upright swan-necks which are typical of this period.

Fig 102: Clock number 428 by Watkin Owen. An early, brass-dialed clock from the period 1776-80. It was quite common in Llanrwst at this period to have square dials in cases with swan-necked hoods. Note the twin hearts in the fretwork frieze.

Fig 103: Clock number 48 by Watkin Owen, c1780. Another fine swan-necked case housing a square dial. This example combines fretwork and parquetry decoration.

Fig 104: Clock number 30 by Watkin Owen, c1785-90. A classic example of a Llanrwst 'architectural' case from this period. Note the geometric fretwork in the frieze and the shaped splats. The brass finials and hood pillar bases and capitals are later.

Fig 105: Clock number 621 by Watkin Owen, c.1780-85 Llanrwst cases invariably stand about 84" high, but this example is a very rare exception, being 8" inches taller. The case is also of very good quality - note how the fretwork in the frieze is repeated below the hood.

the clock cases that housed his clocks, and, indeed, in the clocks of all other makers in the area.

Even in the late 1790s, some strange and very different cases had appeared. These were less well made, with a deterioration in proportions and style and often the cases were constructed of inferior timber. They strongly suggest that new case-makers were offering cases at lower prices. After 1805 this process accelerates.

The most obvious stylistic change is the appearance of what we refer to as the late Llanrwst swan-necked style. Here, a swan-necked pediment is used for the standard 13" and 14" square dial hoods. They feature a combined frieze and pediment of a simplified but rather debased form. A very deep frieze or facia board is used upon which the swan-necked mouldings are then planted. Whilst there are good quality cases in this style, there are many that, increasingly, are lightly built to the point where some are skimpy and unimpressive (see Figure 109, p173).

Other experimental forms begin to appear, all giving the appearance of having been designed to save cost, but it is the new swan-necked form that proves the most popular and, gradually, this replaces most other styles. Once again, it must be emphasised, however, that good-quality cases, following earlier styles, continued to be made well into the century; they do not finally disappear until about 1820. Equally, better-quality cases in the new styles were produced, but these were rather fewer in number.

Other stylistic changes that date from around 1800 can be quickly described. The trunk door begins to shorten, leaving more and more space between its lower edge and the plinth moulding. This space became so large that the case makers began to fill it with a separate rectangular panel. Sometimes, this panel is an applied board that matches the door: sometimes, the outline of a panel is merely inlaid with a contrasting veneer. It is rare for a short door, with a panel below it, to appear before 1800.

The cases begin to become more highly decorated after 1800. Crossbanding re-appears, usually in stained oak but also in mahogany and walnut. Sometimes, pieces of mahogany are now incorporated into oak cases: often this takes the form of a half round moulding of mahogany on the trunk just below the hood. We have already mentioned brass case furniture, apparently introduced by Edward Jones, and increasingly this seems to have been used by case makers in place of gilded softwood. Hood pillar and quarter column bases and capitals, finials and paterae for the decoration of the swan necks, all now occur, with increasing frequency, in brass.

Inlaid designs become more common, again, in this period. The favourite motif on Llanrwst cases had, from the earliest times, been a multi-rayed star made in alternate dark and light veneers. Sometimes, these stars are large and elaborate, having very many points; sometimes they are very simple. Another design that is quite often seen is a strange, curved, propeller-like emblem. These and other similar inlay designs are often interpreted as fertility symbols! These traditional inlays persist during the first two decades of the 19th century. In this period shell inlays, normally associated with the mahogany furniture of the period, from time to time appear on clock cases although it is difficult to be sure whether these are original or more recent 'improvements'.

Cases with swan-necked pediments for arch dialled clocks follow the earlier designs throughout this period, but, increasingly, these incorporate the shorter door with panel beneath and the other, new, decorative features such as brass case fittings.

The oak boards used to construct the better-quality cases remain of consistent quality and colour, but on the cheaper cases the boards are very thin. The nature of the oak seems somewhat different too. Often, it is very straight, and closely grained, and has a greyish cast, quite unlike the typical local timber. This suggests that imported oak was now available and was being used by the Llanrwst case makers.

Distinguishing features of cases from the late Watkin Owen period may be summarised as follows:

> Inferior cases from new makers although good quality cases persist.
> Swan-necked pediments became popular for square-dialled clocks.
> Inlays, cross-banding and decorative timbers and mouldings more common.
> Brass case-ornaments introduced.
> Trunk doors shorten, with separate panel beneath.
> Oak now of inferior quality, some probably imported.
> Timber much thinner and cases much lighter in weight.

THE REGENCY PERIOD AND LATER, c1810-50.

Long-case clockmaking in Llanrwst declined throughout this period, reaching a very low ebb by the 1830s and 1840s. The older style of case that we have so far discussed, finally dies out by about 1820, leaving the late Llanrwst swan-neck style supreme both for square and for arched-dial cases. A steady increase took place in the width of the case trunk, whilst, at the same time, the depth from front to back decreased. The hood and plinth soon became not much wider than the trunk. Overall, the clock acquired a wide rectangular section. Trunk doors were now much shorter, invariably with a panel beneath. Both this panel and the applied plinth panel were, like the doors, heavily cross-banded in dark veneers. The panels eventually disappear, being replaced by inlays giving the impression of panels. Quarter columns shortened with the doors and, increasingly, together with hood pillars, were made of square rather than round section, usually reeded. The swan-necks were carved simply from oak and were decorated with brass paterae. Various inlaid decorative veneers and stringing were used. Bracket feet gave way to simple skirtings, and the overall weight of the case was now very much less that in former times.

This general style was to be virtually standard for Llanrwst-made cases until the eventual demise of the long case after 1870.

Distinguishing features of cases from the Regency period may be summarised as follows:

> Swan-necked pediment virtually standard.
> Trunks ever wider and shallower, front to back.
> Hood and quarter columns reeded and often square.
> Dark cross-banding very common.
> Trunk doors very short with inlaid panel beneath.
> Construction increasingly skimpy.
> Brass case ornaments.

THE LAST PERIOD, 1850-80

To the purist familiar with the classical cases of the 'golden age' of clockmaking in Llanrwst, the cases of the period 1820-50 appear somewhat stereotyped and debased, poor things indeed. But, more dramatic changes were to come.

Fig 106: Clock number 274 by Watkin Owen, c1795-1800. An excellent example of the late Llanrwst architectural style. Note how the cornice mouldings forming the architectural pediment are now integral with the horizontal cornice, not superimposed upon it. The finials are original.

Fig 107: Clock number 271 by Watkin Owen. A clock from the early 1800s, important because the inscription on the dial identifies the maker of the case – Edward Jones. Note the horizontal bands of vertical reeding much favoured by this case-maker.

Fig 108: Clock number 217 by Watkin Owen, c1805. The swan-necks on this case are the most exaggerated that we found. At this date the brass case ornaments could be original but the finials are not.

Fig 109: Clock number 224 by Watkin Owen, c1800-05. A good example of the simplified late Llanrwst swan-necked style which was to persist for as long as cases continued to be made in Llanrwst. This rare, pine case has been stripped but, originally, would have been stained or painted.

Fig 110: Clock number 75 by Watkin Owen. A typical chalk-date. The numbers are usually of approximately this size and in this position. This example reads '1777'.

When, in the third quarter of the 19th century, long-case clocks enjoyed a renaissance, or perhaps more appropriately, a swan-song in Llanrwst, their cases were something to behold. This was the time of the so called 'Yorkshire' case, a big, wide and exceedingly florid affair, much decorated with exotic veneers, inlays, cross-bandings, turnings and appliqués. At the risk of offending proud owners of these clocks it has to be said that, to many people, the cases are somewhat startling to say the least.

There are a few examples that appear to be hybrids between those of the preceeding period and these later Victorian giants. Presumably, these were the response of the local case makers to the new style. They failed to stem the tide of the new imported cases however and it is unlikely that any more cases were made in the town after about 1860.

Cases of the new style were manufactured throughout the north of England at this period, but more particularly in west Yorkshire, Lancashire and North Wales. We believe that most of those, which house clocks sold by Llanrwst retailers, were made in Anglesey. We have located two clocks by Theophilus Davies still bearing the remnants of address labels and railway tickets inside their cases. Both labels indicate that the clock cases were consigned to Llanrwst by rail from Conwy, one apparently via Bangor. The Conwy Valley

Railway from Llandudno to Blaenau Ffestiniog was not to open until the 1880s, so before this date Conwy town was the nearest station to Llanrwst. The mention of Bangor on one of the labels suggests, strongly, a source of origin in Anglesey, the rail crossing from the island being close to that particular town.

Anglesey is, indeed, a very likely place for these cases to have been made. A considerable furniture manufactory had grown up in the Llangefni and Llanerchymedd areas, with its centre at Llangristiolus. The workshops specialised in the production of the rather florid and large furniture that is typical of this period, and much of this furniture still exists in the houses of northern Wales today, perhaps the most typical item being the *cwpwrdd gwydr* or glazed cupboard. As in earlier times, this domestic furniture shares many stylistic and constructional feature with the contemporary clock cases, in this instance the so-called 'Yorkshire' cases.

Several of the examples that we have included in our photographic surveys bear the initials 'WG' branded on the inside of the case in at least two places. We have been told by an old-time watch and clock maker that these are the initials of William Griffith, a large-scale producer of clock cases in or near Llanerchymedd, Anglesey.

The illustration on page 189 and Plate 11 convey a better impression of these cases than can easily be given in words. Usually, they are about 8' in height, whereas the 18th century clocks stood only 7' high. Normally, these late Victorian cases have a softwood carcass on to which the mahogany, rosewood and satinwood veneers have been applied. Fancy inlays and pillars are much favoured: indeed, there are often four instead of two hood pillars. In spite of their large solid appearance these cases are very light in weight and rather flimsily constructed.

Similar cases are to be found throughout much of North Wales, often bearing the same branded initials of 'WG'.

Distinguishing features of cases from this last period may be summarised as follows:

> Wide, florid 'Yorkshire' cases.
> A wide variety of decorative veneers applied to softwood carcases.
> External finish excellent, but construction flimsy and cases very light in weight.
> Cases encrusted with decorative turnings, appliqués and inlays.
> Cases taller, averaging 8' 0".
> The brand 'WG' frequently to be found inside the case.

DATES WRITTEN IN CHALK.

Before leaving the subject of Llanrwst cases, it is important to describe how some unknown person, and our benefactor in no small degree, developed the routine of scrawling the date with chalk inside clock cases and continued to do so for at least thirty years.

Fortunately, we noticed just such a date inside a Watkin Owen clock very early in our survey. Clock cases are often full of various scrawlings, frequently in chalk. Auctioneers have a particular habit of writing lot numbers or recording the names of owners inside clock cases, usually on the back of the door. So do removal and storage contractors. It is more unusual to see chalk inscriptions on the backboard, although scraps of paper recording the history of the clocks and other family matters are often found there. It was chance, therefore, that drew our attention to a large and distinct '1780' written boldly across the backboard inside the clock and located approximately opposite the top of the trunk door. What particularly held our attention was the fact that the figure '8' was written in the 18th century manner. Although this inscription was interesting and agreed closely with our dating of the clock on stylistic grounds, we paid it little more attention at the time. But soon we observed another, and another, until, by the end of our survey, we had found no less than 30 clocks dated in this manner.

These dates appear to have been written originally in thick chalk or some similar substance. Often, all traces of the chalk have now disappeared, leaving a remarkably clear impression or shadow of what was originally written, the surrounding area having, over time, darkened much more than the area covered by the numbers.

There can be no doubt that these dates were inscribed more or less at the time when the case was made. Not only is the script in the style of the time but we have found no anomalous dates: all, without exception, fit in with the progression of dates that we can work out on stylistic grounds. Furthermore, we have found Llanrwst clocks dated in this manner at many different locations all over Scotland, England and Wales. It is hardly likely that any modern person, no matter how expert, could have written them, even if he had a motive for doing so.

Who could have written the dates? We have racked our brains for the answer. Was it the original casemaker? Are all the clocks, so dated, the products of a single workshop? They could be. Or was it someone in Watkin Owen's workshop, or the great man himself? If it was, why did he date only some of the clocks? And why did he date a fine case housing an Owen Evans clock and several more by Moses Evans? We cannot begin to know the answers to any of these questions. We do know, however, that finding these dates was perhaps our greatest piece of good fortune in the entire project. Dated clocks are exceedingly rare: three John Owen cases in our survey have inlaid or carved dates and two by Watkin Owen. One John Owen movement had a date engraved on the front-plate, as had one dial plate by Watkin. Two other clocks had old documents stuck inside, giving the date of their manufacture. These would have been the total extent of dated clocks had not that unknown person been so diligent with his piece of chalk.

Today, when we discover another Owen clock the first thing that we do is to open the trunk door and look for the chalk date. Great is our excitement if we discover one.

The chalk dates were not the only interesting things that we found inside clock cases. We had been told that farmers traditionally kept various valuables inside their clocks but we can inform interested parties that this does not appear to have been borne out by our investigations. We encountered guns and firearms tucked away in this ideal hiding place, including some truly fearsome examples that must have constituted as much of a hazard to the user as to the intended victim. Hooks of various kinds appear inside the clocks, usually to hold the winding key, but on one farm they were particularly large. We were told that they had been inserted during the last war and were used for hanging illegally killed lambs when the Ministry of Food inspector was reported to be in the district. On one never to be forgotten occasion during our survey our arrival at a remote farm house was unexpected and the clock case was stuffed with old bank-notes to the level of the door! Would-be burglars should take note, however, that this was the only time, in more than 500 occasions, that we found anything of substantial value inside one.

Fig 111: Typical lead weights used by the Owens. They invariably have these highly distinctive and unusual conical tops.

Fig 112: An example of original ogee bracket feet of the type used on Llanrwst clock cases throughout the last quarter of the 18th century. This case dates from c1800.

177

LLANRWST CLOCK CASES - STATISTICAL TABLES.

The following statistical tables may help to provide a more detailed picture of the evolution of Llanrwst clock cases.

Fig 113: Case Styles - John Owen

	%	No
Early, flat-topped	17.9	19
Early, caddy-topped	3.8	4
Early, swan-necked	1.9	2
Early, architectual	0.9	1
Early, arched	2.8	3
Llanrwst architectural	21.7	23
Flat-topped	19.8	21
Swan-necked	4.7	5
Arched	0.9	1
Other	2.8	3
Wrong cases	15.1	16
No case	7.5	8
Total	100.0	106

NB: 29% of all original cases were of the 'architectural' type although several of the now 'flat-topped' cases may have started life with an architectural pediment which, subsequently, has been removed to allow the clock to be accommodated beneath a low ceiling.

Fig 114: Case Styles - Watkin Owen

	%	No
Llanrwst architectural	26.6	67
Late Llanrwst architectural	18.7	47
Flat-topped	14.3	36
Swan-necked - square dial	5.6	14
Swan-necked - arched dial	9.1	23
Late Llanrwst swan-necked	6.3	16
Wrong or changed case	17.1	43
Other	0.4	1
No case	2.0	5
Total	100.0	252

NB: Again many of the flat-topped cases may have started life with architectural pediments.

Fig 115: Timbers Used on John Owen Cases

	%	No
Oak	64.2	68
Oak with crossbanding	10.4	11
Yew-tree	0.9	1
Mahogany	1.9	2
No case/ wrong case	22.6	24
Total	100.0	106

NB: 96% of all surviving original cases are oak.

Fig 116: Timbers Used on Watkin Owen Cases

	%	No
Oak	79.8	197
Oak with crossbanding	0.4	1
Mahogany	0.8	2
Fruitwood	0.4	1
Pine	1.2	3
No case/ wrong case	19.0	48
Total	100.0	252

NOTES

1. The Gwydir Castle contents were sold by the Scarborough auctioneers Ward Price & Co on 24, 25 and 26 May 1921. Several copies of the extensively illustrated catalogue are still in the hands of residents in the valley, and there is a further copy in the Ancaster Papers at the Lincoln County Record Office.

2. Gwydir Castle was gutted by fire in 1922 so it may be argued that the dispersal of the contents in 1921 resulted in many of them being saved. Some of the panelling may not have been contemporary with the house, but added in early Victorian times, see: G J Bennett, *A Pedestrian Tour through North Wales*, published by Henry Colburn, London, 1838, p308.

3. The Wynn Papers contain many references to the family obtaining luxury items in London.

4. Whilst not dealing specifically with Welsh furniture, the interested reader will find an excellent account of the manufacture of 'joined' furniture in *Oak Furniture, The British Tradition* by Victor Chinnery, published by the Antique Collectors Club Ltd, Woodbridge, Suffolk.

5. See Chapter VII.

6 W T R Pryce and T Alun Davies, *Samuel Roberts, Clock Maker*, published by the Welsh Folk Museum, Cardiff. Chapters 8 and 9. See, particularly, p311.

7. Llanrwst Churchwardens' Accounts for 1794. Clwyd County Record Office PD/69/1/77.

8. The Vestry Minutes for 1794, Clwyd County Record Office PD/69/1/192, specifically refer to it as a "Riga plank".

9. The contract document has survived. It is in the Lincoln County Record Office.

10. This does not, of course, include clocks that have been re-housed in cases from other places and other periods. These 'marriages' become easy to identify with a little practice and are not infrequent.

11. Library of the University College of North Wales, Bangor, Mostyn MS1440.

CHAPTER IX
Sundials, Watches, Victorian Clocks, Alterations and Fakes

SUNDIALS

We have scoured the Vale of Conwy in an effort to locate a sundial by a Llanrwst maker but, regrettably, without success. Sundials were made quite frequently by clockmakers in the 18th century, but, usually, only if there was an engraver in the workshop. A knowledge of the theory and the mathematics of sundials and the ability to engrave were all that were necessary for their production; the manufacturing processes involved were of a relatively minor nature. Other Welsh clockmakers certainly produced sundials; for example, Samuel Roberts of Llanfair Caereinion and the Ratcliffes of Wrexham.

We have seen that the Llanrwst makers were not themselves skilled as engravers and until about 1790, their clock dials were engraved elsewhere, mostly in far off Lancashire. It was not altogether a surprise, therefore, that we were unable to locate a Llanrwst sundial, either in the Valley or, indeed, anywhere else in North Wales. The inhabitants of the district, when they needed a sundial, would have had to purchase it from a professional sundial and instrument maker, either direct or through an agent, who could well have been the local clockmaker.

As our search progressed we began to realise that, repeatedly, we were seeing the work of a Welsh dial-maker, who, as far as we could discover, was unrecorded. There is a large sundial in the churchyard at Conwy which, unfortunately, the sea air has corroded until it is virtually illegible. Fortunately, Bezant Lowe, in his invaluable work *The Heart of Northern Wales* published in 1912 [1] reproduces the inscription on this dial in full. It reads:

Erected
by the Corporation
of
Conway
Robert Wynn, Junr Esq. Alderman
Hugh Williams and John Nuttal, Bailiffs,
1761
Meredith Hughes, Fecit Lat 53 20

There is another dial in a Conwy Valley churchyard signed 'M Hughes fecit 1766' and in Bolton, Lancashire, the dial from Penloyn, signed 'M Hughes fecit 1759'. At this stage we had no idea where Meredith Hughes lived and worked. Then, we were fortunate enough to be invited to a large house in Clwyd to see a John Owen clock. There, on the lawn opposite the front door, was a truly magnificent and complex sundial which would, amongst other things, record the time in various parts of the world by rotating a section of the dial. It was engraved with the monogram of the family for whom it was made originally and the motto 'ex hoc momento pendet aeternitas'. It was signed 'Meredith

Hughes de Bala fecit 1769'. That so accomplished a dial-maker should have been located in Bala is something of a surprise. We consulted the parish registers [2] and found reference to a Meredith Hughes but nothing more. Certainly, he merits further research and, hopefully, more of his dials will come to light.

There are still plenty of sundials in North Wales although, sadly, they are vulnerable to theft and disappear all too frequently. This is why we are deliberately vague about the locations of those that we have recorded. We suspect that many more are in people's homes, lovingly polished each week with the rest of the family brass. We saw just such a dial signed 'R Davies 1795' that was originally at Ty Isa near Glanconwy. We have found an immense slate sundial, nearly a yard across, also made in 1795; and, perhaps, the finest of all, an octagonal dial signed 'Hen Wynn fecit'. Henry Wynn was Master of the Clockmakers' Company in 1690 and was dial-maker to Charles II. There is one of his dials at Windsor. The dial we found is still in the possession of the North Wales family for whom it was made.

POCKET WATCHES

Perhaps the greatest disappointment of our clock survey was the tiny number of pocket-watches by Llanrwst makers or retailers that it yielded. As we travelled around North Wales examining long-case clocks we always enquired of their owners whether there were any old watches in the house as well. Sometimes these were produced, but all too often they were not by Llanrwst makers. More usually, we were told that there was an old watch somewhere in the house, but that it could not found. We remain convinced that there are still plenty of Llanrwst watches in the backs of dressing-table drawers or in old trunks in the loft. Perhaps, as public awareness and the values of the watches increase, more will come to light.

There is no doubt that all the Llanrwst makers would have sold and repaired pocket-watches, including John Owen. The inventory of Owen Evans, clockmaker of Llanerchymedd in Anglesey, who died in 1782, [3] shows that he possessed watchmaking tools as well as those specifically for clockmaking. Also, he had a considerable stock of spare parts for watches, including verges, fusee chains, case buttons, hands, chain hooks and no fewer than 6 dozen watch glasses. Obviously, he had plenty of watches brought to him for repair. There is no reason to suspect that the Owens of Llanrwst were any different.

It is doubtful, however, if watches were ever actually made in Llanrwst. By the middle of the 18th century, watchmaking was a highly organised and specialist industry and one of the great centres where watchmaking was concentrated was in south Lancashire, at Prescot and Liverpool in particular. Prescot specialised in the manufacture of ebuchons; that is the production of unfinished watch movements. Watchmakers, everywhere, including those with illustrious names, obtained their ebuchons from the Prescot area which were then finished in their own workshop. But nearby Liverpool specialised in the finishing of watches, which were then sold, via wholesalers and agents, to the so called watchmakers for retail purposes. They were supplied complete with the name and workplace of the retailer inscribed on the movement; possibly too, with the retailer's own numbering sequence.

It has been suggested that the Owens could have bought ebuchons and finished them themselves, but this is not supported by the few early Owen watches that have survived. A watch expert who examined the Llanrwst watches that we have found, did not hesitate in

Figs 117 & 118: A silver, verge watch by Watkin Owen, unusual in that the top-plate is significantly smaller than the bottom. The case was hall-marked in London in 1799/1800. This watch is reputed to have belonged to the driver of the Holyhead mail coach.
[Welsh Folk Museum]

Figs 119 & 120: A silver, verge watch by Watkin Owen, c1805. The watch has a replacement dial and has been re-cased.
[Welsh Folk Museum]

Fig 121 (left): A silver, verge watch by Watkin Owen, numbered 109, the case hall-marked in London in 1791-92. Probably a Liverpool watch.
[Welsh Folk Museum]

Fig 122 (right): A silver, verge watch by John Jones, numbered 305, the case assayed in Birmingham in 1814-15.

Figs 123 & 124: A silver, pair-cased, verge watch by David Owen, the case assayed in Birmingham in 1838-39, the year in which David Owen appears to have left Llanrwst.
[Welsh Folk Museum]

Figs 125 & 126: A silver, pair-cased lever watch by Robert Williams, the case hall-marked in London in 1860-61. The escapement is of the English table roller type. Probably a Coventry watch.
[Welsh Folk Museum]

Fig 127 & 128: A silver, pair-cased lever watch by Griffith Owen, the case hall-marked in Birmingham in 1847-48.

Fig 129 & 130: Victorian and early 20th century dial clocks like these examples are to be found in many chapels in and around the Conwy valley. Griffith Owen seems to have secured the lion's share of this market.

declaring that three of the examples by Watkin Owen were Liverpool made watches. In any case, the Owen workshops would not have been able to apply the fine engraving which all the watches exhibit.

Furthermore, it is interesting to note that although south Lancashire was also a centre of watch case making, with much of the production carrying the Chester hall-mark, Llanrwst watch cases bear London and Birmingham hallmarks too. It is not until the end of the 19th century that they are consistently found in Chester hallmarked cases. This reinforces the view that watches were purchased from large wholesalers offering a very wide choice of stock.

By about 1820, it is clear that, in Llanrwst, pocket-watches had surplanted the long-case clock in importance. Clockmakers came to be known more frequently as watchmakers, and, as the surviving watch case papers show, they carried a large stock of watches in a wide variety of designs. All of them repaired and regulated watches and this would have been their 'bread and butter' business.

Just how many watches they handled is typified by a story related to us by Mr W Scriven Williams, son of Owen Williams, watchmaker and jeweller in Llanrwst at the turn of the present century. On his father's death, Mr Williams, himself an optician, had the task of clearing up his father's shop and workroom. In the latter he found a large number of watches that had been repaired but which their owners had failed to collect. Having advertised these in the local press with only partial success, Mr Williams decided to present the remainder to the Welsh Folk Museum at St Fagan's. The National Collection thus obtained no fewer than 10 fine watches bearing the signature of Llanrwst clockmakers or retailers, and many more from elsewhere.

What then happened to all those watches which have not survived to our own times? Sadly, most would have been scrapped, sometimes because they were old but just as often for the value of the silver and gold in their cases. We have been given two early but damaged verge movements that carry the names of makers in North Wales. These surviving movements had been wrenched out of their cases by a tinker at the door, who had given their owners a few shillings for the cases. But there must still be many surviving watches that lie tucked away and forgotten by their owners. Recently they have increased in value and, today, are worth much more as complete watches than they are for the value of the bullion in their cases. Let us hope many more come to light; perhaps even a watch by John Owen!

A list and brief description of most of the Llanrwst pocket-watches that we have located may be found in Appendix III, p266.

BAROMETERS

We have received reports of a good quality banjo barometer signed by Watkin Owen of Llanrwst. Unfortunately, we have been unable to trace it. We, ourselves, have seen a 20th century banjo barometer signed 'David Jones, Llanrwst'.

It is unlikely that barometers were ever made in Llanrwst. Instead, any signed by Llanrwst makers would have been obtained from a specialist maker or wholesaler elsewhere and then sold in retail shops in the town.

VICTORIAN CLOCKS

The decision was made early in our research project to restrict our detailed survey to long-case clocks that had been made in Llanrwst. This resulted in us imposing a somewhat arbitrary date line of around 1825. When we came across later clocks these were photographed but full technical details were not recorded. In consequence, details of a considerable number of later made clocks were recorded photographically and from this information some interesting conclusions can be drawn.

We have already described how the manufacture and sale of long-case clocks declined in Llanrwst reaching a low point in the period 1825-45. We saw very few clocks from this period - certainly not more than twenty in total. From the mid-1840s onward, however, there seems to have been something of a re-kindling of interest in long-case clocks, and a very marked change in their style, especially of the cases. It is the period of large, florid clocks in cases that, frequently but misleadingly, are called 'Yorkshire' cases.

The dials from this period are rather coarsely painted. Biblical, allegorical or pastoral scenes prevail, but ruins and scenes from nursery rhymes are popular, too. Occasionally, a dial arch will be well painted: we have seen several dials featuring English abbeys and churches that fall into this category. Most, however, are much cruder. Increasingly, in this period the dials are fitted direct to the movements without the use of the intermediate false-plate, and, if there is a false-plate, usually it is devoid of any maker's name. It seems likely that both movements and dials were bought from a single source, hence there was no requirement for the false-plate. As the years progress, square dials become much less frequent, the arched dial becoming almost universal.

The movements continue to be of good quality but of standard design and without any special distinguishing feature that might indicate where they had been made. It is common for dealers and repairers to describe all as having been made in Birmingham, but, as we have already seen, this is unlikely. It is much more likely that these movements were made for wholesalers and specialist suppliers by self-employed clockmakers who worked in considerable numbers in Staffordshire, Lancashire and elsewhere. One feature seems to be common to most movements of this period; the knops on the pillars are flattened and not rounded.

It is the cases, however, that distinguish these later Victorian clocks. The use of the word 'florid' to describe them is often an understatement, and it has to be suggested that these clocks do not accord with modern taste. If, stylistically, they often tend towards the grotesque, it is nevertheless possible to admire the skill of the craftsmen that produced such impressive clocks at very modest cost. The methods used in their construction are very distinctive of this period because most of these large wide cases are clothed in exotic veneers over softwood carcases. The veneers are thin and the carcases flimsy, but always, the external finish is excellent. A very wide range of different inlays, turnings and applied decorations are used to the point where the cases appear to be heavily encrusted. Although the cases of these clocks are very large, it is always a surprise to discover how light in weight they are compared with the solid oak cases of a hundred years earlier.

The best Llanrwst clocks of this period usually bear the name of Griffith Owen or Theophilus Davies, but occasionally, too, that of Robert Williams. This type of clock was sold in huge numbers all over North Wales but styles were very similar as, undoubtedly, most makers purchased them from common sources.

This renaissance in the long-case clock seems to span the years 1845-80. After 1880 very few, if any, long-case clocks were made, and the names of the late Victorian makers in Llanrwst do not appear on long-case dials. Instead, they seem to have concentrated on dial-clocks for use in the growing number of new chapels, schools and shops. We have not seen a Llanrwst dial-clock earlier than about 1840, but from then onwards, they appear in considerable numbers, especially in chapels. Griffith Owen must have used his chapel connections to obtain the lion's share of this particular market. The majority are small drop-dial clocks with good, English-made fusee movements. Later in the century, increasingly, American and German drop-dial clocks begin to compete successfully against the more expensive English clocks. There are even one or two so-called Vienna regulators bearing the names of Llanrwst retailers on their dials: Griffith Owen and Owen Williams are the names most usually found on these clocks.

ALTERATIONS AND FAKES

Very few fakes were found during our survey. As would be expected, however, there were a significant number of 'marriages', sometimes of movements to unrelated dials, but, more usually, of an old dial and movement to a later case. Some indication of the frequency with which these are found is given in part two of this book. Usually these marriages are readily identifiable, and anybody wishing to purchase a 'right' clock is advised to consult a reputable dealer or take advice from some other qualified source.

False-plates attached to brass dials, winding squares not lining up to the centres of their holes in the dial or the winding holes themselves enlarged or mutilated are clear warning signs that a movement may have been changed. There are no sure identifications of a later

Fig 131: A long-case clock by Robert Williams, c1860. The eyes of the lion in the arch are connected to the pendulum and swerve from side to side in a truely unnerving fashion!

case other than stylistic ones, but these are clear and obvious to anyone familiar with Llanrwst clocks. Fortunately, the incidence of these marriages is still small in the context of the total number of surviving clocks by Llanrwst makers.

Sometimes Llanrwst clocks are found in heavily carved cases. Although the carving is often of excellent quality, it is unlikely to be original. There was a craze for 're-carving' plain pieces of furniture in Victorian times, and all the carved cases that we have seen owe their decoration to the Victorians. They did not confine their activities to oak cases: we have seen an arch-dialled John Owen clock in a fine mahogany case, the door of which has been heavily re-carved.

Occasionally, the Victorians went even further and completely re-built and re-styled a long-case clock with astonishing results. They took an ordinary long-case clock with a square brass dial and an oak case and dismantled it. An arch with an ornamental boss was then added to the square dial and the dial itself was re-waxed with red and blue wax. Every inch of the case was heavily carved, the designs usually incorporating religious or medieval scenes with heraldic shields and helmets prominent in the designs. The original door was discarded, the new one being much thicker to give the wood-carver more scope.

189

Fig 132: John Owen would have difficulty in recognising his very ordinary square-dial clock beneath all this Victorian Gothic re-building and re-carving.

Of necessity, the hood would have had to be completely re-made to accommodate the new arched dial. Finally, the entire case was stained black or nearly so. The resulting clock, which its original maker or owner would be unlikely to recognise, would then grace some neo-gothic entrance hall or study looking, for all the world, like a prop from a Frankenstein film! Just such a remade clock is shown in Figure 132. Not many of the clocks in our survey have undergone such a complete transformation as this one but several appear to have been modified to reach intermediate stages.

There are a few completely faked clocks in existence, and, sadly, these are still being produced. A family we met had lost their Watkin Owen painted-dial clock to burglars. They went back to the source from which the clock was purchased and asked for another Watkin Owen clock. In a surprisingly short time they were provided with a replacement. It was a genuine enough clock, but the original maker's name had been erased from the dial and Watkin Owen's applied in Letraset: a cheap and shoddy fraud. The names of Llanrwst makers are sometimes engraved on old, plain, brass dials by anonymous makers to enhance the value of the clocks. We have seen two clocks purporting to be by Moses Evans of Llangernyw where this has been done. Although the number of clocks involved is very small, we have reason to believe that this particular form of faking continues.

NOTES

1. W Bezant Lowe, *The Heart of Northern Wales*, Caxton Press, Llanfairfechan, 1927, Vol I, p303.

2. The registers for Llanycil and Bala are in the Gwynedd Archives Service office at Dolgellau.

3. Welsh Folk Museum Archives; Will and probate inventory of Owen Evans, Llanerchymedd, Anglesey.

CHAPTER X
Special Clocks

In this chapter we examine, in some detail, six clocks which are special either on grounds of their technical complexity or historical interest.

THE MUSICAL CLOCK

Finding this clock provided us with perhaps the most exciting day in all our years of research into Llanrwst clocks. We had been to see the late Mr Bob Owen, *Per Nant*, [1] at that time Llanrwst's resident bard and local historian. During our discussions he asked us whether we had been to see his old friend Mr Bill Thomas of Plas — who had several clocks. We had not, so, a few days later, we telephoned Mr Thomas, explained who we were and asked whether we might be allowed to see the clocks. Bob Owen's name did the trick and we were asked to tea the next day.

Plas — is a large, rather faded, house built on the hillside about six miles from Llanrwst. It enjoys splendid views towards the Carneddau range. We were met by our elderly hosts and conducted to a large front room where a huge tea was spread on an immense table. Portraits of Thomas ancestors stared out at us somewhat gloomily from the walls and in one corner a splendid, venerable and rather oily grandfather clock ticked and creaked in a decidedly rheumatic fashion. The name on the dial was Watkin Owen: our visit had not been in vain.

However, any further inspection of Watkin Owen's handiwork had to take second place to the tea; and, soon, we were being plied with buttered *bara brith* and sardine sandwiches watched, enviously, by several large cats. Our host, who was rather hard of hearing, only contributed to the conversation now and then but always to good effect; he was a witty man with a decidedly mischievous twinkle in his eye. Suddenly, he made his most rivetting contribution so far: "The John Owen clock in the other room" he said, "strikes the hours OK, but I can't make it do the quarters any more".

Only in our wildest dreams had we ever expected to find a three train chiming clock by a Llanrwst maker, so rare are they in Wales. Suddenly, it seemed that we were only two doors and a hallway away from one. "Have some more *bara brith*, and what about a cake?" said Mrs Thomas.

Our kindly hosts were never to know (we hope) how interminable the remainder of that tea seemed, before we felt able to ask with ill-restrained excitement if we could have a look at the other clock. The suspense was not over, however, because the key of the room could not be found and when, finally, we entered it was to find all the curtains closed, the light bulb broken and the room in darkness! But the curtains were soon drawn and there was the clock standing in the darkest corner, only its top two-thirds showing above the books and packing cases stacked around it. In the dial were the tell-tale three winding holes, symmetrically placed: we had found a genuine three train clock, not a later Victorian conversion. The signature on the dial was `John Owen, Llanrwst'.

Fig 133: Clock number 16. The Musical Clock. Although this clock is so grand in every other respect, it is quite diminutive, standing a little under 84" high. The quarter columns on the plinth are a very rare feature.

Fig 134: The hood and dial of the Musical Clock clearly show the lavish decoration. The serpent sound-fret in the frieze is backed with red flannel and surmounts a parquetry, chequer-pattern band. The flambeau finials and column capitals are modern replacements closely modelled on a few remnants of the original ones.

Fig 135: The dial of the Musical Clock. The curved slot to the right of the seconds disc, now blanked off, once housed the lever for changing from simple chiming to the tune. The entire date disc revolves around the winding square. The spandrels are Large Lady with Fan Head-dress. The hands are modern replacements.

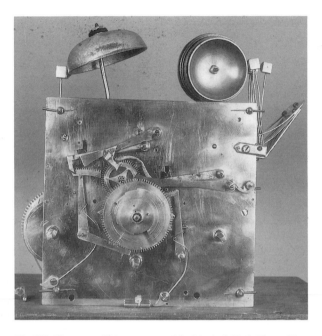

Fig 136: The seven pillar movement of the Musical Clock. The striking train is on the left, the going train in the middle, and the now inoperative chiming/musical train is on the right.

Fig 137: The wheelwork of the Musical Clock. The pallets and scape wheel have been replaced.

Fig 138: The front-plate of the movement of the Musical Clock, a battlefield fought over by repairers ill-equipped for the task.

Fig 139: Side view of the movement of the Musical Clock, showing the Latin inscription.

Subsequently, through the great generosity of our hosts, we were allowed to borrow the clock and the following description is based on our examination of it in our workshop.

We will probably never know who bought the clock from the young John Owen and his case-maker. We can be sure, however, that his instructions must have been quite specific: he wanted to own the best, the most prestigious, the most outstanding example of horological craftsmanship in the district. The expense must have been of secondary consideration. It is perhaps surprising, therefore, that the clock is quite diminutive. It stands a bare 84" high even on its somewhat over-large modern feet. Perhaps the ceilings in the house where it was destined to stand would not allow for anything taller.

The case is a tour-de-force by the country craftsman who made it. It is made of mid-coloured oak and is very heavy. The doors and the panel on the plinth are all cross-banded with walnut. The heavily fluted quarter columns on the trunk are repeated on the plinth. The method of making these quarter pillars is very unusual. Normally the bases and capitals would be made separately and joined to the columns at their extremities. On this clock, however, the joint is well down the column and the first inch or so of the fluting is integral with the capitals and bases. This highly distinctive feature appears on one or two other cases, obviously the work of a single case-maker.

The trunk door is exceptionally narrow, an early feature. In its centre is a parquetry panel inlaid with a curved 'propeller' device surmounted by a rather strange bird of ill-defined species; a crow or chough perhaps? This panel also contains the initials 'HR' and the date '1752'. At the foot of the plinth panel there is a parquetry rayed sun, again surmounted by a similar peculiar bird.

The hood is of broken arch design and has arched, glazed side windows through which the movement can be seen. Below the cornice of the arch is a fretwork frieze in the form of a serpent behind which we found incredibly dirty, red flannel of doubtful originality. The serpent frieze is immediately above a parquetry band of alternate dark and light divisions. The hood pillars are turned and are now surmounted by gilded wooden capitals, which are exact replicas of the single worm-eaten original capital that was still in place. The bracket feet are modern replacements but these are rather too large. Altogether, this is, by far, the most elaborate case that we have found on a Llanrwst clock. Nevertheless, the lasting impression is that it should have been larger. Certainly, the hood seems out of proportion: it is a bit too large for the trunk and its plinth.

The complexity of the dial matches the case. In the arch the moon-phase disc is engraved in brass and silvered. The quality of the engraving is good. The moon-face is cheerful, and it is decidedly less gormless than other examples that we have seen. The chapter-ring is of the usual design for the period, with quarter-hour divisions on its inner edge and the fleur-de-lys motif as half-hour markers. The dial centre is very crowded. It is decorated with concentric matting and has a recessed seconds disc above the hands and a matching date disc below them of very unusual design. The whole date disc revolves, recording the date by a static pointer. The central winding square is located in the centre of the date disc, requiring the latter to be friction-spring mounted. To the right of the seconds disc is a curved slot that once accommodated the lever to change from the tune to simple chiming or back again. A matching dummy slot has been engraved on the other side of the dial centre to preserve a balanced appearance. Until the movement can be fully restored the empty slot has been blanked off. All the hands and pointers are modern replacements. The spandrels are a large and intricate version of the Lady with a Fan Headdress pattern. The maker's name is engraved in capitals, somewhat crudely, on the dial-plate itself, at the 6 o'clock position. The dial measures 18^1/$_2$" x 13^1/$_4$" x 13^1/$_4$".

Turning now to the movement, all three trains are contained between the brass plates which measure 8" x 7^1/$_2$" and are 2^3/$_8$" apart. Looking at the movement from the front the striking train is on the left, the going train is in the middle and the chiming train is on the right. There are seven pillars which are unusual because they are plain without any knop at their centres.

Sadly, the movement has been mangled by numerous incompetent repairers over the years, all of them, evidently, ill equipped for the tasks confronting them. It is true that a thoroughly competent clockmaker has, at some time, provided a new scape wheel, pallets and chiming great wheel, but his work is the exception. The front plate has become a wasteland of empty holes, home-made detents and bodged adjustments. The clock has long since ceased chiming and it will demand the skills of an expert clock restorer to return it to full working order. The nest of six bells seems to be original, and, if the chiming train is turned manually, some sort of tune is discernable, but missing pins have rendered this unrecognisable. Perhaps, the most charming and appropriate feature of the movement is the beautifully engraved quotation on the hammer guard plate; `Sic transit gloria mundi' [2] - an apt comment on the movement in its present condition.

Nothing that can be said detracts from the importance of this clock: it is one of the rarest and most complex ever produced in Wales. We have consulted the Llanrwst registers and those of neighbouring parishes in an effort to decipher the initials 'H R' together with the date '1752' on the trunk door. Perhaps, it was a marriage clock and 'H' and 'R' were the initials of the happy couple; perhaps 'H R' are the initials of the man who commissioned the clock for his own delectation and agrandisement. So far we have been unsuccessful in our search. Mr Thomas could not remember how his family had acquired the clock, although he thought that his ancestors had bought it perhaps a hundred years previously.

Sadly, our host has recently died, the last Thomas of Plas —. He provided us with one of the rarest clocks we were to find, and with much good humour and kindness. His family had contributed greatly to the history of the district over the past two hundred years and his house was full of mementos of their residence, including the wonderful musical clock.

THE TITLEY CLOCK

A friend rang up one day: "Would you be interested in a John Owen clock with a coat-of-arms on the dial, centre seconds and maintaining power?" and then, as an afterthought, "It's in Bolton". That is how we first met Mr and Mrs Williams who lived on the outskirts of Bolton, and their marvellous clock. Not only is the clock a fine and fascinating specimen in its own right, but it is also the only Llanrwst clock for which we have a reliable provenance back to the date when it first left John Owen's workshop.

Mr Williams inherited the contents of Penloyn, a substantial house situated on a small rise on the northern edge of Llanrwst town. The house has always been an important one and can be traced back in the local records to the early 17th century and beyond. From our point of view the house is of particular interest because it was purchased by Peter Titley, the leading apothecary, doctor and surgeon in the town following his arrival there from Denbigh in about 1765. We have mentioned this first Peter Titley earlier in this book. He built up considerable estates in the town and was to become landlord of Tyn-y-pwll, the house and workshop used by the Owen family in Denbigh street. [3] He was succeeded by a son, also called Peter, who continued to live at Penloyn as, until recent times, did succeeding generations of the family. For the Llanrwst historian it is worth noting, in passing, that in 1833 Admiral Wyatt Watling married Martha Hughes Titley, the first Peter's grand-daughter. The Admiral was to give his name to one of the most important streets in the town, built in the middle of the 19th century, much of it on land owned by the Titleys.

To return to our clock, one of its most notable features is the large coat of arms engraved on the arch of the dial. They, in fact, are the heraldic bearings of the thirteenth Noble Tribe of Wales, the tribe of Ednowain Bendew, Lord of Tegaingle, who is said to have been chief of the fifteen tribes in 1079. [4] The origins and authenticity of the Fifteen Noble Tribes of Wales seem to be much challenged, and this is no place to review those arguments. Pennant, who wrote a detailed account of the Tribes [5], listed the extant descendants of Ednowain Bendew as the Lloyds of Wygfair, the Foulkes of Mertyn, the Griffiths of Rhual, the Hughes of Halkyn and of Bagillt and Griffith of Plas Issa, Caerwys. It seems doubtful that Peter Titley could have even been related to any of these families, and thus aspire to the armorials as of right. However, in one respect, the Noble Tribes are rather like the Scottish clans: people have, over the years, claimed kinship with them on the flimsiest or even non-existant grounds. We know that when Peter Titley came to Llanrwst he embarked on building up an estate and attained a position of considerable importance in the town. Adopting the coat of arms of the Thirteenth Tribe, if indeed he had no right to it by birth, would have been in keeping with his social aspirations. We know that he did so because much of the domestic silver from Penloyn dating from late Georgian times, was also in the house in Bolton. A large percentage of it has the same boar's head motif engraved upon it as appears on the clock.

Therefore, there is good reason to believe that this particular clock was made by John Owen in the early 1770s for Peter Titley, and that it has been in the family ever since, for most of the time at Penloyn.

As with the Musical Clock, Peter Titley must have agreed with John Owen that his clock should be as special and as impressive as the pair of them could devise. Certainly they succeeded in this objective.

To the horologist, the most extraordinary part of the clock is the dial. This measures $18^{1}/_{2}$" x $13^{1}/_{2}$" x $13^{1}/_{2}$" which is, in no way, remarkable, but the dial-plate alone weighs no less than $9^{1}/_{2}$lbs! It achieves this astonishing weight because it exceeds $^{1}/_{4}$" thickness at its centre, tapering away to slightly less than $^{1}/_{8}$" at its edges. Quite why this dial-plate was cast in this fashion is difficult to imagine. Possibly because of its huge weight, the dial is not attached directly to the movement by means of four conventional dial feet: instead it is attached to a brass false-plate, which, in turn, is fixed to the movement. This false-plate is made of sheet brass and is in the form of a large x-shaped cross attached to the dial-plate by small screws. The screw holes at the extreme corners of the dial are clearly visible in Figure 141 (p202). It is an interesting thought that the estimated date of this clock is in the early 1770s and, perhaps, it is significant that in 1772 the first painted dials were advertised by Osborne and Wilson of Birmingham. Is it possible that John Owen and his dial-maker had seen the publicity or even one of the new dials and incorporated features of the innovation in Peter Titley's clock - including the one-piece dial and the false-plate?

The dial is notable for a number of reasons. It is a one-piece dial, an early example of this

Fig 140: Clock number 64. The Titley Clock, c1770. A very rare and imposing example of a mahogany case made in Llanrwst. It is made of solid Cuban mahogany and is very heavy.

Fig 141: The amazing dial of the Titley Clock. It weighs more than 9lbs and is 1/4" thick at its centre. The decoration is a marvellous example of the Good Engraver's art. The arms are those of the Thirteenth Noble Tribe of Wales.

Fig 142: The extraordinary, brass false-plate which carries the dial of the Titley Clock. It is difficult to understand why it was thought necessary to use a false-plate, unless it became necessary because of the extreme and variable thickness of the dial.

Fig 143: The movement of the Titley Clock, viewed from the side. Note the maintaining-power detent.

Fig 144: The movement of the Titley Clock, showing the extra motion-work wheel required because of the centre seconds hand; also the maintaining-power lever and counter-weight.

form. It has no date indication which is most unusual; perhaps, because of its thickness, making a neat date opening in this particular dial presented real problems. Finally, the engraved designs are truly remarkable and very beautiful.

Needless to say, it is evident that this is the handiwork of the Good Engraver mentioned earlier. The chapter-ring is twelve sided, the half-hour markers intricate and fine. But it is the dial centre which is so unusual. It seems certain that the engraver was influenced by Chinese porcelain plates and dishes decorated 'in the Chinese taste'. Chinese porcelain destined for the English market was, usually, heavily decorated; in the period 1720-50, when the famille-rose style was at its height, plates, dishes and saucers were virtually covered with decoration including numerous intricate diaper borders around the edges, a feature copied by the Good Engraver to frame the seconds disc on his Exotic Plant series of dials. 'Chinese taste' porcelain, however, was much more lightly decorated, often with a single branch of blossom wandering naturalistically across the plate, sometimes extending over on to its reverse. The engraver has produced a similar design in the centre of this dial; indeed the whole design is free, asymetric and with a hint of chinoiserie. The dial is a beautiful example of this engraver's craftsmanship and artisitic talent and, yet, it is interesting to note that the maker's name is off-centre. What is more, John Owen, as noted in earlier examples, has drilled the winding holes through his own name.

The hour and minute hands shown in the illustration appear to be original; the sweep centre seconds hand is modern. Only one other clock by John Owen with centre seconds has been found. In this latter case the seconds hand appears to be original. It is a curious affair with a large cranked counterweight.

The movement to which this extraordinary dial is attached is also of considerable interest. It measures $6^3/4$" x $5^1/2$" with $2^5/8$" between the plates. It has five pillars. Originally, it had a dead-beat escapement as is usual when centre seconds hands are fitted. The 'scape wheel was originally mounted between the back plate and a bridge. Later, the centre seconds hand and the 'scape wheel must have proved troublesome because it was converted to an anchor escapement and the bridge was dispensed with, the 'scape wheel arbor being now mounted, conventionally, between the plates.

The repeat-spring is very unusual for an Owen clock: it is mounted horizontally across the top of the front-plate, a variation forced on John Owen by the presence, on the front-plate, of the additional wheel required to drive the minute hand on a centre seconds movement. This would have fouled a repeat-spring in the more usual place at the right of the front-plate and mounted vertically.

The final, and most unusual feature of this movement, is the maintaining mechanism, necessary to to keep the clock going during winding. It is somewhat primitive but surprisingly effective. It consists of a long, horizontal, counterweighted steel lever with a detent attached. When the string, hanging down inside the case, is pulled, the detent engages with the teeth of the third wheel and the counterweight is sufficient to drive the escapement during winding. This very primitive mechanism is reminiscent of the method often used in the movements of turret clocks.

It would be surprising if a clock, such as this one, were to be housed in an ordinary case: indeed it is not. The stately and somewhat sombre case is made in solid Cuban mahogany. The timber is thick and the case is very heavy. Mahogany was very rarely used in Llanrwst; we have only found two other cases made in this exotic timber. Initially, it was assumed that the case had, in all likelihood, been bought from Liverpool or Chester where the use of mahogany was much more usual. But, eventually, it was realised that its design was virtually identical to one or two other cases in oak which, without doubt, had been made in Llanrwst. John Owen's case-maker, therefore, must have sent away to Liverpool or Chester for the mahogany planks from which this special order was executed. No concessions, however, were made to the use of the much costlier and more fashionable mahogany. The somewhat stylised, standard, oak design was followed down to the last detail. The clocks stand 86" high.

Undoubtedly, the Titley clock is the most interesting and most unusual of all the clocks found during our survey.

THE OWEN HUGHES CLOCK

At first glance the reader may question the inclusion of this clock in the chapter: it is, after all, a fairly ordinary arched, painted-dial clock with moon-phase indication. Nevertheless, this clock is crammed full of interest, to the local historian as well as to the horologist, and we make no apologies for selecting it. The clock may be dated about 1780 and for Llanrwst, at least, is an early example of a painted dial, perhaps the earliest so far located. Most painted dials of this period were fitted to Watkin Owen's clocks without the use of the usual iron false-plate. This is an exception but, infuriatingly, the false-plate bears no maker's name. There is a faint shadow of one but today this is illegible, almost as if it

Fig 145: Clock number 121. The five pillar movement from the Owen Hughes Clock. It gives the lie to the assertion that the wheel-work is never scribed on the front-plates of Watkin Owen movements. The moon and date wheels are modern replacements.

had been deliberately obscured. We suspect that the dial was by Osborne, but Osborne and Wilson dials of this period are, usually, very similar in style and layout. Other early signs are the half globes, the four similar corner designs and the straight minute hand. And, of course, the square date aperture of the kind normally found on brass dials. This form of date indication on a painted dial is unusual and must have been costly. Nevertheless, it features on all of Watkin Owen's early painted dials. He, or his clients, must have been very conservative - although it can be said in their defence, that this was altogether a more positive and legible method of recording the date than the disc and lunette opening found on most painted dials at this time. The brass date ring is waxed and silvered, exactly as it would be on a brass dial, but in this case rotates on very well made rollers, something never seen on Llanrwst brass dials.

The reader may already have noticed a peculiarity of this particular dial: the winding hole on the right is significantly higher than the left. This is not a particularly rare feature on Owen clocks. We have observed several others including a very early example by John Owen. In only one instance have we seen the left-hand, striking train winder higher than the going. This is not surprising because there are more wheels to be accommodated in the striking train and, therefore, less room to arrange the train. It is difficult to understand why the winding holes should be arranged asymetrically. It could be carelessness, but this would have been easy to correct providing the plates had not already been drilled. Perhaps there is a clue on this dial: the date ring is unusually small in diameter. Confronted with a smaller than usual date ring, the clockmaker may have found that planting the arbors and winding squares in their more usual position resulted in one of the winding squares fouling the teeth of the date ring. Moving it upwards would provide the necessary clearance even at the expense of some lack of symmetry in the layout of features on the dial.

The problem does not end there, however. Who cut the holes in the dial? There is evidence to suggest that the dials were delivered without the winding holes having been cut, [6] and that this operation was carried out by the clockmaker, who also fitted the brass winding hole bushes thus giving a tidy finish to the holes. If this actually is what happened, then we are left with the inescapable conclusion that the swag of flowers that incorporates both winding holes was added in Llanrwst: and very competently this was done, too. We can only think that Watkin Owen was sensitive about the untidily placed winding holes, and that the flowers were added as camouflage: or maybe, it was his client who had it done.

Did the same artist add the name Owen Hughes that is written in red on the arch above the moon-phase indicator? A name added in this way is usually that of the clock's first owner, and this seems likely in this case. Indeed, we can identify him: he was a well-to-do tenant farmer who lived just outside the town.

In the early 1780s the Gwydir Estate commissioned an estate atlas of maps and plans and this, and a much smaller contemporary copy, have survived. [7] The maps show that the farm of Henblas, totalling some 159 acres, was let to Owen Hughes and contemporary rentals record that the annual rent was £38 0s 0d. Henblas still exists today, seven hundred feet above the town, on the foothills to the east before they finally give way to the moorlands of Hiraethog and Denbigh. [8] Henblas, and its neighbouring farm Brynsylldy, have a particular place in local history because Sir John Wynn, in his *History of the Gwydir Family* [9] records how his ancestors acquired Henblas and built Brynsylldy, and how both

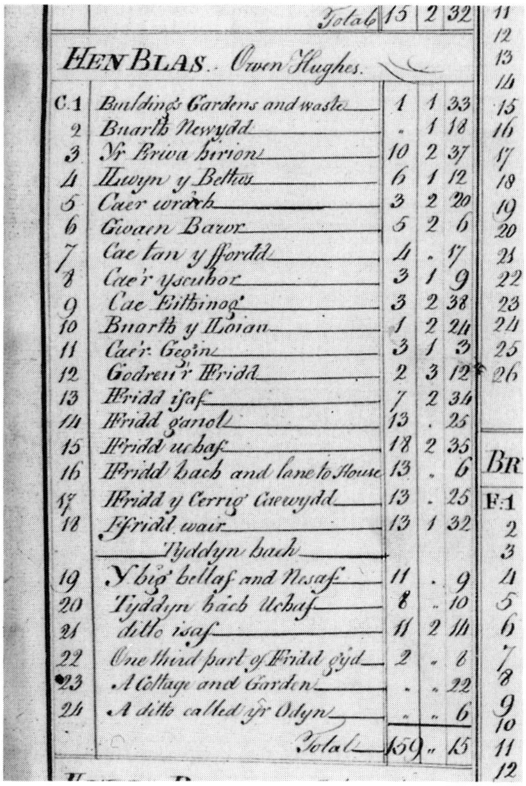

Fig 146: An extract from the Gwydir Estate Atlas, c1780 which gives full details of Owen Hughes' farm Henblas. [Trustees of the Grimsthorpe & Drummond Castle Trust Ltd]

HEN BLAS. *Owen Hughes.*

Total 15 | 2 | 32

C.1	Buildings Gardens and waste	1	1	33
2	Buarth Newydd	.	1	18
3	Yr Briwa birion	10	2	37
4	Llwyn y Bettws	6	1	12
5	Caer wrach	3	2	20
6	Gwaen Bawr	5	2	6
7	Cae tan y ffordd	4	.	17
8	Cae'r yscubor	3	1	9
9	Cae Fithinog	3	2	38
10	Buarth y Lloian	1	2	24
11	Caer Geoine	3	1	3
12	Godreu'r Ffridd	2	3	12
13	Ffridd isaf	7	2	34
14	Ffridd ganol	13	.	25
15	Ffridd uchaf	18	2	35
16	Ffridd bach and lane to House	13	.	6
17	Ffridd y Cerrig Caewydd	13	.	25
18	Ffridd wair	13	1	32
	Tyddyn bach			
19	Y big bellaf and Nesaf	11	.	9
20	Tyddyn bach Uchaf	8	.	10
21	ditto isaf	11	2	11
22	One third part of Ffridd gyd	2	.	6
23	A Cottage and Garden	.	.	22
24	A ditto called yr Odyn	.	.	6
	Total	159	.	15

survived the Wars of the Roses unscathed. He quotes a Welsh rhyme:

Hardlech a Dinbech pob dôr
Yn Cunnev
Nanconway yn farwor
Mil a phedwarcant mae Jor
A thrugain ag wyth rhagor

which has been translated, somewhat awkwardly, as follows:

At Hardlech and Denbigh every house was in flames,
and Nantconwy in cinders; 1400 from our Lord, and
sixty and eight more". [10]

We will let Sir John complete the story:

In that expedition Jevan ap Robert lay one night at the house of Rhys ap Einion at Henblas, who was maried to his cosen Catherine daughter of Robin Vaughan; and setting forth very early before day unwittingly carried upon his finger the wrest [11] of his cosen's harpe, whereon (as it seemeth) he had played over night, as the manner was in those days, to bring himselfe asleepe. This he returned by a messenger unto his cosen, with this message with all, that he came not into

Denbigh land to take from his cosen as much as the wrest [11] of her harpe: whereby it appeareth, that by this means neither her house, nor any of her goods were burnt, wasted, hurt or spoyled, Thus both her houses, Henblas and Brinsyllty, escaped the Earle Herberte's desolation, though the same consumed the whole burrough of Llanrwst, and all the vale of Conway besides, to cold coals, whereof the print is yet extant, the very stones of the ruines of manie habitations, in and along my demaynes, carrying yet the colour of the fire . . .' [12]

Henblas survived the Wars of the Roses but not the rebuilding of Victorian times from when most of the present buildings date.

There are other mentions of Owen Hughes in the Llanrwst archives. He was, for instance, churchwarden in 1785 and, obviously, he was a man of some substance in the community. Just the sort of man who would have wished to have a clock that was slightly above average and who could have afforded to pay for it.

In other respects this clock is not remarkable. The movement is interesting because the wheelwork is fully scribed on the front plate which contradicts, convincingly, the held view that Watkin Owen movements never reveal any such scribing. The handsome, slender case has had a very hard life and it has required much loving care to return it to its present condition. The little dentil fret below the hood is a pretty detail as are the scalloped pads above and below the quarter column bases and capitals. The hood pillars are in yew and the quarter columns seem to be of another exotic hardwood, possibly padouk.

At first sight a conventional clock, but, in reality, one which is brim-full of interest.

THE WATKIN OWEN BRACKET CLOCK

Welsh bracket clocks are rare: indeed, 18th century Welsh bracket clocks are so rare that less than ten have, so far, been recorded. Judging by the engraving of the dial this example squeezes into the 18th century by about five years or so.

As the reader will recognise, the dial, which measures $8^1/4$" x $8^1/4$" x $11^3/4$" is engraved by the Urn Engraver who worked for Watkin Owen during the 1790s, and who was, in all probability, resident in Llanrwst working for the Owens full time. Note how the winding holes are incorporated into the design. Obviously, the engraver knew where they were going to be or maybe he received the dial-plate with them already drilled. In other respects the dial exhibits a certain lack of practice in engraving small dials like this one. Observe the rather unsatisfactory way the 'grass seed-head' swirls cut across the more formal curved motifs either side of the strike/silent circle in the arch. The hands are modern replacements; by this date it is more likely that non-matching serpentine hands would have been superseded by matching diamond-pattern hands.

The seven pillar verge movement is large. It measures $8^1/2$" x $6^1/4$" is very robust and, it has to be said, somewhat crude. It gives every indication of having been made by someone unpractised at making bracket clock movements. The stop-work and spring barrels are massive. As an experienced clockmaker friend commented: "Quite large enough to accommodate month going springs". The clock barely manages to go for 8 days, however, because the capacity of the fusees does not match that of the spring barrels. The wheels, too, are large and the construction of the 'scape and contrate wheels most unusual. The rims and spokes have been made separately and then soldered together: a neat job, but not the usual way of doing it. There are signs, too, that because it has been altered slightly, as has been the repeat work, the geometry of the strike work was not entirely satisfactory in

Fig 147: A Watkin Owen bracket clock, c1795, featuring the work of the Urn Engraver. The case was originally 'scumbled'. It is now partially veneered with walnut.
[Welsh Folk Museum]

Fig 148: The front-plate of the Watkin Owen bracket clock. It has no typical Owen features, and was probably bought-in.
(Welsh Folk Museum)

its original form. Altogether, the movement exhibits many signs of improvisation and, clearly, is the work of someone not used to fusee movements.

The movement exhibits no trace of any Owen design features. In particular, the strike-work is strictly conventional. Equally, it is clear that the movement did not come from one of Watkin's regular suppliers in Lancashire or Cheshire: it is far too crude. There is little doubt, in fact, that it comes from Wales. If Watkin Owen's own clockmaker was not responsible for it, then maybe this movement is the work of Maurice Thomas of Caernarfon or one of the Wrexham makers.

The case is in a somewhat distressed state. The front and sides are veneered in walnut but the base and top are painted or 'scumbled' on pine. [13] It had always been assumed that, originally, the entire case was veneered. But closer examination reveals a surprising fact. The holes in the side of the case for the strings to activate the repeat mechanism have been veneered over, indicating that the case had originally been painted in what is usually known as 'scumble-work'. This is somewhat surprising for a clock that must have been very expensive when it was first made.

We have heard numerous rumours that other Owen bracket clocks exist, but, so far, we have been unable to confirm their authenticity.

THE TOWN HALL CLOCK

The Owen family tree discussed at length in Chapter II records John Owen as the "Maker of the Old Town Hall Clock", and it has always been assumed that the turret clock illustrated on page 213 is that clock. Certainly, this clock was in position in the gable-end of the town hall when the building was demolished, to ease the passage of modern traffic through the town square, some twenty five years ago.

The original building is said to have been built by Mary Wynn of Caermelwr in 1661 or by Sir John Wynn's son, Maurice, in the same year. According to Bezant Lowe, [14] it was subsequently burned down and rebuilt early in the 19th century by Lord Willoughby D'Eresby, Baron Gwydir, although no documents relating to this re-building seem to have survived. This may, however, be the reason for the little family tree referring to the "Old Town Hall", to distinguish it from the new building. We can only assume that the clock was rescued and re-installed in the re-built hall: the present clock is certainly old enough, as we shall see.

The clock is not signed by its maker nor has it any feature that would enable us to say, positively, that it had been made by John Owen. But there is no reason to doubt that he was the provider of the clock; we hesitate to say maker, again for reasons that will become clear.

We know when the clock was installed. It was in 1761 or 1762. In the Gwydir Estate rental the agent John Williams records the following disbursement:

> Paid Your Grace's Contribution towards erecting a new clock on the Town Hall at Llanrwst by your Grace's Order . . . . £5 5s 0d. [15]

If only Williams had realised how much more he could have told us by adding a few extra words! Who was the money paid to? What was the total cost? Did the use of the word "new" imply that there was a clock in the town hall already? Unfortunately, the

Fig 149: Llanrwst Town Hall in the early 1930s. The John Owen turret clock is in position in the gable end. Sadly, the building has been demolished in recent years to make way for modern traffic.

Gwydir agent had a long and comprehensive rental to write, and he was required to produce at least two copies, so he was not in the habit of recording more than the basic essentials.

The use of the word 'new' is, nevertheless, thought provoking. If the clock erected in 1761/62 was a replacement, who made the earlier one? Maybe "Maker of the Old Town Hall Clock" implies that he made the old clock, not the new one. In the absence of any other documentary evidence, however, all must be regarded as conjecture. Suffice to say that John Owen was clearly competent to make turret clocks. Why else would the churchwardens of Conwy have employed him in 1746 to repair their clock. [16] It would, surely, have been unlikely that anyone else would have been employed in 1761 to erect the new town hall clock in Llanrwst.

It is time now to turn to the clock itself. After its removal from the town hall, it was stored in the local council yard for some years. Fortunately, the council refused various offers to buy the clock, and, in due course, it was sent to the Welsh Folk Museum for safe keeping. We asked our friend Adrian Dolby, himself something of an expert on turret clocks, to examine this clock and let us have his conclusions. His first observation was a surprise: the clock was significantly earlier than 1761, at least those parts of it that are original. It has to be said that the clock has been the subject of numerous alterations, additions and subtractions and is far from complete at the present time. There are numerous empty holes and repairs both skilled and crude. If the clock is, indeed, earlier than 1761-62, then either it is not the clock that was installed in that year, or, the clock installed in 1761 was an existing clock from somewhere else. This seems perfectly likely.

211

Turret clocks, especially those in churches, were regularly upgraded at this period, and it would have been perfectly possible for John Owen to have obtained an existing clock for the town hall. The townspeople need not have known that the new clock was not altogether the handiwork of their clockmaker. A coat of new paint and much polishing of brass wheels would have dispelled any doubts.

The second conclusion to be drawn from the examination of the clock is that, originally, it was single handed. The motion work now attached to the clock is relatively modern in appearance and must have been added during the last one hundred years or so. Furthermore, it is clear that this is an addition. There is, for instance, no set-hand dial or mechanism. [17] Instead, a single spring bearing on the end of the 'scape wheel arbor allows the 'scape wheel to be disengaged from the pallets and the hand to be set. With considerable care it must be added; allowing the hand to run free would have had spectacular results as the huge stone weight plunged earthwards! Clearly, the present anchor escapement is a replacement, but it is likely that the clock always had an anchor escapement.

The installation of the clock in 1761 was not the end of the matter. Fortunately for us, at that time local charities provided for the sustenance of 6 widows of the town, and for the apprenticeship of poor boys. These had been endowed by the Wynn family of Gwydir and were administered by the Gwydir agent. Any surplus funds had to be applied to the maintenance of the town hall, and the account book for these charities has survived. [18] In between details of the apprenticeships are the following details, dated 1765:

Expenses in Erecting a Cupola over the clock to hang the Bell

	£	s	d
Carrying the stones		5	-
Richard Jones, mason 39 days work at 1s	1	19	-
Richard Jones, labourer 37 days at 10d	1	10	10
William Griffiths for timber and work		3	6
Tho: Owen, Smith for work to the clock case		18	-
Richard Pierce & John Hughes, slaters for work done		6	-
John Williams for carrying gravel & slates		10	-
	5	18	4

This entry is interesting as the bell now with the clock is inscribed - "Founder, T Rudhall 1767". T Rudhall was a bell founder from Gloucester. It is not clear whether the cupola was erected two years in advance of the arrival of the bell or whether the present bell replaced an earlier one.

It also appears that the building of the cupola was an elaborate and time consuming operation, if the hours worked by Richard Jones, the mason, and his labourer, are anything to go by!

Apparently, the cupola replaced a tower, because, in 1757 and 1758, £12 5s 0d. was spent from the charity fund in making a new tower for the town hall - the old one had, in all probability, been blown down, a regular occurrence. This work included the supply and erection of a new gilded copper weather vane that had been supplied by John Hughes for 3

Fig 150 & 151: Views of the front and rear of the movement of the John Owen turret clock. The clock was originally single handed and dates from the first half of the 18th century. It has been much altered over the years, and is now in need of extensive restoration. In the meantime, it is held for safe-keeping in the Welsh Folk Museum, St Fagans.
[Welsh Folk Museum]

213

guineas. In 1773 it was blown down again together with the cupola and had to be "fixed up" by Richard Pierce. This new tower, and, presumably, the one that it replaced predate the installations of the clock in 1761-62, lending support to the suggestion that there had been an earlier clock or market bell or both.

These are the first of a series of entries in the charity book and the Gwydir rentals concerning repairs to the clock, to the cupola and to the weather cock. In 1781, 11s 10^1/2d. was paid for "putting up and cleaning the Town Hall Clock".

Figure 149 shows a cupola, housing the bell, once again in position on the Town Hall. It is surmounted by the weather cock consisting of the Gwydir Eagle. Despite all these vicissitudes the weather-vane has survived and is with the clock at the Welsh Folk Museum in St Fagans.

There is, from time to time, talk of rescuing the clock from St Fagans and re-erecting it in the town. So far no entirely suitable position has been found and the clock movement itself will require much careful and skilled restoration.

THE JOHN LLOYD DRESSER

Finally, amongst these special clocks we have included a Welsh dresser with a clock incorporated within it. The clock is signed by Moses Evans, Llangernyw. Unfortunately, we do not know the name of the joiner who collaborated with Moses Evans in the making of this interesting piece of furniture. Clocks built into dressers or cupboards should always be regarded with some caution because, frequently, they are a later marriage of long-case clock and dresser or cupboard. No such doubts need exist about this excellent example, perhaps the finest of its sort in existence.

The dial false-plate carries the inscription 'Wilson, Birmingham'. The chapter circle consists of Arabic tumbling numbers, an early example of this switch from the Roman numerals that, hitherto, invariably had been used. The dial corners feature roses and poppy-like flowers contained in raised, gilded 'comma' borders. In the arch is a good-quality painting of the dove returning with the olive branch in its beak, contained in a circular black and gilt border. The diamond pattern hands are original. The most interesting feature of the dial is the addition of the inscription 'John Lloyd 1797', each letter being painted radially just inside the hour chapters. Thus, we are provided with an accurate date for the dresser and, presumably, the name of the man for whom the dresser was made originally. So fine a piece of furniture must have been made for a man of some substance and the obvious place to look for such a person living in Llangernyw parish is the substantial residence Hafodunos.

For centuries, Hafodunos had been the home of the Lloyd family. John Griffith in his monumental work *Pedigrees of Anglesey and Carnarvonshire Families* [19], records that there was, indeed, a John Lloyd at Hafondunos in 1797, who died in 1815 at the age of 66. It is, of course, mere speculation that this was the client of Moses Evans, but this seems to be a distinct possibility.

The quality of the dresser is exceptional, and it has survived in remarkably good condition. It is made throughout from deep honey coloured oak, which, over the decades, has developed a lovely patina. The clock case element is elaborate, more so than for any ordinary long-case clock, and, unusually for a Llanrwst clock case, features a shell inlay in the trunk door.

The dresser rack has 'bellied' ends that proclaim its origin in the Llanrwst area together

Fig 152: The John Lloyd Dresser Clock, dated 1797, by Moses Evans of Llangernyw. Note the 'bellied' ends of the rack denoting its origin in the Llanrwst area.
[Welsh Folk Museum]

with a row of spice drawers, including a dummy one in the clock trunk. To accommodate the clock weights the drawers in the centre of the base do not reach to its full depth, but are stopped short to leave adequate clearance. It is very interesting to note that the dresser incorporates design features that are identical to those found on contemporary clock cases, especially the reeded quarter columns and the ogee bracket feet. The drawer handles are turned oak and are original. It is quite unusual to find a break-fronted dresser at this period: they are more often later.

Altogether this is a marvellous piece of furniture and it is fitting that it should be in the national collection at St Fagans.

Notes

1. *Per Nant* was Mr Owen's Bardic name. Literally it means 'Nightingale of the Valley'.

2. "O, how quickly doth the glory of the world pass away!" Attributed to Thomas a Kempis (1380-1471) in his *Imitatio Christi*. This translation by Anthony Hoskins.

3. We do not know when, exactly, Peter Titley purchased the freehold of Tyn-y-pwll, but the Mostyn estate disposed of much of its property in the town in the last years of the 18th century as several documents in the Mostyn papers in the library of the University College of North Wales, Bangor record. That Peter Titley did acquire the property is confirmed by surviving Land Tax records for 1825. Clwyd County Record Office ref: QSD/Land Tax 1825.

4. Thomas Pennant, *The History of the Parishes of Whiteford and Holywell*, printed for B and J White, Fleet Street, 1796, p 308 *et seq*.

5. *Ibid*.

6. Brian Loomes, *White Dial Clocks*, 2nd Edition, published by David & Charles. Chapter 5. See p77.

7. In the Ancaster Papers at the Lincoln Record Office, 4/ANC/4/6.

8. Henblas ('The Old Place' or 'The Old Hall') is a very common house name in Wales. There is at least one Henblas to be found in most parishes. In this context we can be reasonably sure that we have identified the right Henblas because, here, it is coupled with the farm Brynsylldy which is less than a mile away.

9. Sir John Wynn, *The History of the Gwydir Family*, published by Woodall and Venables, 1878, p54 *et seq*. This has been published on several other occasions, using various source manuscripts. The first publication was in 1770, edited by the Hon Daines Barrington, the second in *Barrington's Miscellanies* in 1781 and the third in 1827, edited by Miss Angharad Llwyd.

10. This translation appears in one of Barrington's (see note 9 above) footnotes. Even he considered it a very awkward translation because he quotes another from the same source "in the stile of Sternhold and Hopkins".

11. Daines Barrington, in a footnote, explains a 'wrest' as follows: "The wrest of a harp is the hollow iron with which the strings are tuned; this term is still used by the harpsicord tuners for an instrument they use for the same purpose". See, Sir John Wynn, *Ibid*.

12. Sir John Wynn, *op cit*, p55.

13. Technically, to 'scumble' is to alter the appearance of a coat of paint by applying a further very thin coat of opaque or semi opaque paint to produce a mottled appearance. In this instance the effect is reminiscent of the patterning of walnut or burr-walnut.

14. W Bezant Lowe, *The Heart of Northern Wales*, Caxton Press, Llanfairfechan 1927, Vol 2, p292.

15. The Gwydir Rental for 1761-62 is at Grimsthorpe Castle.

16. See Chapter II.

17. The set-hand mechanism on a turret-clock allows the hands to be set accurately without being able to see the dial(s). Instead, the position of the hands is shown on a small dial on the movement - the set-hand dial.

18. Lincoln County Record Office 4/ANC/4/7.

19. John Edwards Griffith, *Pedigrees of Anglesey and Carnarvonshire Families*, printed originally in 1914 for the author by W K Morton and Son Ltd, Horncastle. Reprinted in 1985 by Bridge Books, Wrexham.

CHAPTER XI
Conclusion

It only remains to ask what conclusions can be drawn about the Llanrwst clockmakers. In what way were they, in the context of their times and our heritage of their clocks, special or significant?,

The first and now rather obvious conclusion is that the history of clock making, as opposed to clock retailing, in the town is, in reality, the history of the Owens - John, Watkin, William and David. With the honourable exception of Moses Evans, they totally dominated the clockmaking market not just in Llanrwst but in a very large area of North Wales with Llanrwst at its centre. Indeed, in the 18th century, most if not all of the other so called makers in the area should have their credentials closely investigated because we found much circumstantial evidence to suggest that they were either retailers, agents, employees or ex-employees of the Owen workshop. If nothing else, this leads us, inescapably, to the conclusion that the Owens were very successful commercially, securing for themselves unchallenged market-leadership in the area, although not, apparently, any great material wealth.

In the context of Wales as a whole, it seems likely that the Owens were the most prolific family of clockmakers who ever lived and worked in the principality. None of the other Welsh clockmaking dynasties such as the Hampsons of Wrexham, the Bowens of Swansea, the Thomases of Caernarfon or the Winstanleys from the Holywell area seem to have matched the Owens in the sheer number of clocks produced, over a period of nearly a century.

In other respects the Owens were not so remarkable. Their clocks, whilst of excellent quality, were neither very fine nor innovative. Their output, numerically, may not have been matched in Wales but certainly was by other clockmaking families and workshops elsewhere in the kingdom: we have listed several in these pages. So, we cannot claim that the Llanrwst workshop was exceptional, nationally, in either context.

It might be imagined, certainly, that the clocks produced by the Owens deep in North Wales would be distinctively Welsh. We certainly embarked on this project assuming this would be the case. After all, Samuel Roberts of Llanfair Caereinion produced distinctive, vernacular clocks a few miles from the border with England. Surely the Owens, working 40 miles deeper into Wales, would produce even more highly distinctive Welsh clocks? Surprisingly they did nothing of the kind, certainly so far as the dials and movements were concerned. Rather they proved to be an enclave of the highly organised and integrated clockmaking of north-west England and North Wales with its centre in Lancashire and Cheshire. It says much for the Owens' commercial and organisational skills that they could operate so successfully thus, whilst depending on such extended lines of communication. We must conclude that communications in the second half of the 18th century in this part of Britain were a good deal more efficient than they are often given credit for.

Before we are accused by our Welsh readers of being irretrievably Anglo-centric we are delighted to confirm that the cases into which the Owens fitted their clocks are unmistakably of Welsh, indeed of Llanrwst origin. The case-makers followed design trends to be seen elsewhere but stamped their output with the individuality, personality and pride which was a feature of the vernacular furniture produced in the area throughout the 18th century.

The Owens, we are agreed, were very successful craftsmen but craftsmen nevertheless. Tempting as it is to do so, we cannot call them industrialists. They did not live to see or participate in the results of the industrial revolution with its factories, mass production and suppression of individual skills. But the pre-industrialism in which they participated was organised and effective beyond any point that we had imagined when we embarked on this project, and this does not apply to the Owens alone amongst the 18th century Welsh clockmakers - it seems typical of most of them – albeit few were as accomplished practitioners of this form of production as the Owens of Llanrwst.

In one respect, however, the Owens of Llanrwst are, we believe, exceptional and we alluded to this on the very first page of this book. No other family of 18th century clockmakers can command more awareness today in the area in which they worked two hundred years ago. Even more importantly to us, their clocks are still to be found in abundance in the Conwy Valley and throughout North Wales because they are still cherished to an exceptional degree by the descendants of the people for whom they were made originally. The clocks are handed down from father to son and, to this day, it is not unusual for a father with more than a single child to seek out more clocks so that each of his offspring can be endowed with a family clock. Visiting so many Welsh homes, we soon realised that, whereas much of the old vernacular furniture has been replaced by its modern, mass-produced equivalent, the dressers and, particularly, the clocks have been retained. It would be difficult to over-estimate the importance to our project of this fact. If we have any basis for being regarded as authoritative it must be because of the exceptionally high percentage of the Owens' output we were able to locate and inspect in so relatively short a time. Long may this adherence to their clocks by the people of North Wales continue.

Many times during the past ten years of more or less continuous involvement with the project we have felt very close to the Owens, the men, and would not have been too surprised to turn round one day and see John and Watkin looking over our shoulders. We are sure that, if they had been there, they would have been shaking their heads at our stupidity in failing to comprehend what would have been simple and obvious to them. If we are fortunate to meet them in the hereafter we will shake their hands as old and respected friends - and then fall to asking them for the answers to all those questions that we have posed in these pages and failed, so signally, to answer satisfactorily.

PART TWO
The Clock Survey

CHAPTER XII
Methodology

Introduction

From the very earliest days we realised that the examination of surviving clocks by Llanrwst makers would be a crucial source of material for our research. It was easy to embark on the process as we had several friends in the valley who had Llanrwst clocks in their houses. A telephone call, or a knock on the front door, was all that was required to get the clock survey under way. Furthermore, our friends had their own networks of friends or relations with clocks. A few more telephone calls and in no time we had seen a dozen clocks. At this rate, we thought, we might find 50 or even 100 clocks altogether. Little did we know!

Now ten years, at least 30,000 miles and nearly 600 clocks later, we have had to call a halt to our survey. New addresses and telephone numbers arrive nearly every week but the survey has had to be suspended, at least for a period, to allow the results of our researches to be analysed and for this book to be written.

If authorship came more easily to us it would be very tempting to write a book about writing a book! This would enable us to recount all our adventures over five years of spending weekends and evenings driving to every district and community in North Wales, and further afield, to inspect clocks. Adventures we had aplenty; some funny, some not so funny, some incredible, some fascinating but all, with very few exceptions, enjoyable. We have made countless new friends, and today are hailed in the streets of most towns and villages in North Wales by erstwhile hosts wanting to know when the book will be published. The survey resulted in us becoming exceedingly expert on the highways and byeways of Wales. It is our boast that we have travelled virtually every mile of road in Gwynedd and Clwyd, and a good many more miles without the assistance of roads at all!! A Range Rover came in very handy on occasions, especially when visiting houses or cottages that had no road or track leading to them at all, or when the tracks became so steep as to be impassable with any ordinary car.

The survey was not without its hazards, perhaps the most dangerous being hostile dogs and Welsh cream teas. The Welsh sheepdog will usually retreat, albeit noisily, if spoken to firmly - even in English. We encountered a few, however, invariably on remote farms, miles from anywhere, which would have sent the hounds of the Baskervilles scurrying back to their kennels. Fortunately for us, this fearsome minority were usually chained up but always with the length of chain nicely adjusted so that the beast's fangs snapped together within a bare half-inch of our anatomy as we edged towards the front door. We seemed to live a charmed life and thus grew careless, giving a fat little pug-dog in a smart Cheshire drawing room an undeserved opportunity to draw first blood.

The afternoon teas did us much more damage. We would not for a moment wish to impugn all those kind ladies who laid on such wonderful spreads for us, even if these always seemed to be designed to immobilise rather than merely refresh. We were reasonably healthy and could do justice to sandwiches, buttered bara brith and incredibly sticky cream cakes, but only once in an afternoon. Confronted by the third such offering within the space of a couple of hours we usually wilted, and we hope that we have not offended our hostesses.

Altogether, our clock survey provided us with some very happy and exciting times and we can thoroughly recommend the process to anyone contemplating their own horological research project.

The Method

In the early days our inspections were limited by uncertainty as to what we should be recording. Later on it became apparent that the sheer numbers of clocks to be inspected necessitated a carefully planned but limited initial inspection.

Each clock inspection was made up of two distinct elements, the completion of a detailed written survey form and a complete photographic record.

Our survey forms are reproduced in Appendix II (p264). The forms themselves have proved very satisfactory and, if we were starting all over again, we would only make a few minor improvements. There was a time when we thought that the photographs made it unnecessary to record so much detail in writing, but we soon learnt that this was a profound mistake. No matter how good the photographs, they were never as reliable as a carefully recorded visual inspection with measurements. There was some debate as to whether the forms should be amended so as to facilitate computerisation, especially as several researchers have recently demonstrated some impressive benefits of computer analysis of vernacular furniture. For a number of reasons we decided to rely on a hand compiled record but we acknowledge that we may have missed certain opportunities as a result. In the event, we used a computer after all - to facilitate the statistical analyses contained in the technical commentary that follows. We devised a simple data-base in which to store the technical and stylistic features of the clocks. This was done by means of Lotus Symphony software and an IBM personal computer.

Two reasons for retaining a simple format are worth mentioning. Firstly, the survey form doubled most efficiently, both as a record and as a check list of items to be inspected. Without a check list it would be virtually impossible to record data in a comprehensive and consistent manner. Secondly, the form could be completed by clock owners themselves with a minimum of explanation. Thus, dealers and clock owners overseas were able to send reliable information on clocks which we were quite unable to inspect ourselves.

It was necessary to have separate forms for brass and painted dial clocks. Otherwise, the standard format proved perfectly satisfactory, not just for recording long-case clocks but also for the relatively few bracket and wall clocks that came to our attention. If these had been more numerous we would have designed special forms for them.

No less important was the photographic record. All the clocks were photographed insitu, without any attempt to move them or otherwise make them more photogenic in appearance or setting. Throughout the survey Canon AE1 35mm cameras were used, fitted with Canon dedicated flash equipment. A 28mm wide angle lense was essential to obtain full-length shots of long-case clocks in their owner's homes because there were few opportunities to stand far enough away to use longer lenses. The Canon 28mm lense proved very satisfactory indeed, giving sharp images with very little distortion.

Kodacolour 100 film was used throughout. With the equipment used, this resulted in most shots being taken at F5.6 and 1/60th second. Because the camera was synchronised for flash at 1/60th second and the lense performed well at F5.6 there was little advantage in using faster film.

A series of shots was taken of each clock, including the dial with the hood removed, the dial with hood insitu, the complete clock in full length and close-ups of the mouldings under the hood, the mouldings on the plinth and any other distinctive features. Finally, the clock movement itself was photographed in close-up from both sides, the 28mm lense allowing us to fill the camera frame with detailed images of the movement. It was never possible to take full frontal views of the clocks or their dials. Invariably, this resulted in excessive reflection of the flash from the polished case or dial, with the resulting loss of much detail. Standing approximately 5 degrees to either side effectively overcomes this difficulty.

Only on rare occasions were we defeated. Clocks standing on small landings, halfway up flights of narrow stairs, were exceptionally difficult to record on film, as, obviously, were clocks too high for the room in which they stood, especially if the ceiling was beamed. Many clocks had lost their feet or pediments because they were too tall, but owners sometimes took more radical steps to overcome the problem. We were to see one or two clocks standing in wells excavated in the floor. This solution effectively removed the need to mutilate the clock, but in one case, the well lived up to its name and flooded in wet weather with rather unhappy results to the clock's nether regions. In only one instance did we see the top of a clock projecting through the ceiling into the room above which overcame the owner's problems of accommodating a tall clock but effectively frustrated our efforts to get a full length shot!

Every clock was given a reference number at the time of the inspection and this number was, from that moment on, our means of identification. Early in the project we invested in a Canon Databack for our camera with a view to imprinting the appropriate reference numbers on all negatives and resulting prints. This was only partially successful; from time to time we forgot to re-set the Databack with the serial number: this led to considerable confusion and the device itself consumed expensive batteries at an alarming rate.

We had to make an early decision as to how much detail was to be recorded in our survey. It was decided that an over-riding requirement, at least for initial inspections, was to limit the time required to around half an hour. Apart from the need to include a large number of clocks in our survey, we felt that we should not impose ourselves for longer than absolutely necessary on clock owners - especially those who may have felt uneasy about letting relative strangers into their homes. We could, after all, return at a later date, if the initial visit proved insufficient to make a proper and full record. In the event, this rarely happened.

Having set ourselves these objectives, the nature of our examination was easy to decide. We would not have time to use studio-type lighting for the photography nor would we be able to contemplate removing the dial and movement from the clock. Richard Cave-Brown-Cave, during the course of examining clocks by the Barbers of Winster, had to remove the dials because the Barbers numbered and dated so many of their clocks on the front-plate of the movement. The Llanrwst makers did not do this so that we were not confronted with such an urgent need to inspect the front-plates. For this we were very grateful. Not only is the process time consuming but, undoubtedly, it would have got us into all kinds of trouble. The clocks were usually still going but some only just: removing the hands and dial would have been the last straw! We would have had to retain the services of a competent clock repairer virtually full time to get each of the clocks going again. Even removing the case hood often created vibrations that stopped the clock, although, fortunately, we were able to cajole a majority into resuming their duties at the end of our inspection.

We had to make an arbitrary decision as to what constituted a Llanrwst clock, thus qualifying for inclusion in our survey and for the allocation of one of our numbers. It was decided that an original Llanrwst dial had to be present. Thus, whilst a dial plate bearing the signature of a Llanrwst maker but without movement or case was counted as a clock, a Llanrwst case or movement on its own, without a dial, was not.

Upon completion of each clock inspection, a small printed self-adhesive label was stuck inside the clock (with the owner's permission), usually on the back of the trunk door. On this label we wrote the number that had been allocated to the clock and the date of our inspection. The original reason for the label was to ensure, so far as possible, that the clock could be identified by its number and that the number itself would be inside the clock at all times. Subsequently our labelling system assumed a practical significance for an entirely different reason: it enabled us to avoid driving considerable distances to inspect clocks that we had already seen. Clocks change hands quite frequently: without the label, we, as well as the new owner, might be unaware that the clock had already been included in our survey.

Confidentiality was an important consideration throughout the survey. Over the last few years the value of long-case clocks, indeed all clocks, has increased enormously. One of the less happy results of this is that clocks are a target for burglars and unscrupulous so-called antique dealers who knock on peoples' doors. Clock owners can be excused, therefore, for being very cautious about contacting us, let alone inviting us into their homes to see their valued possessions. Quite a number, we know, have decided not to contact us for just these reasons, and we fully understand the caution underlying their decision. Fortunately for us, however, many more came forward and provided us with the great wealth of material which is at the heart of this book. In no small measure our friends at the Welsh Folk Museum were responsible for this. They publically endorsed our project and, on a number of occasions, appealed for assistance on our behalf. Without the Museum's close involvement with us, many fewer clock owners would have been prepared to come forward. It should be emphasised, however, that this support was not given lightly. We discussed and agreed a code of conduct with the Museum relating to amongst other considerations, the matter of confidentiality, the keeping and protection of records, and the actual conduct of the survey. The Museum further required us to given an undertaking that the survey would not be used as an opportunity to try and buy the clocks that we had seen. All these precautions we regarded as appropriate and essential for the protection of clock owners and for the furtherance of a research project such as ours. As a matter of interest we were never offered a clock to buy during any of our visits of inspection by the home owner. Dealers were rather different! Everyone, however, wanted an estimate of the value of their clock and we could only do our best to indicate current market prices. We felt it important to do this, not least because the clocks were, frequently, badly under-insured.

We would not wish to suggest that a clock survey should be other than great fun and very rewarding. We believe, however, that such a project cannot be undertaken without careful pre-planning, meticulous implementation and, at every stage, scrupulous consideration and respect for the clock owners themselves.

A final practical note. A torch is useful for illuminating the murky interiors of clocks; so is a steel tape with which to record the dimensions of dial, movement and case. A good supply of spares in the car is essential; we managed to leave behind a trail of torches and tapes in various houses all over North Wales.

Clocks in the survey

In all, we have traced approximately 460 clocks by John, Watkin, William and David Owen. However, we have not been able to inspect them all, mainly because some were reported to us after we had already decided to call a halt to our inspections so that this book could be prepared. In spite of this, clock owners have continued to contact us and our numerous helpers keep on finding us more and more clocks. We would like to take this opportunity of apologising to all those owners who have contacted us but whom we have been unable to visit. We very much hope that they will understand why we have been unable to respond to their invitations to inspect their clocks.

At the time of writing the position is as follows:

Fig 153: *Owen clocks included in the survey*		
MAKER	CLOCKS LOCATED	CLOCKS INCLUDED IN THE SURVEY
John Owen	125	106
Watkin Owen (with brass dial)	165	150
Watkin Owen (with painted dial)	120	102
William Owen	35	30
David Owen	15	12
Total	460	400

Since our definition of a clock allowed even a dial-plate, on its own, to be included, it is interesting to observe the status of the clocks included in our survey.

From Figures 153-156 it can be seen that approximately three quarters of all the clocks are, substantially, in their original condition, *ie* the dial, movement and case all appear to belong to each other and are relatively unaltered. More interesting, perhaps, is the fact that more of Watkin Owen's brass dial clocks have been interfered with than those of his father, John. In particular many more of Watkin's brass-dial clocks have been re-cased - 22% no

Fig 154: John Owen – brass dials

STATUS	%	TOTAL NO
Substantially original	74.5	79
Ditto, but case re-carved	0.9	1
Clocks extensively re-built	1.9	2
Dial only	3.8	4
Dial & movement only	2.8	3
Dial & movement in wrong case	12.3	13
Dial with wrong movement in wrong case	2.8	3
Dial with wrong movement	0.9	1
Total	100.0	106

Fig 155: Watkin Owen – brass dials

STATUS	%	TOTAL NO
Substantially original	72.0	108
Ditto, but case re-carved	0.7	1
Clocks extensively re-built	0.7	1
Dial only	0.7	1
Dial & movement only	0.7	1
Dial & movement in wrong case	22.0	33
Dial with wrong movement in original case	2.7	4
Dial with wrong movement in wrong case	0.7	1
Total	100.0	150

Fig 156: Watkin Owen – painted dials

STATUS	%	TOTAL NO
Substantially original	85.3	87
Dial only	1.0	1
Dial & movement only	1.9	2
Dial & movement in wrong case	8.8	9
Dial with wrong movement in original case	2.9	3
Total	100.0	102

less - whereas only 12% of John's clocks are now in wrong cases. Perhaps less surprisingly, Watkin's painted-dial clocks have attracted relatively little attention from the 'improvers' and botchers, because 85% of them are still in original condition.

Changed movements are rare, only twelve in all. This figure might have been much higher had the Owens produced 30-hour clocks.

To be strictly accurate, we have no way of knowing when a dial or movement has been re-housed in a case of typical Llanrwst manufacture and of the right period. There must be one or two of these lurking undetected amongst our statistics.

Location

The map on page 228 shows where we found clocks by John and Watkin Owen.

It is far from clear whether any significant conclusions can be drawn from the present location of the clocks. It is likely that the maps tell us more about the movement of people from the Llanrwst area during the past 200 years than the original locations of John and Watkin Owen's customers. Certainly, the heavy concentration of clocks in Llandudno, Rhos-on-Sea and Colwyn Bay would seem to result from the migration of people from inland villages to these relatively recent towns - all of which are substantially 19th century: retiring to a house or bungalow on the coast has long been a common, almost standard convention amongst the country people of North Wales.

Certainly, the maps confirm the marked reluctance of the people of North Wales to part with their clocks. Rather, it is a firm tradition to pass them on to their children, and it is only when the children have left Wales, taking their treasured heirlooms with them, that the clocks have become increasingly scattered. Dealers and collectors, it is true, have transported others, and there is a small, but steady, outflow as holiday visitors and tourists to Wales buy clocks in antique shops and take them home with them at the end of their holidays. As interest in clocks continues to increase, so too will this latter trend so that we were lucky to conduct our survey when we did when there was still a heavy concentration of clocks in their native North Wales. There was a time when long-case clocks could be bought for a few pounds: dealers from Holland and Germany, in particular, are reported to have bought Welsh clocks `by the van load'. It is difficult to obtain a true estimate of the numbers of clocks that have vanished overseas in this way but there is some indication that 30-hour clocks, which were the least valued by the Welsh people, may have been prominent in this export trade and the same may apply to the large Victorian clocks in 'Yorkshire' cases. Perhaps this may have contributed to the relative scarcity of 30-hour clocks today.

There is plenty of evidence to show that 18th century clockmakers sold a preponderance of their clocks to customers living in a 25 mile radius or a day's ride of their workshop, although the topography and population density of the area would have had a considerable influence on just how extensive was the market hinterland served by a particular clockmaker. Clockmakers sold clocks further afield by means of agents of one sort or another who obtained orders on behalf of a clockmaker in their own particular areas. Pryce and Davies record that Samuel Roberts extended his market in this way as did many other recorded clockmakers. So prolific were the Owens, especially in the period 1770-1800, that it seems certain that they must have established agents or other sales outlets much further from Llanrwst than the traditional 'day's ride'. It is tempting to try and identify where these sales outposts may have been from the present whereabouts of

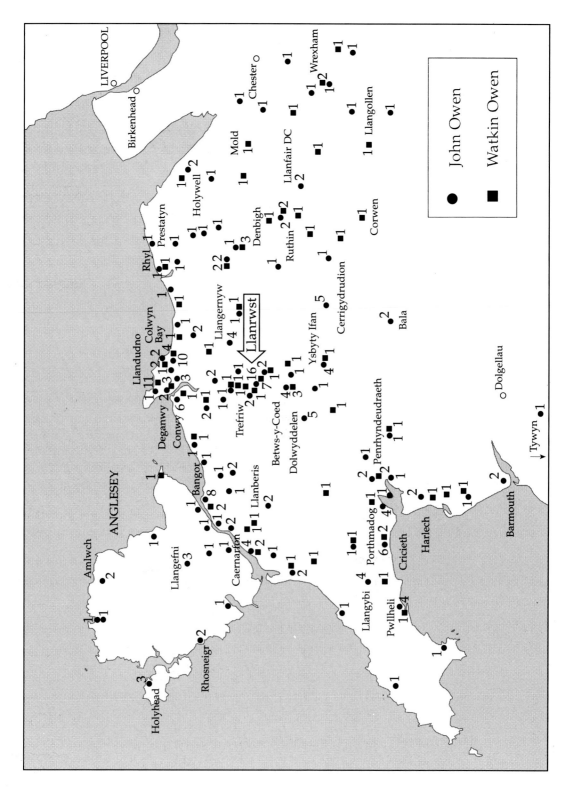

the clocks. Perhaps there are more clocks in the immediate area of Denbigh and on the southern coast of the Lleyn peninsula than can be accounted for solely in terms of population movements. This must be mere speculation, however, not least because most clocks that we have located had been moved to their present locations within living memory. It was one of the surprises and disappointments of the survey to discover how rare it was to be told that a clock was still in the house where it had always been. Instead, most people knew how and when, approximately, the clock had arrived. On the hearsay evidence that we have collected, we estimate that less than 1% of all the clocks could be standing, today, in the original houses for which they had been made. There is some evidence on the other hand, that clocks had moved just once, their owners tracing them back to the farms in the Llanrwst area where, it was claimed, they had always been hitherto. We have encountered the same pattern with dressers and *cypyrddau tridarn*, which only emphasises the need for an urgent study of these important items of Welsh vernacular furniture before their original whereabouts becomes impossible to establish.

Beyond these somewhat generalised conclusions, we hesitate to draw any more profound conclusions from the location maps, tempting as it is to try and do so.

THE CLOCKMAKERS OF
LLANRWST   PROJECT

Reference No. ....

Date ....

Surveyed by ....

In collaboration with the Welsh Folk Museum, St. Fagans, Cardiff.

Fig 158: The Project Label (actual size). One of these was invariably inserted on the back of the trunk door of clocks that we surveyed. The eagle symbol, which became the 'logo' for the project, was taken from the weather vane on the old Town Hall (the vane is now in the Welsh Folk Museum, St Fagans).

CHAPTER XIII
Technical Commentary

Introduction
This brief commentary is intended for the more technically-minded reader, restorer, repairer or horologist who may be interested in the finer details of Llanrwst dials, movements and other components, especially those diagnostic features that may assist in identifying the output of the Llanrwst workshops. We have already made the point on numerous occasions throughout this book that the Llanrwst makers were closely integrated into the remarkably uniform clockmaking crafts of north-west England and North Wales and purchased components mostly from sources in Cheshire and Lancashire. We have, therefore, tended to concentrate on the distinguishing features rather than giving detailed description of the various individual components that apply to the work of most contemporary clockmakers in the region. In preparing this section we have relied more on our own photographs rather than our written records in describing the components. By this means we seek to keep as close as possible to original sources, ie the movements themselves.

The commentary describes and illustrates the output of the dominant Owen workshop. Only Moses Evans produced a substantial number of movements that differed significantly from the work of the Owens.

Brass Dial-plates
The brass dial-plates on Llanrwst clocks are usually approximately 12" x 12" in John Owen's early period (c1745-55). Thereafter 12" dials are rarer, giving way to 13" dials which persist until the end of the brass-dial period in about 1805. There are a few 14" dials from about 1770 onwards but these, too, are rare. Interestingly, Llanrwst plates are usually over-size, 12" plates measuring 12¼" x 12¼" or thereabouts and 13" plates averaging approximately 13³/₈" x 13³/₈".

All Llanrwst brass dial-plates so far seen have the north country cut-outs (see Figure 159, p231). Most expert commentators seem to agree that these cut-outs are cast in, not cut out from a solid sheet. It is not easy to deduce this, however, by examining the dials, because the apertures are usually trimmed with a coarse bladed piercing-saw or a coarse file.

The purpose of these cut-out apertures is not completely clear. Everyone seems to agree that significant quantities of expensive brass are saved thereby and this seems to be difficult to contest. However, we believe that there was also a real, practical benefit. The process of matting the dial-centres invariably stretched the brass causing the dial centre to bow and to become shallowly saucer-shaped. This then, had to be flattened by heating and hammering the sheet until it was once again flat. We believe that this process would have been much easier when only the spokes had to be heated and hammered to get rid of the bowing. Certainly the spokes almost always show the colouration and hammer marks suggesting this method. Later, when the dial centres were no longer matted, the dial makers persisted with cut-outs.

Otherwise, the dial-plates on Llanrwst clocks are remarkably consistent and of good

Fig 159: The back of a typical Llanrwst brass dial – the design of which changed little over the years. The date-ring rotates in slotted brackets, not rollers.

Fig 160: The back of an early painted dial from a Watkin Owen clock c1780. Unusually, early Llanrwst painted dials retained the brass-dial method of date indication.

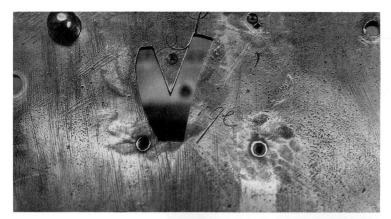

Fig 161: The engraved doodles, Sam and George, were applied before the vee-shaped aperture for the strike-work detents was cut. Samuel and George were Watkin's elder brothers.

Fig 162: One date aperture too many! John Owen overcame the problem by hiding one of them with his nameplate (see Figure 24, p68).

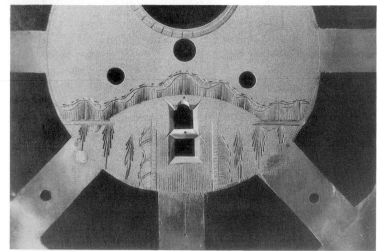

Fig 163: Open oval spandrels enjoyed a brief vogue on Llanrwst clocks in the mid 1790s.

quality, suggesting practised and specialist manufacture. Only at the very end of the brass dial period do we find badly cast plates with prominent casting faults. It is possible that, by this time, the few brass dial-plates required were being produced in Llanrwst. Prior to this date however, the high and consistent quality of the plates suggests specialist manufacture, probably in south Lancashire or Cheshire.

These brass dials are fixed to the movement by means of four dial feet, riveted to the plate, usually, but not invariably, under the chapter-ring.

Dial Centres

The dial centres are matted until about 1770 when the first dials with plain, un-matted centres begin to appear. Matted dial centres are rarely seen after 1775. Only rarely do the early Llanrwst dials have any engraving superimposed on the matting. When this feature does occur, the engraving is usually an embellishment around the date aperture. Sometimes a flame-like motif is engraved around the edge of the dial centre adjacent to the chapter-ring.

By the end of the 1750s, however, the acanthus engraving motif in one or other of its numerous forms becomes virtually standard, being cut deeply into the matted centre and this continues until around 1770, when this form of decoration gives way to plain dial centres with various forms of engraved decoration. Thereafter, the engraved designs take many forms and are discussed in more detail in Chapters III and IV.

The original matted dial centres would have been scratch brushed and lacquered; the plain, engraved dial centres were probably always silvered. It is difficult to be certain on this latter point because only a few of the dial-plates still show signs of old silvering. However, we are of the opinion that these were all silvered because their legibility would have been so poor without, nullifying the engraver's efforts.

The various types of decoration used on the dial centres of brass dialled clocks made by the Owens are listed in the following tables:

Fig 164: John Owen – dial centre decoration

TYPE OF DECORATION	%	TOTAL NO
Plain, matted	17.0	18
Matted with engraved designs around date apperture	12.3	13
Matted concentrically	2.8	3
Matted with engraved designs usually, but not always, with acanthus leaf motifs	46.2	49
Plain, un-matted, with 'Exotic Plant' engraving	15.1	16
Plain, un-matted, with other engraved designs	6.6	7
Total	100.0	106

NB: 52 (or 49%) of the dials were executed by the 'Good Engraver', the remainder by several unidentified engravers.

Fig 165: Watkin Owen – dial centre decoration
(all but one dial had plain, not matted, centres)

TYPE OF DECORATION	%	TOTAL NO
Cornucopia design series	8.0	12
Cornucopia + Pimpernel	4.0	6
Cornucopia + Little black arrows	0.7	1
Pimpernel design series	12.7	19
Pimpernel + Little black arrows	1.3	2
Little black arrows design series	1.3	2
Little black arrows + Pimpernel	1.3	2
Acanthus swirls	10.0	15
Chequer-board	4.0	6
Fine grass swirls	4.7	7
Formal shapes + Pimpernel	0.7	1
Formal shapes	11.3	17
Exotic Plant series	1.4	2
Urn design series	15.3	23
Grass-seed-head design series	12.0	17
Other	12.7	18
Total	100.0	150

NB: The 'Good Engraver' provided Watkin Owen with only 4 dials. Another engraver then provided most of Watkin's dials until about 1790. He was responsible for the Chequer-board, Cornucopia, Pimpernel, Little black arrows Acanthus and Fine Grass swirls and many of the Formal designs. In the early 1790's the 'Urn Engraver' took over and engraved all the remainder of Watkin's brass dials. Between them these three engravers provided 95% of all Watkin Owen's brass dials.

Makers' names

The maker's name is, in the early years of John Owen usually on a separate, variably-shaped, silvered plate that is riveted to the dial-centre, but the maker's name sometimes appears around the arch when moonphase indication is present. The signature on these plates is invariably executed in a rather shaky, spidery hand, and was, we believe, engraved by John Owen himself this being his only contribution to the engraving of the dials. He continues to sign his own dials even when the signature begins to be located on the chapter-rings.

It was in the late 1760s that he ceased this practice and from then on his name was applied by the dial-engraver. We have seen two or three dials dated around 1770 where the whole of the engraving looks as if it was executed in the Llanrwst workshop, but, by this time, the engraver may have been Samuel Owen, or his brother George. We know that both of them practised engraving on the movement plates, although never, interestingly enough, on the dials. As we have argued elsewhere in this book we have no doubt that the dials were engraved far away, which is why Samuel's and George's doodles never appeared on the backs of the dials. They had ample opportunity to practise their skills on the movement plates, whereas the dials arrived in the workshop complete, by-passing them.

Winding holes

On the earlier clocks winding holes were ringed. If this ringing was applied by the engraver, then the clockmaker must have used the completed dial to locate the spots where the winding barrels had to be planted, because, invariably, the winding squares are in the centre of the winding holes. Alternatively, the clockmaker may have applied the ringing once he had located the winding holes, and we believe that this is the most likely explanation. Ringed winding holes began to give way to plain ones in the mid-1750s and disappeared altogether a few years later.

In all cases, the winding squares are neatly centered in the winding holes, and the holes themselves are neatly formed and finished. On Llanrwst clocks distorted winding holes or winding squares that are badly centred are a reliable indicator of a changed movement.

Seconds dials

All but two of the Llanrwst 8-day clocks seen in the survey have a seconds dial. Of these two, one has no seconds dial whatsoever, whereas the other has a strange circular decoration which, obviously, started out as an engraved seconds dial, but was aborted before the dial was completed. The movement has no extension to the 'scape-wheel arbor, on which a seconds hand could be mounted.

Until the early 1790s, seconds dials on Llanrwst clocks are usually engraved on separate discs fixed behind the main dial-plate to render them recessed or countersunk. Thus, it was possible to ensure that the seconds hand does not project above the main dial-plate, so reducing the chances of it fouling the main hands. Whether, in fact, the seconds dials are recessed for this reason or for decorative purposes remains uncertain.

The seconds disc has two 'ears' - usually at 15 seconds and 45 seconds - which are used to rivet the discs to the main dial-plate. On a few dials small, obviously contemporary screws have been found securing the seconds disc. It may be that, originally, many more were attached with screws but these have been lost and replaced by rivets.

On one or two very early John Owen dials, the seconds disc is fitted flush with the main dial plate, the fixing ears being attached to the back of the disc. Quite why this was done is difficult to imagine. It may be that this separate disc was used so that it could be silvered and then fixed into a dial centre that was all-over matted otherwise. Subsequently, it must have been decided that a countersunk disc improved the overall appearance of the finished dial and, moreover, that this was easier and quicker to achieve.

From about 1770 one batch of dials has seconds apertures with scalloped circumferences that look most decorative.

Throughout the brass-dial period, however, the occasional dial has the seconds ring engraved on the main dial-plate. In the early 1790s when a new, probably Llanrwst-based engraver, began to engrave all the Owen dials, he preferred to engrave the seconds ring on the dial-centre. From this date the countersunk disc suddenly disappeared and was never to reappear. Maybe this resulted from the need to keep down costs in an increasingly competitive market.

Separate, annular seconds rings pinned to the dial centre appear only occasionally on Llanrwst clocks, usually before about 1765. We have found two clocks by John Owen with a centre-seconds hand. One has lost its original seconds hand; the other has an original but rather strange cranked and counter-weighted hand.

Some idea of the types of seconds indication used on brass-dialled clocks by the Owens is given in the following tables:

Fig 166: John Owen - Seconds Indication - Brass dials

TYPE	%	No
Recessed disc	83.0	88
Flush disc	0.9	1
Superimposed disc	0.9	1
Superimposed annular ring	5.7	6
Engraved on dial centre	4.7	5
Centre seconds	1.9	2
None (including a 30hr movement)	2.8	3
Total	100.0	106

Fig 167: Watkin Owen - Seconds Indication - Brass dials

TYPE	%	No
Recessed discs	62.7	94
Engraved on dial centre	36.7	55
Planted annular ring	0.7	1
Total	100.0	150

Chapter-Rings

There is nothing remarkable or unusual about the chapter-rings on Llanrwst dials. They are pinned to the dial-plate by means of four, short, rounded feet, riveted into the ring. These feet sometimes have to be filed flat at the end to clear moonwork if this is present. Usually it is the foot that goes through the top right-hand corner of the movement (when viewed from the front) that has been flattened.

Throughout the survey we recorded the width of the chapter ring band which can be as little as 2¹/₁₆" or as much as 2¹⁵/₁₆". However, we are unable to detect any distinctive pattern or trend in these variations, except to state that the widest coincides with the trend towards minute numbers of exaggerated size in the 1770s, for the obvious reason that these large minute numerals require the widest rings.

We have never found any doodling nor any interesting inscriptions on the back of any of the chapter-rings. Usually, there are a couple of short lines or a cross somewhere on the back of the ring where the engraver has tested his engraving tool before commencing work. Similar practice marks are also found on the dial-plate itself.

Two small register or securing holes are usually found on the inside edge of the ring, most often at 12 o'clock and 6 o'clock. Presumably, these were used by the engraver to secure the ring in the jig used for marking out the Roman chapters.

The minute circles on all dials until about 1770 are strictly conventional, *ie* two concentric circles divided into minutes by radial divisions. The only unusual variation seen is the waxing-in of alternate minute divisions to give a chequer pattern. This feature is found on a few dials in the very early period (see Frontispiece).

After 1770, stylistic changes occur as the conventional minute circle described above gives way to large individual dots for the minutes. The last full minute circle disappears around 1780. There are a few dials with a transitional arrangement: two complete concentric circles enclosing the dots that mark the minutes.

Most of John Owen's earlier dials have quarter hour divisions on the inside of the chapter-ring as well as the conventional minute divisions. We have no record of single-handed clocks by the Owens, or by any other Llanrwst maker.

Half-hour Markers

The half-hour markers follow conventional trends but persist rather longer in Llanrwst than elsewhere. Their evolution can be divided into three main periods. The first is from 1745 to 1765 when the commonest motif in use is the fleur-de-lys or derivations of it. Then, especially with the advent of the Good Engraver, the half-hour marker enters a period when its design is much more interesting, original in design and artistic, and its execution is often beautiful and accomplished. A characteristic of the dials executed by the Good Engraver with Acanthus engraving on matted centres is that the half-hour markers echo the designs used in the centre of the seconds discs. When the same engraver embarks on his Exotic Plant series of dials in about 1772, however, the half-hour marker goes into decline and frequently is no more than a simple lozenge or group of dots. After Watkin Owen took over his father's workshop and used a new engraver to execute his dials, half-hour markers of a much simplified and crude star-like design reappear and continue to the end of the 1780s. These late half-hour markers seem to appear at random on approximately one third of the dials during this period and may have been optional extras.

We have never seen half-quarter markers on any Llanrwst dial.

Spandrel Ornaments

The brass spandrel ornaments used on Llanrwst dials are the same as those used throughout British clockmaking but either the town's remoteness or the conservatism of its clockmakers and their clients resulted in the various patterns coming into fashion approximately ten years later than in the larger towns of England. Thus, the Four Seasons design is not seen much before 1755, the rococo designs appear about 1760 and the question-mark design does not become common until around 1780.

Llanrwst spandrel ornaments are usually of excellent quality. The castings are clean and sharp, and have been meticulously cleaned of casting rag. We believe that the castings must have been obtained from specialist suppliers in England, and given to outworkers in Llanrwst to clean up. Only occasionally is a poor set of spandrels seen, for which there could be several explanations - the most likely being that they are replacements. There was, however, a short period in the late 1790s, right at the end of the brass dial period when there was a sudden and drastic deterioration in the quality of the spandrel ornaments: older designs reappear, the castings are of inferior quality, and, almost

Fig 168: Spandrel Ornaments - John Owen

PATTERN	%	No
Bird & Urn	7.6	8
Cherub and Crown	1.9	2
Cherub and Bridge	4.7	5
Cherub and Posy	4.7	5
Four Seasons	1.9	2
Lady with Fan Headdress (Large)	3.8	4
Flowers and Scrolls	8.5	9
Shells and Scrolls	12.3	13
Castle Gateway	5.7	6
String of Pearls	6.6	7
Starfish	5.7	6
West Country	3.8	4
Large Cherub's Head	7.6	8
Lady with Fan Headdress	10.4	11
Question-mark	2.8	3
Branches	1.9	2
Replacements etc	9.4	10
None	0.9	1
Total	100.0	106

Fig 169: Spandrel Ornaments - Watkin Owen

PATTERN	%	No
Large Lady with Fan Headdress	0.7	1
Flowers and Scrolls	2.0	3
Shells and Scrolls	2.0	3
Star-Fish	0.7	1
Large Cherub's Head	2.0	3
Lady with Fan Headdress	6.7	10
Question Mark	57.3	86
Open Oval	7.3	11
Palm in border	0.7	1
Late Bird and Urn	3.3	5
Late Lady with Fan Headdress	2.7	4
Engraved	5.3	8
Other and Replacements etc	8.7	13
None	0.7	1
Total	100.0	150

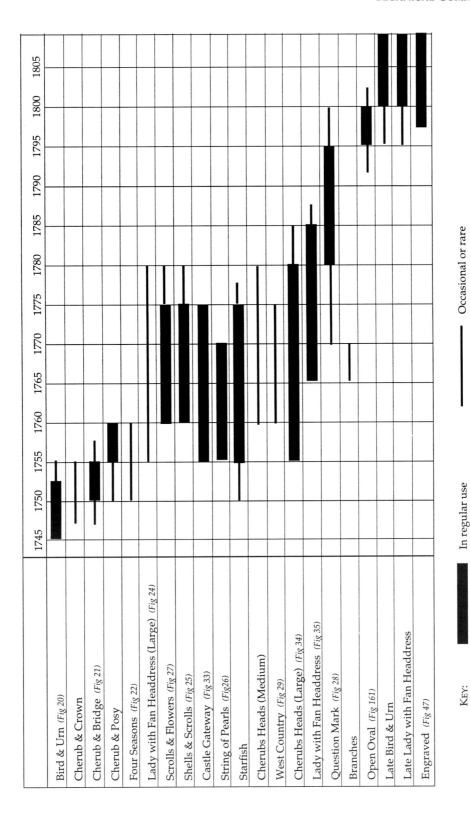

Fig 170: Approximate dates of brass spandrel ornaments on the clocks of John Owen and Watkin Owen, and other Llanrwst makers, 1745-1805.

invariably, these corner pieces seem too small for the dials. The most likely explanation is that this resulted from cost cutting - a feature of this period. The possibility that the castings were produced locally using old spandrels to make the moulds seems to be precluded by the reduction in size.

Many, if not most, of the original fixing screws have long since been lost and replaced, but original screws, when present, are usually small, with a thin, domed octagonal top, approximately 5 or 6 BA in size.

We have never seen anything to suggest that the spandrel ornaments were ever gilded. Subsequent polishing may, however, have removed all trace of any original gilding that may have been applied to the ornaments on some of the grander clocks. In general we conclude that most of the spandrel ornaments used by the Llanrwst clockmakers would have been polished and lacquered.

Figures 168 and 169 show the relative frequency with which the various spandrel patterns were used by John & Watkin Owen. Figure 170 gives the dates at which the various patterns of spandrel ornaments were used. It is very unusual for designs to appear on Llanrwst clocks that do not conform to the general chronological progression indicated by the table. When this does occur it may simply be because the clockmakers used or re-used some old designs that suddenly became available, or they may be later replacements.

The method of indicating the approximate dates we have borrowed from Loomes, because we cannot improve upon it. Once again we warn against dating a clock merely on the basis of a single feature, *eg* the spandrels. The dates we give are approximations only, and, as we have stated elsewhere, anomolous or 'out-of-date' spandrels are encountered from time to time.

Date Indication

We have only found one Llanrwst brass-dialled clock without date indication - the Titley clock discussed in Chapter X. Otherwise all brass dialled clocks have date indication; all, but a handful, taking the form of square or circular aperture in the lower part of the dial centre behind which the engraved date ring rotates, moving on once every twenty-four hours to display the date. We have found five dials where there is a larger lunette or semi-circular opening in the dial with a rotating engraved disc displaying the date by means of a pointer. This was not the preferred method on Llanrwst clocks, however, and the dials on which it occurs are usually anomolous in other respects perfectly genuine but, from a stylistic point of view, not part of the normal production. Perhaps these particular dials were experimental, or bought-in from alternative suppliers to relieve a production bottleneck.

The detailed design of the date aperture itself is almost infinitely variable. Some are square, some circular, some trapezoidal. Some have a wide bevel with elaborated corners, others have no bevel and are completely plain. It is true to say that trapezoidal apertures are relatively infrequent, as are circular ones until about 1792 when Watkin Owen's new dial engraver produced circular apertures exclusively until the end of the brass dial period.

The toothed date-ring is a very standard product varying throughout the period only in diameter, but, even then, such variations as do occur are small. The rings usually have two small register or retaining-pin holes at 180 degrees to each other - probably used when cutting the teeth on the inner perimeter or when engraving the numbers or both. The

Fig 171: Methods of Date Indication - John Owen - brass dials

TYPE	%	No
Square aperture below hands	77.4	82
Trapezoidal aperture below hands	8.5	9
Circular aperture below hands	7.6	8
Lunette opening and disc	3.8	4
Revolving circular disc	1.9	2
None	0.9	1
Total	100.0	106

Fig 172: Methods of Date Indication - Watkin Owen - brass dials

TYPE	%	No
Square aperture below hands	53.3	80
Trapezoidal aperture below hands	14.0	21
Circular aperture below hands	31.3	47
Lunette opening and disc	0.7	1
Pointer on engraved dial	0.7	1
Total	100.0	150

Fig 173: Methods of Date Indication - Watkin Owen - painted dials

	%	No
Lunette	89.2	91
Square box	10.7	11
Total	100.0	102

numbers were waxed and the ring was silvered. It seems clear that these date-rings were supplied with the dials.

The date-rings are mounted in deeply slotted brackets of brass, rivetted to the back of the dial plate. There are three brackets: two fixed rigidly at, approximately, the 4 o'clock and 8 o'clock positions whilst the third, mounted at the twelve o'clock position just above the seconds disc, will rotate sufficiently to allow the date-ring to be removed. This third revolving bracket usually has a long cutaway on its lower edge to allow it to clear the seconds disc. We have never seen the date-ring on a brass dial mounted on roller-discs as was the earlier or better practice elsewhere. Interestingly, the only time Llanrwst date-rings are mounted on these roller-discs is on the early painted dials of the 1780s. Whilst, in theory, the roller-discs should allow the date-rings to rotate more freely, the fixed brass brackets seem to work just as well.

Fig 174: Makers of painted dials for Watkin Owen

DIAL MAKER	%	No
Not known	27.5	28
Finnemore	1.0	1
Hobson & Todd	1.0	1
Keeling	1.0	1
Osborne	1.0	1
Owen & Price	8.8	9
Owen	2.9	3
Wilson	52.0	53
Walker & Finnemore	3.9	4
Walker & Hughes*	1.0	1
Total	100.0	102

* *NB. Since Loomes indicates that Walker & Hughes did not go into production until after 1809, this clock, on which the signature is illegible, may be by William Owen. Alternatively it could be a very early Walker & Hughes dial.*

Fig 175: Painted dial centres - Decorative motifs/themes

	%	No
Plain	20.6	21
Flowers	10.8	11
Floral swags	3.9	4
Birds	39.2	40
Cartouche around signature	12.8	13
Cottages	1.9	2
Pears	1.0	1
Ruins	1.9	2
Shells	1.9	2
Sheep	1.0	1
Ships	1.0	1
Swans	1.0	1
Formal scrolls	2.9	3
Total	100.0	102

Fig 176: Painted dials - Corner Arrays

	%	No
All corners the same	39.2	40
Opposite corners the same	5.9	6
Upper corners and lower corners the same	54.9	56
Total	100.0	102

Fig 177: Painted dials - Corner Decoration		
	%	No
Raised, gilt, spandrel designs	3.9	4
Birds in raised, gilt borders	1.9	2
Flowers alone	9.8	10
Flowers in raised, gilt medallions	1.9	2
Strawberries and flowers in raised gilt comma borders	11.8	12
Shells	4.9	5
Landscapes in circular vignettes	1.9	2
Formalised flowers	2.9	3
Martial symbols	2.9	3
Formal designs	4.9	5
Peacock feathers	1.0	1
Windmills	1.0	1
Formal fans	9.8	10
Flowers in gilt fans	1.9	2
Shells and nuts	1.0	1
Flowers in flat borders	1.9	2
Flowers in raised, gilt comma borders	36.3	37
Total	100.0	102

Occasionally, dials are found where the date-ring is prevented from moving when free of its actuating detent, by a piece of springy wire mounted in the foot of one of the adjacent dial feet and bearing against the back of the ring. It is possible that this was standard practice but that most of the wires have been lost. We confess that we did not check this during our survey.

Dial set marks

On many dials of the mid-period the various components comprising the set ie the plate, the chapter-ring, the seconds disc and the date-ring carry similar marks to identify each item as belonging to a set of components. The marks are either scratched vertical dashes, or dots made with a drill. We have seen up to four such marks indicating, we believe, that there were at least four dials in a batch delivered to the engraver. To save time the engraver would doubtless wish to do all the dial centres together, then the chapter-rings and so on. The small identifying marks would enable him to reassemble the completed dials quickly and easily - another instance of batch production.

One-piece Dials

We have found seven clocks by Watkin Owen fitted with so-called 'one-piece' or 'all-over silvered' square dials. These can be dated towards the end of the brass dial period about 1798-1805. One other one-piece dial, much earlier in date, arched and signed by John Owen occurs on the Titley clock described in detail in Chapter X.

All these one-piece dials have the spandrel ornaments, chapter-ring and seconds disc engraved directly onto the dial-plate. The only moving part is the date-ring which is conventionally mounted on rivetted brass brackets. Often the quality of these one-piece dial-plates is poor with very obvious and extensive casting faults. It is possible that these dials were produced in Llanrwst, hence the very variable quality. Invariably these dials were silvered: without silvering their legibility would have been very poor.

It is widely accepted that one-piece dials mark the end of the brass clock dial and, in the face of the all-engulfing tide of white or painted dials, represent the swan-song of the dial engraver. Certainly, the designs closely ape the so-called white or painted dials.

White or Painted Dials

The white or painted dials used on Llanrwst clocks from about 1780 onwards were obtained from the same dial makers who, by this date, supplied clockmakers everywhere. These dials have no distinctive features which might identify them as coming from Llanrwst, other than the signatures of the local clockmakers that made the movements. We do not intend to provide any technical commentary on them, therefore, as we have with the more distinctive and individualistic brass dials. Details of their construction and decoration are fully covered in *White Dial Clocks* by Brian Loomes which deals with this important topic in an authorative and convincing manner and in great detail.

As a footnote, and an exception to prove the rule, we found a single dial late in our survey on which an unmistakable representation of Llanrwst bridge was painted. The clock was by David Owen and was probably produced in the 1820s (see Figure 60, p102). Figures 174-177 provide statistical details of the dialmakers and the designs which they used.

Hands

As with the spandrel ornaments, the design of the hands on Llanrwst clocks follows a standard chronological progression more or less in line with clocks elsewhere in England and Wales.

The popular designs, too, are virtually identical to those used elsewhere and probably came from the same specialist producers. The Llanrwst clockmakers could have manufactured their own hands but we suspect that they did not, certainly from the time of the significant increase in production after 1765.

Hands are unlike spandrel ornaments in one respect however: far fewer of the original ones have survived. This is hardly surprising because clock hands are relatively delicate and subject to much more handling, especially when setting the clock to the correct time. For this reason, far more hour hands have survived than have minute hands because they are not handled to adjust for correct time. Even fewer original seconds hands have survived: this must be because they are so delicate and can be broken very easily.

Clock repairers and bodgers rarely seem to have bothered to ensure that replacement hands are of the correct pattern. Fortunately for us, the result is that most replacement hands are quite obviously out of keeping with the dial, often ludicrously so. Today, conscientious restorers will use replacement hands that are close replicas of the original ones and, in consequence, there is more difficulty in distinguishing them. Present-day restorers tend to be in a hurry, however: rarely do they fettle their steel blanks as industriously as did the 18th century craftsmen so that replaced hands tend to be much more clumsy in appearance and not as fine as the originals, even if the designs are the same.

Fig 178: Hour & Minute Hand Status

	John Owen		Watkin Owen	
	No	%	No	%
One or both replaced	42	39.6	77	30.6
Apparently original	64	60.4	175	69.4
Total	106	100.0	252	100.0

NB. Once again we must caution that we may be unable to distinguish replacement hands of the correct period and type, or even very good modern replicas, so that, in reality the 'one or both replaced' category is bound to be understated.

Fig 179: Hour & Minute Hands - Patterns

	John Owen Brass Dials		Watkin Owen Brass Dials		Painted Dials	
	No	%	No	%	No	%
Early tapered, straight minute	2	3.1				
Early slender, straight minute	6	9.4				
Crossover hour, straight minute	27	42.2				
Other hour, straight minute	29	45.3	34	32.1	2	2.9
Serpentine			56	52.8	14	20.3
Matching Diamond			16	15.1	46	66.7
Other Matching					7	10.1
Total	64	100.0	106	100.0	69	100.0

Figure 180 (p246) shows the main patterns of hour and minute hands found on Llanrwst clocks, together with the dates when they were used. There are other patterns, especially from the period 1755-70, which may be original but these were not used in sufficient quantities for us to be certain: they could be old hands that have been transferred from other clocks. It is only when large numbers of similar hands are found on clocks of a given period that we can be sure that they are mostly original.

There are very few features of hands that are peculiar to Llanrwst but the one or two that do occur are worthy of attention.

We have seen apparently original hands on some of the very earliest clocks by John

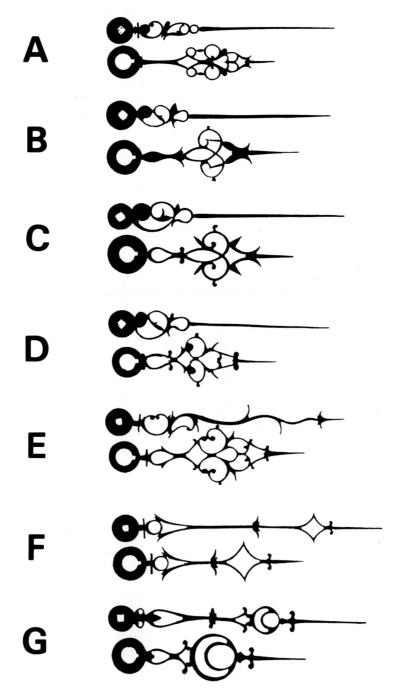

Fig 180: Hour & Minute Hands – Standard Patterns Used in Llanrwst
A: Early slender hour, straight minute, 1745-55. B: Crossover hour, straight minute, 1750-75. C: Crossover hour, late form, 1770-76. D: Standard hour, straight minute, 1760-85. E: Serpentine minute, 1780-95. F: Matching diamond pattern, 1785-1810 G: Victorian brass, 1850-80.

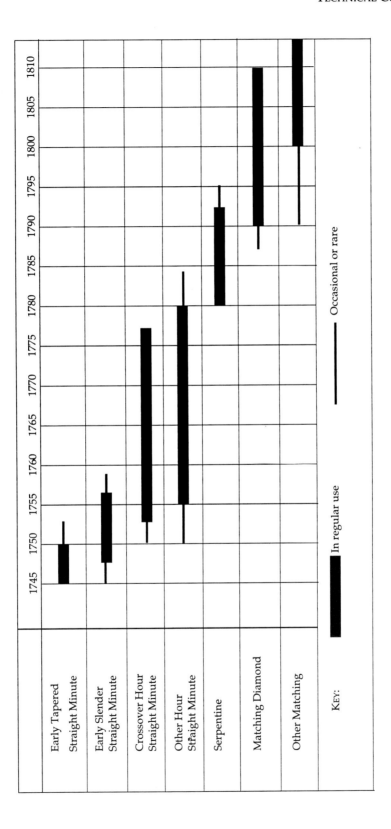

Fig 181: Approximate dates of of patterns of hands on Llanrwst clocks, 1745-1810.

Owen which are as different from his later production as the clocks themselves. These hands are relatively crude, not the finely executed products of an established town or city clockmaker. Their distinguishing feature is that they are very much thicker at the base than at the tip, tapering evenly between the two. A typical example is the hands on the dial shown in Figure 20 (p64). The most distinctive feature, however, is the often extreme length of the minute hand on clocks by John Owen, especially his earlier ones (see Figure 21, p64). It was good London practice for the minute hand to reach exactly to the outside edge of the minute circle. Country clockmakers were not so particular and allowed themselves some margin of error. John Owen, however, did not think it amiss for his minute hands to extend nearly to the outer edge of the chapter-ring! The earlier the clock the longer the minute hand was likely to be. This cannot have been a feature approved of by Watkin Owen, because, as soon as he took over his father's workshop, the practice ceased. Watkin's assumption of control did, of course, coincide closely with the general introduction of serpentine minute hands and these can look even more out of place if they are too long.

Incidentally, many restorers must have been sorely tempted to bring horological respectability to minute hands on John Owen's clocks with one snip of their pliers. We have no idea how often they may have succumbed!

Frequently, hour hands are found to be fixed accurately by a pin extending out of the arbor of the snail-wheel on which they are mounted. The pin fits into a notch on the boss of the hour hand. This feature may well be original to Owen clocks. Fixing the hour-hand more firmly in position by tapping the hole formerly occupied by the locating pin and using a small screw to complete the job seems to be a later modification.

Seconds hands that are original are so delicate that it seems a miracle that so many have survived. The hand is filed to needle fineness in marked contrast to the large circular boss - so fine, indeed, that rust has probably accounted for the demise of as many as has breakage. Restorers usually do not dare to emulate this fineness even if they have the patience and skill.

Some original seconds hands are rivetted to their brass pipe, others are hard-soldered.

The Movements

The movements used on the Owens' clocks may be categorised as follows:

Fig 182: John Owen movements		
TYPE	%	No
Typical John Owen movements with 4 pillars	67.0	71
Ditto but with 5 pillars	14.2	15
Other types but original	9.4	10
Original, special movements	1.9	2
Wrong, replaced movements	3.8	4
Dial only, no movement.	3.8	4
Total	100.0	106

Fig 183: Watkin Owen movements		
TYPE	%	No
Typical Watkin Owen movements with 4 pillars	2.4	6
Ditto but with 5 pillars	92.1	232
Other types but original	1.6	4
Wrong, replaced movements	3.2	8
Dial only, no movements	0.8	2
Total	100.0	252

The Plates

Size: As a general statement the earliest Llanrwst clock movements seem to have been the largest. Thereafter, the average size of the movement plates steadily diminished until by about 1810 the movements were at their smallest. If there was ever such a thing as an average or standard size it would be for the plates to be $6^1/2$" x $5^1/4$" and to have approximately $2^1/2$" between them. Until about 1760, however, individual movement plates were sometimes as large as 7" x $5^1/2$". We do not believe that this steady reduction in size of the movement was peculiar to Llanrwst. Llanrwst makers were, we are sure, following general trends. These trends probably reflected the steady reduction in the significance of the craft aspects of clockmaking in the face of hard commercial and competitive facts of trade that demand cost cutting wherever possible. Had not the craft of clockmaking been so inately conservative due to the apprenticeship system, this process could well have occurred more quickly and resulted in even smaller movements.

Unfortunately, we never systematically recorded the thickness of the plates, but we are confident from more random observations that this was also reduced.

Occasionally, when the clock embodied special mechanical features the plates would be much larger - for example the three-train Moulsdale clock. The only significantly smaller plates recorded were on the 30-hour example.

All the back-plates have a polished finish on both sides. The back face of the front-plate is finished similarly. It is impossible to tell whether the original makers actually polished the plates, but they certainly achieved a finish as standard that could receive a full polish if required. Any vertical graining of the outside face of the back-plate has, we feel, been applied by restorers.

By contrast, the front face of the front-plate is invariably left with a cast and planished finish. It is never filed, stoned or polished, except to remove excessive unevenness.

Typically, the circular aperture at the top of the backplate, through which the pallet arbor and crutch protrude, is round with its edges filed to remove the sharp edges. Sometimes, this has been enlarged, usually by means of a crudely cut 'vee', presumably to accommodate an over-large replacement crutch.

Apart from the pivot holes the only other opening on the plates is the curved vee-shaped aperture high up and slightly off-centre on the front plate. It accommodates the two detents, the one on the lifting-piece and the other on the hook - a feature of the Owen's 'two-piece lifting detent' strike-work. The opening was located by using dividers or some similar device and, invariably, the circular scribing marks that delineated the curves of the vee are present.

Fig 184: A typical pillar from a John Owen movement – plain, without decoration.

Fig 185: A very rare example of a decorated pillar from a John Owen movement.

Fig 186: We have never seen any decoration on a pillar from a Watkin Owen movement. This is a typical example.

Fig 187: Tapered pilars became virtually standard in Llanrwst in the 1790s.

STRIKING SIDE   GOING SIDE

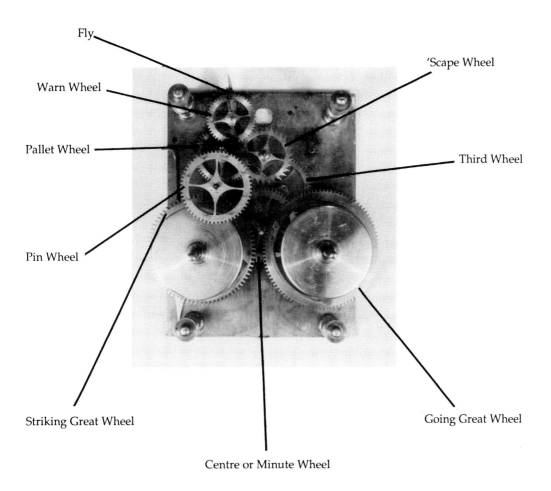

Fly

'Scape Wheel

Warn Wheel

Pallet Wheel

Third Wheel

Pin Wheel

Striking Great Wheel

Going Great Wheel

Centre or Minute Wheel

Fig 188: The wheel work of a typical Owen movement, in this case by John Owen.

Oil-sinks: Many Llanrwst movements now have oil-sinks but we are confident that these have been added by restorers or repairers and that these were not a feature of the movement in its original state.

Repairer's graffiti: Repairers have always been in the habit of scratching their names and the date on the movement plates - usually, but by no means invariably - on one of the faces of the front-plate. These scratchings are often interesting and can give some indication of the provenance and travels of the clock.

The Pillars

The pillars on Llanrwst clocks have few, if any, distinguishing features.

We have found decorative, turned fins on the pillars of only two Llanrwst movements, both very early, non-typical examples. Otherwise, the pillars are of standard design with a round knop in the centre and two half knops at either end. Usually, they are quite devoid of any other decoration or distinguishing feature. On a few John Owen movements, however, we have seen simple scribed-line decoration on pillars. We have never seen any decoration on pillars used in the clocks of Watkin Owen, nor have we ever been able to discern any progressive or distinctive design trends on any Llanrwst movement pillars. The only exception is the introduction in about 1790 of a pillar that tapers substantially from the middle to both ends and which features much smaller, narrower knops. This design was adopted by the Owens for most of their production from the last decade of the eighteenth century but so it was, too, by other makers in the Llanrwst district *eg* Moses Evans. We conclude that the new design was inaugurated by a specialist supplier of components used by all the Llanrwst clockmakers.

On the three-train Musical Clock the movement pillars are devoid of the central knop. Possibly, in an otherwise cramped movement, this provided improved clearance.

We have never seen latched pillars on any Llanrwst clock.

The Wheelwork

With rare exceptions the wheelwork in Llanrwst movements is very standard and featureless and is of the type that occurs throughout the north-west. Typically, the quality is quite excellent: there are few casting faults or blemishes, the crossing-out of the wheels is neat and accurate and the regularity and profile of the tooth-cutting consistent and good.

Indeed, if there is any feature of Llanrwst wheelwork that we have come to recognise it is the relative absence of poor crossing-out, non-radial teeth and the various other signs of slip-shod craftsmanship seen, not infrequently, on movements by makers from elsewhere. Of course, Llanrwst makers were not perfect, but the blemishes that we have seen occur only as exceptions. There is some variation but not much. Typically, the crossing out leaves a fairly wide rim on the wheels, but, occasionally, this rim is significantly narrower. George Jackson left very narrow rims indeed - almost dangerously so, but the sample of his movements that we inspected is very small.

Our comments on the excellence of Owen movements, in particular, do not apply to a few of the very early movements signed by John Owen. One or two of these are very rough, but we argue elsewhere that these were bought-in by him from another maker.

Fig 189: Another rare example of decoration on an Owen movement, this time by John. The twin scribed lines have been applied to the arbor bosses of the lifting piece and hook.

Arbors

There is little to say about the wheel arbors. On the earlier movements these tend to be thicker in the middle, tapering towards the ends, but this was a universal feature, not specific to Llanrwst. Again, the arbors are well finished. When turned from pinion wire, it is rare to see any remaining residue of the pinion teeth left on the arbor. By the last quarter of the 18th century, the arbors have lost their tapers. The exception is the large minute or centre wheel which, of necessity, becomes thicker at the point where it goes through the frontplate and is squared to receive the friction spring.

Pivots

Pivots on Llanrwst clocks are usually quite fine (thin) but otherwise they are unexceptional.

Wheel Collets

On some of the earliest movements wheel collets are of the early, domed type. Thereafter a plain, stepped collet (see Figure 191, p256) becomes standard on all Llanrwst clocks.

Going Train

Wheel-Count - We have been able to check some fifty Llanrwst movements in all - these came from all periods and makers - for their wheel-counts. We found all of the movements to be identical and conventional:

Main Wheel	96 teeth
Pinion	8 leaves
Centre Wheel	60 teeth
Pinion	8 leaves
Third Wheel	56 teeth
Pinion	7 leaves
'Scape Wheel	30 teeth

Great-Wheel Assembly - The great-wheel assembly and its associated barrel are conventional in design. Invariably the slip washers are fixed in position by pins; screws are later 'improvements'. The washers are almost always undecorated, but, occasionally, these have one or two scribed concentric circles close to their rims but only on movements by John Owen.

Clicks - The steel clicks never have tails which makes them difficult to disengage with the great wheel assembly in position. They are fixed by means of an integral threaded foot to the rim of the great-wheel.

Click-Springs - Typical click-springs are shown in Figure 195 (p258) and are rivetted to the rim of the great-wheel. Click-springs of other patterns or click-springs fixed with screws are probably not original.

Barrels - The barrels are usually marked with a W (watch) and S (striking) to identify them, but was this done by the maker or a subsequent repairer?

Minute, Third and 'Scape Wheels - These have no distinctive features.

The Pallets - Again, there are no distinctive features on the pallets of Llanrwst clocks. As a general guide John Owen's pallets are lighter and more likely to be in the shape of a horse-shoe, whilst Watkin Owen and the later makers used pallets that are much flatter and heavier, following the fashion of their period. However, pallets have often been replaced, usually quite expertly - so, it can be difficult to identify original pallets with complete certainty. We have not been able to identify a particular style of pallet with any individual craftsman and, therefore, we suspect that the blanks were bought in by the clockmakers. There also seems to be random variation in the geometry of the completed pallets, although it is possible that the Llanrwst makers generally favoured a good lusty swing to the pendulum *eg* 6-7" from one side to the other when measured at the rating-nut.

Crutch

The soft iron crutch on Llanrwst clocks, much lighter in construction than its modern commercial replacement counterpart, is riveted to the pallet arbor by means of a neat block. So neatly, indeed, that the rivet is virtually invisible.

Back-cock - Invariably the back-cock is of conventional design, without decoration. Today, steady-pins are usually present but we suspect that these are later additions.

The Striking-Train

Wheel Count - As with the going-train the striking-train wheel counts that we have checked are conventional and similar:

Great Wheel	78 teeth
Pinion	8 leaves
Pin Wheel	56 teeth
Pinion	7 leaves
Pallet Wheel	56 teeth
Pinion	7 leaves
Warn-wheel	48 teeth
Fly-pinion	7 leaves

Great-Wheel Assembly - Apart from the fact that the striking great-wheel is slightly smaller than the going great-wheel, the wheel assemblies are identical in all other details to the going-train equivalent.

Pin Wheel - In most Llanrwst movements, the pin wheels, their arbour and pinions are very large and robust.

Pallet Wheel - The extension of the pallet arbor that projects through the front-plate is tapered and squared to receive the gathering pallet. Occasionally, the projecting end of this arbor has been threaded to take a tiny nut to retain the gathering pallet. This seems to be a modern modification: the original pallets always have a friction fit.

WarnWheel - This light and small wheel has a pin mounted in its outer rim by means of which the train is locked when the detent on the hook collides with it. During the warning process this pin drops from the detent on the hook to the detent on the lifting piece.

The Fly - The fly has no special distinguishing feature.

The Hammer - The lever fixed to the front end of the hammer arbor is lifted and released by the pins of the pin wheel. Typical Owen strike-work will only run, when assembled so that the hammer lever is virtually in contact with the next pin to activate it when the train is locked. The hammer itself is mounted usually at the rear end of the arbor, but sometimes it may be in the middle of the arbor. Otherwise, the hammer and its arbor are devoid of decoration or elaboration.

The Bell
Bells on Llanrwst clocks are of the conventional design. After about 1800 the occasional one can be found inscribed 'AINSWORTH WARRINGTON'. Ainsworth was a major supplier of clock components at this time - especially, it seems, of bells. The bell stake is secured to the outside of the backplate adjacent to, and often almost touching, the back-cock.

Strike-Work
We have discussed the form and operation of the Owen brand of strike-work in considerable detail in Chapter III. From about 1750 until around 1815 the Owen family used the same strike-work mechanism and layout, the only changes throughout this period being of a stylistic nature. It is true that in the mid-1770s the workshop switched to using brass instead of steel for the rack, hook and lifting piece, and Watkin Owen, by dispensing with the blade-spring operated repeat mechanism, was able to modify the lifting piece slightly. Otherwise the basic essentials remained unaltered.

The strikework components are often beautifully made, and this gives us the impression that the workshop craftsmen relished making them. Most of the other components may have been bought in, in the rough, seriously restricting opportunities for individualism and the display of craftsmanship. Invariably, the geometry of the strikework is excellent and its operation elegant and efficient.

Towards the end of the 18th century, and in the early years of the 19th, when journeymen and apprentices left the Owens to establish their own businesses, they took with them the Owen strikework although their rendition of it was often clumsy.

Fig 190: A set of screws and studs from a John Owen movement and dial. The small octagonal screws at the top secure the spandrel ornaments. Watkin Owen screws and studs were vertually identical.

Fig 191: The collets used to secure these wheels to their arbors are of the standard design invariably used by the Owens. The scribed line decoration, however, is a very rare feature.

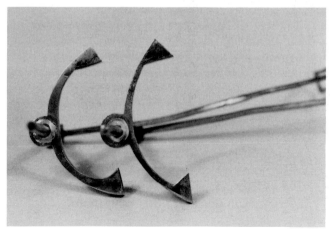

Fig 192: Two sets of pallets from a John Owen movement showing the earlier horseshoe shape. Both have been re-faced.

Repeat-Work

Typical John Owen repeat work may be seen in Figure 14 (p57). The blade-spring in this case is a great rarity because it appears to be original, one of only three that we have found.

Why so many of the blade-springs have been removed and discarded is something of a mystery. We suspect it is because sooner or later the original Owen blade-springs became bent, interfering with normal striking or preventing it altogether. We suspect that the springs were bent by frustrated clock owners pulling the string too hard during the warning phase (approximately the five minutes before the hour) when the mechanism is prevented from operating. Whatever the cause, most repeat blade-springs today are modern replacements. More usually all that remains of the original ones are the screw and steady-pin holes where once they had been fixed. These may be found in the lower right hand quarter of the front-plate, quite close to the edge of the plate, on all John Owen movements, and on a few by Watkin Owen.

Another mystery related to the repeat-work is the fact that the upward forked extension of the lifting piece carries two pins between which the blade-spring rises. This enables the repeat-work to be activated by pulling the blade in either direction, to the left or to the right. But, since the cord attached to the top of the spring seems always to have hung down inside the case, and was never carried outside through a hole in the side of the case-hood, it is very difficult to see why this bi-directional provision was necessary.

It seems clear that Watkin Owen soon came to this same conclusion. He dispensed with the repeat blade-spring and contented himself with drilling a simple hole in the now single upward extension of the lifting piece. To this hole he attached the activating cord. This much simpler arrangement works just as well, simplifies the mechanism and obviates the danger of a bent blade-spring.

Horizontal repeat springs that depress the extension of the lifting-piece are only seen on the earlier clocks of John Owen and on the Titley Clock (Figure 144, p203) where the additional motion-work wheel occasioned by the provision of centre seconds renders the usual vertical placement impractical.

Motion-Work

The motion work on Llanrwst clocks is conventional and without any distinguishing features. The cannon wheel and minute wheel are always crossed out.

The studs that carry both the strike-work and the minute wheel are threaded and screwed into the front-plate. Riveted studs are the work of a later repairer.

Moon-Work

Over the 100 years or so of Llanrwst clockmaking the various workshops used just about every form of moon-work ever devised. We suspect that the mechanisms were often, if not always, bought in 'in the rough' from specialist wholesalers. This accounts for the wide variety of moon-drive mechanisms that we have seen.

Unfortunately, much of the drive mechanisms have long since been discarded by repairers who either did not understand them or, more likely, were only paid "to make it go". The easiest way of doing this was to discard moonwork, datework and anything else that increased the load on heavily worn movements.

On one or two very early movements by John Owen the moon-work has disappeared almost entirely. This seems, originally, to have consisted of a moonwheel mounted on a

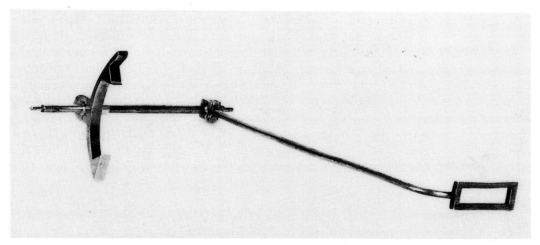

Fig 193: (above): Pallets from a Watkin Owen movement. At this later date, the pallets were flatter and broader (compare with Fig 192, p256).

Fig 194: The going and striking barrels and main wheels from a movement by John Owen, but typical of any Owen movement. Note the slip-washer arrangement which holds the assembly together.

Fig 195: Typical Owen winding clicks and click-springs.

Fig 196: In the 1770s, the minute numbers were often disproportionately large as in this example. No fewer than seven large holes (drilled in this dial centre to allow the fitting of an electric movement) have been filled by an expert restorer.

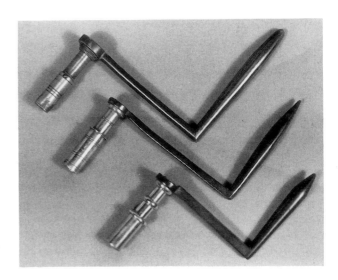

Fig 197: Typical keys of the types issued with Llanrwst clocks.

hollow brass arbor fitting over the extension of the 'scape-wheel which carries the second hand. The wheel itself would have engaged with the large pinion on the snail-wheel and activated the moon disc via a pin or detent mounted on its rim.

Later, John Owen changed to the long articulated lever system which moves the moon disc on one tooth when it is depressed by a pin on the date-wheel. Later, on clocks by Watkin Owen, William Owen and Moses Evans the moon-wheel is mounted on a stud arbor in the top right hand corner of the front-plate. This wheel engages, somewhat precariously, with the snail-wheel and carries two pins to engage with the toothed edge of the moon disc. When this type of moon-drive is present the stud arbors and bosses of the lifting piece and hook of the Owen strikework have to be shortened to make way for the moon-wheel. On movements by Moses Evans the top right hand corner of the front-plate is virtually empty and the moon-wheel causes fewer problems.

As for the moon-discs themselves, they follow the contemporary conventions. The earliest John Owen moon-disc we have found has gilded stars on a dark blue ground surrounding the two moon faces. On at least two of John Owen's early clocks, however, the moon-disc is engraved, waxed and silvered, not painted - see, for instance, the Musical Clock. From about 1770, a painted landscape scene displaces all or half of the gilded stars on their dark blue ground, whilst on the painted dials dating from about 1780 a painted landscape scene alternated with a maritime scene - usually of a warship in full sail. Rather curiously, on the Owen Hughes clock [see Chapter X], the warship seems to be in the process of being blown-up!

The rim of the arch above the moon-disc was used for various purposes. On John Owen's very early moon-phase clocks he affixed his nameplate there. Later he preferred an improving motto, choosing, invariably, `He appointed the man for seasons' from Psalm 104. Watkin also favoured this although, occasionally, he used the rim of the arch for his signature, and, on two occasions, for the name of the purchaser. We have never seen 'High Tide at Liverpool', 'Conwy' or 'Trefriw Quay' or anything similar. This is somewhat surprising because lower down the valley tidal information would have been of considerable significance.

The Weights

Two typical pairs of Owen weights are shown in Figure 111 (p177). Weights of this distinctive shape were used from about 1755 onwards. We have assumed that they were made locally. We have no hard evidence for this but their shape is highly distinctive and unusual.

The weights are variable in size and weight but, usually the going weight is 12 lbs +/- 1 lb with the striking weight 14 lbs +/- 1 lb. Occasionally, they appear very much larger but we suspect that this is because 'plums' of lower specific gravity are concealed within. Certainly, on one occasion, we have found an extra large weight to be full of fragments of cast-iron. The fragments appear to have come from a high quality circular vessel of some type - possibly one of the crucibles used for melting the lead?

The hooks for attaching the weights to their pulleys are very variable in form, indicating that any available wire or rod was used. Often, these are very crude.

We have been unable to form any firm opinion as to when cast-iron weights were introduced but we think not before about 1810.

The weight pulleys on Llanrwst clocks have no distinguishing features, but it is interesting to note that the iron or steel hoop changes to brass at about the same time that there was a general change to brass components in the Owen workshop in the 1770s. This suggests that the hoops were made and fitted in the workshop even if the pulley wheels themselves were amongst the ready-made components that had been bought in.

Pendulums

The brass-faced pendulum bobs on the earliest Llanrwst clocks are also the smallest. Until about 1765, the bobs are about $3^1/_2$" - $3^3/_4$" in diameter. Thereafter they become larger, usually measuring 4" - $4^1/_4$". In the 1770s a few clocks seem to have been given pendulums with bobs that are even larger, measuring as much as 5" in diameter. But these over-sized bobs, which are very heavy, never seem to have been numerous.

We are unable to be sure when cast iron bobs took over from the brass-faced, lead ones but we do not think it was much before 1820.

The 18th century pendulum rods are made of relatively thin iron or steel wire or rod, much thinner than the modern equivalent. The pendulum-bob slide is either of iron or brass and, again, is very slender by modern standards. At the other end of the pendulum wire the brass crutch blocks, too, are much smaller in all their dimensions than those available today. We think it is unlikely that we have seen many original suspension springs, and, even if we have, we have been unable to identify them. If we had to hazard a guess, we would say that, once again, they would be very narrow *eg* about $1/_8$" to $3/_{16}$" in width.

Keys

Figure 197 (p259) shows three old keys which we believe to be 18th or early 19th century in origin and of the type issued with Llanrwst clocks.

Appendix I
CLOCKS IN THE CONWY VALLEY BEFORE 1745

There were, of course, clocks and watches in the Conwy Valley before John Owen established himself in Llanrwst but there are very few references to them. We have already seen that one of John Owen's first major commissions was to renovate the Conwy church clock in 1746 which must mean that this clock had been in situ long enough for it to have become dilapidated. Unfortunately, few Conwy church records have survived and we have no idea who made this clock or when. It is unlikely that any other church in the valley had a turret clock at this time, and, indeed, few have today.

Most other clocks or pocket watches prior to 1745 would have been owned by the wealthier inhabitants and before 1700 by the very wealthy who would have bought them in London.

The Wynn Papers contain some passing references. The inventories of the possessions of Sir John Wynn do not appear to include either a clock or a pocket watch but these documents are very difficult to decipher so there may be one concealed behind Maurice Wynn's scrawl. As an aside because he lived in London, not at Llanrwst, Sir Richard Wynn, who died in 1649, had no clock either, but he did have a 'Weather glass'. [1]

The second Sir Richard Wynn who, following the introduction of the pendulum in about 1660, lived at a time when London clockmakers and their clocks were in the ascendancy, had much more involvement with them. In 1661 he had a dispute with his cousin Christian Grosvenor over financial matters and this involved, inter alia, a gold clock which the lady was refusing to part with until her gold watch was returned. Obviously, matters became very heated because Christian's father-in-law, Richard Grosvenor, wrote to Sir Richard Wynn in an attempt "to make peace amongst you". [2] Probably, because it was in gold and because there would hardly have been time in 1661 for a pendulum clock to have found its way to North Wales, the clock in question was a table-clock.

A year later, in 1661, John Williams wrote to Lady Sara Wynn [3] about money matters and, once again, there is a reference to a clock this time valued at £30. Probably he is referring to the same clock.

In 1667, Sir Thomas Cholmondley sent a fascinating letter to Sir Richard at Gwydir, mostly concerning the activities of the Dutch fleet off Gravesend. However, he starts off by telling Sir Richard that, as requested, he has sent him "a watch from Mr. Aspinwall . . . with an open face and the day of the month". [4] Josiah Aspinwall was a very well known London watchmaker of this period, who may have come originally from Lancashire.

Most tantalising of all Sir Richard's dealings with clocks and clockmakers, was his habit, when visiting London, (in order to take his seat in parliament) of lodging in the house of Edward East the famous London clockmaker who was to become Master of the Clockmakers Company and Clockmaker to the King. [5] Whether he bought clocks and watches on these visits we shall never know, nor indeed why he chose to lodge with East.

No clocks appear to have survived from this very early period. In 1737, an Inventory [6] of

Upper Gwydir House - by then full of worn-out furniture and hangings - refers to "One pendulum with brass weight, a broken line . . ." which is recorded as being in the Stone Parlour and this is all we are told. The description is not particularly helpful. At that time, all clocks with a long pendulum were apt to be called a 'pendulum', so this one could have been a long-case clock, hooded wall clock or lantern clock, but perhaps the first is the most likely. The fact that this clock had a brass weight suggests a London origin where good quality clock weights were usually encased in brass.

In 1921, when the contents of Gwydir were sold there was a lantern clock by Jeremy Gregorie included amongst the items catalogued for the sale. [7] Obviously this was a particularly fine example because it was surmounted by silver ornaments, a very rare feature. Perhaps, Sir Richard Wynn brought this clock home with him after one of his trips to the capital, - but this is only conjecture and it may have arrived at Gwydir much later. The same sale included two other clocks, a long-case by Moses Evans (in the kitchen) and, in the Oak Parlour, "An interesting and very *Early Brass Dial Hanging Clock* in Repousse brass work frame".

This was almost certainly the German clock which was tended and wound by contract by various clockmakers during the first half of the 19th century. It can be seen in one of the illustrations to the catalogue and, indeed, in certain photographs appearing elsewhere. It was a German or Austrian wall clock called a *telleruhr* and would have been made sometime during the 18th century. A feature of these clocks was that the small bob pendulum swung in front of the dial.

NOTES

1. Calendar of Wynn Papers No 1897.
2. Ibid No 2314.
3. Ibid No 2343.
4. Ibid No 2509.
5. Ibid Nos 2236 and 2241.
6. Lincoln County record Office ANC/X/A/16.
7. Catalogued by Ward Price & Co of Scarborough.

Appendix II
the Survey Questionaires

CLOCKMAKERS OF LLANRWST		BRASS
	Ref. No.	
	CLOCK INSPECTION REPORT - BRASS DIAL	

Inspection by:	Date:	Long-case/8 day/30 hour	Bracket

Name& Address of Owner:

Tel. No:

Makers Name & Place of Origin:	Location of Signature:

DIAL	APPROX. DATE:

Square/Arched	Dial Dimensions:
Moonwork etc:	
Seconds Dial:	
Date Indication:	
Dial Centre:	
Spandrels:	
Chapter Ring:	
Description of other features:	

HANDS	Matching/Non-Matching	Original Hour	Yes/No
		Original Minute	Yes/No

Brief Description of		
Hand Design:	Hour:	Minute:
Other Hands:		

MOVEMENT	Dimensions	(Plate size x inside plates)

Strike-work:
Repeat-work:
Other Features:

CASE	Style:	Height:

Hood Pillars:	Capitals:
Quarter Columns:	
Door Shape:	
Finials:	
Wood:	
Other Features:	
Comments:	

CLOCKMAKERS OF LLANRWST	PAINTED

Ref. No.

CLOCK INSPECTION REPORT - PAINTED DIAL

Inspection by:	Date:	Long-case/8 day/30 hour	Bracket/Dial

Name& Address of Owner:

Tel. No:

Makers Name & Place of Origin:	Location of Makers Name:

DIAL	APPROX. DATE:

Square/Arched	Dial Dimensions:
Moonwork etc:	
Seconds Dial:	
Date Indication:	
Dial Centre:	
Dial Corners:	
Falseplate: Yes/No Dial Maker:	
Description of painting & other features:	

HANDS	Steel/Brass	Matching/Non-Matching	Original Hour	Yes/No
			Original Minute	Yes/No

Brief Description of		
Hand Design:	Hour:	Minute:
Other Hands:		

MOVEMENT	Dimensions	(Plate size x inside plates)

Strike-work:
Repeat-work:
Other Features:

CASE	Style:	Height:

Hood Pillars:	Capitals:
Quarter Columns:	
Door Shape:	
Finials:	
Wood:	
Other Features:	
Comments:	

Appendix III
LLANRWST WATCHES LOCATED IN THE SURVEY

1. A silver pair-cased verge watch by Watkin Owen, Llanrwst. The movement is numbered 109, and has a Tompion-type regulator and round pillars. The pierced and engraved cock features Prince of Wales feathers.
The outer case is now covered in shagreen, but shows signs of an original tortoiseshell cover. This outer case is not original. The inner case is probably by James Richards of London and was assayed there in 1791-2. The movement is probably from Liverpool. The dial is a later replacement. From the Evans Roberts collection; now in the Welsh Folk Museum, No 17. 64/3.

2. A silver pair-cased verge watch by Watkin Owen, Llanrwst. A Liverpool watch with, unusually, a top-plate smaller than the bottom. The dial has been replaced but otherwise this is a fine watch. Tompion-type regulator and round pillars; finely engraved and pierced cock. Movement numbered 4303. Silver pair-case by James Richards of London, hall-marked in London in 1799/1800. This watch once belonged to the driver of the Holyhead mail-coach. It is now in the Welsh Folk Museum, No 34.758/84.

3. A silver pair-cased verge watch by Watkin Owen, Llanrwst, the movement numbered 4420, c1805. Tompion-type regulator and round pillars but with a later dial and in a much later case with maker's mark 'JL' assayed in Birmingham, 1836-7. This watch is in the Welsh Folk Museum, No.44.100.

4. A silver pair-cased verge watch carrying the name `William Owen. Llanrwst', the movement numbered 8449. Bosley-type regulator. Dial with Arabic numerals. This watch has a very large pendant. This is a Liverpool watch, in a case by William Hull of Liverpool, and assayed in Birmingham in 1810-11. This watch is in the Welsh Folk Museum, No 44.99. Donor Sir Leonard Twistin-Davies KBE.

5. A silver pair-cased watch by John Jones, Llanrwst; movement numbered 305. A very thick watch but of good quality. The movement with Bosley regulator and round pillars. The cock finely pierced and engraved, incorporating the head and shoulders of a man, side view, in a medallion surround. The dial with vertical Arabic numerals. The case was assayed in Birmingham in 1814-15 and bears maker's mark `WH'. In private ownership.

6. A silver pair-cased verge watch by John Jones, Llanrwst; the movement numbered 470. Very similar to the preceding watch, but movement with Tompion regulator. Again, a very fine cock incorporating the head and shoulders of a man in an elaborate surround. In private ownership.

7. A silver pair-cased verge watch by D Owen, Llanrwst; the movement numbered 11241. The movement with Bosley type regulator is of Liverpool origin. A fine but less elaborate cock than on the earlier watches. A very heavy and thick watch, the case bearing the same number as the movement. The case was assayed at Birmingham in 1838-9; the maker's mark `EB' refers possibly to Edward Brown of Coventry. Presented by W Scriven Williams to the Welsh Folk Museum, No 67.468/18.

8. A silver pair-cased lever watch by Robert Williams, Llanrwst; the movement numbered 2468. The escapement is of the English table roller type. Probably a Coventry watch. The two-piece dial incorporates a small recessed seconds dial. The case was assayed in London in 1860-61; the maker's mark is 'HR'. Presented to the Welsh Folk Museum by W Scriven Williams, No 67.468/10.

9. A silver pair-cased lever watch by Griffith Owen, Llanrwst; the movement numbered 8655. The case was hall-marked in Birmingham in 1847-8. Case maker 'JK', the wholesaler (?) 'TBRB'. A strange watch with all the outward appearances of a verge. In private ownership.

10. A silver pair-cased watch with compensated lever escapement by Griffith Owen, Llanrwst; the movement numbered 9244. The silver pair-case with maker's mark 'JK', the wholesaler (?) 'TBRB'. Assayed at Birmingham 1848-49. Presented to the Welsh Folk Museum by W Scriven Williams. No 67.468/5.

11. A silver pair-cased lever watch by Griffith Owen, Llanrwst, the movement No. 243. The pair-case hall-marked Birmingham 1847-8, the maker's mark 'JH' [possibly John Helsby of Liverpool] and wholesaler's initials (?) 'R&B'. Presented to the Welsh Folk Museum by W Scriven Williams No 67.468/17.

12. A silver hunter watch by Robert Parry, Llanrwst, the movement numbered 2865. The heavily jewelled movement has an un-cut compensated balance. A Coventry-made watch of high quality. The silver case bears the maker's mark 'IH' and was hall-marked in London in 1863-64. Presented to the Welsh Folk Museum by W Scriven Williams No 67.468/2.

13. A silver watch with compensated lever escapement by G. Owen, Llanrwst; the movement numbered 18100. The fusee movement has a very high quality balance with gold timing screws; the escapement is of the English table-roller type. A rather strange watch, early in style. The case made by 'RG' of Liverpool and assayed at Chester in 1893. Presented to the Welsh Folk Museum by W Scriven Williams No 67.468/7.

14. A silver watch with compensated lever escapement carrying the name Griffith Owen & Son, Llanrwst, the movement numbered 317028. The movement with reversing going barrel. A Lancashire Watch Company watch from Prescot, with case by T P Hewitt, hallmarked at Chester 1899/1900. Presented to the Welsh Folk Museum by W Scriven Williams No 67.468/16.

15. A silver lever watch by G Owen & Son, Llanrwst, movement numbered 121227. Casemaker 'IJTH', with hallmark from Chester, 1897. In private ownership.

16. A silver lever watch by J Parry Jones, Berlin House, Llanrwst, the movement numbered 42857. In private ownership.

17. A silver pocket chronograph by G Owen & Son, Llanrwst. The silver case is hallmarked Chester 1904/5; the maker's mark is given as 'AW'. Sadly, this fine watch was inadvertently immersed in the highly acid water from the local supply for a period of many months. When we found it, little more than the case and dial remained! In private ownership.

18. A silver lever watch inscribed 'Thomas Jones, Conway', the movement numbered 9906. In private ownership.

19. A silver lever watch by G Owen & Son, Llanrwst, movement numbered 22188. Heavy, gnurled case. In private ownership.

20. A silver lever watch by G Owen, Llanrwst, movement numbered 18923. A two piece dial with recessed seconds dial. Dial marked 'ENGLISH LEVER'. In private ownership.

21. A silver lever watch by Griffith Owen & Son, Llanrwst, the movement numbered 149567. Two piece dial with recessed seconds dial. Assayed at Chester in 1903/4. In private ownership.

22. A silver lever watch by G Owen & Son, the movement numbered 22784. The case bears the maker's mark 'AW', and was assayed in Chester in 1904/5. In private ownership.

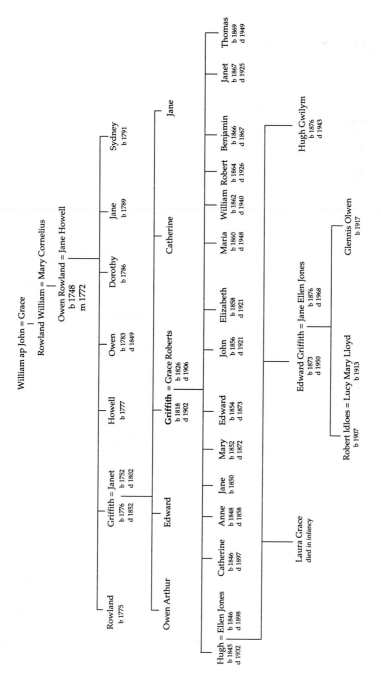

William ap John = Grace

Rowland William = Mary Cornelius

Owen Rowland = Jane Howell
b 1748
m 1772

Rowland
b 1775

Griffith = Janet
b 1776   b 1752
d 1852   d 1802

Howell
b 1777

Owen
b 1783
d 1849

Dorothy
b 1786

Jane
b 1789

Sydney
b 1791

Owen Arthur

Edward

Griffith = Grace Roberts
b 1818   b 1826
d 1902   d 1906

Catherine

Jane

Hugh = Ellen Jones
b 1845   b 1846
d 1932   d 1898

Catherine
b 1846
d 1897

Anne
b 1848
d 1858

Jane
b 1850

Mary
b 1852
d 1872

Edward
b 1854
d 1873

John
b 1856
d 1921

Elizabeth
b 1858
d 1921

Edward Griffith = Jane Ellen Jones
b 1873   b 1876
d 1950   d 1968

Maria
b 1860
d 1948

William
b 1862
d 1940

Robert
b 1864
d 1926

Benjamin
b 1866
d 1867

Janet
b 1867
d 1925

Thomas
b 1869
d 1949

Hugh Gwilym
b 1876
d 1943

Laura Grace
died in infancy

Robert Idloes = Lucy Mary Lloyd
b 1907   b 1913

Glennis Olwen
b 1917

Family Tree of Griffith Owen, Clockmaker of Llanrwst. [R Idloes Owen]

Select Bibliography

AIKIN, A, *Journal of a Tour through North Wales and part of Shropshire*, (London, 1797).

BALLINGER, J, *Calendar of Wynn (of Gwydir) Papers*. (National Library of Wales, 1926).

BENNETT, G J, *A Pedestrian Tour through North Wales*, (Henry Colburn, London, 1838).

BENNETT, J AND VERNON, R W, *Mines of Gwydir Forest*, (Gwydir Mines Publications, Cuddington, 1989).

BINGLEY, REV W, *North Wales including its Scenery, Antiquities, Customs and some sketches of its Natural History delineated from two excursions through all the interesting part of that country during the summer of 1798 and 1801*, (T N Longman and O Rees, London, 1804).

BRUTON, E, *The Longcase Clock*, 2nd Edition (Granada Publishing, London, 1977).

BYNG, Hon J, *The Torrington Diaries 1781-1794,Vol III* (Eyre and Spottiswoode, London, 1936).

CATHRALL, W, *The History of North Wales*, (J Gleave & Son, Manchester, 1828).

CAVE-BROWN-CAVE, B W, *Jonas Barber Clockmaker*, (The Reminder Press, Ulverston, 1979).

CHINNERY, V, *Oak Furniture, The British Tradition*, (Antique Collectors Club Ltd, Woodbridge, 1979).

DODD, A H, *A History of Caernarvonshire 1284 - 1900*, (Caernarvonshire Historical Society, 1968. Reprinted by Bridge Books, Wrexham, 1990).

EVANS, REV J, *A tour through part of North Wales in the year 1798, and at other times*, (J White, London, 1800).

GRIFFITH, J E, *Pedigrees of Anglesey and Carnarvonshire Families*, (W K Morton & Son Ltd, Horncastle, 1914. Reprinted by Bridge Books, Wrexham, 1985).

HEWITT, P A, 'The Deacon Family of Leicestershire Clockmakers', Part II, *Antiquarian Horology* Vol XVI, No 4, (1986).

LOOMES, B, *Yorkshire Clock Makers* , (Dalesman Publishing Co, 1972).

LOOMES, B, *White Dial Clocks, the Complete Guide* , (David & Charles, Newton Abbott, 1981).

LOOMES, B, *Grandfather Clocks and Their Cases* , (David & Charles, Newton Abbott, 1985).

LOWE, W B, *The Heart of Northern Wales* , (Caxton Press, Llanfairfechan, 1927).

NICHOLSON, G (Ed), *The Cambrian Traveller's Guide*, 2nd Edition, (Longman Hurst, Rees, Orme & Brown; Sherwood, Neely and Jones; and B & R Crosby & Co, London, 1813).

PEATE, I C, *Clock and Watch Makers in Wales*, (The Welsh Folk Museum, Cardiff, 1975).

PENNANT, T, *Tours in Wales*, (London, 1810).

PENNANT, T, *The History of the Parishes of Whiteford and Holywell*, (B & J White, London, 1796).

PRYCE, W T R & DAVIES, T A, *Samuel Roberts Clock Maker*, (The Welsh Folk Museum, Cardiff, 1985).

SEABY, W A, 'James Wilson, Clockmaker of Belfast', *Antiquarian Horology*, Vol XIV, No 2 (1983).

SMITH, A, 'An Early 18th century Watchmaking Notebook', *Antiquarian Horology*, Vol XV No 6 (1985).

SMITH, A (Ed), *A Catalogue of Tools for Watch and Clock Makers by John Wyke of Liverpool*, (c1770), (University Press of Virginia, Charlottesville, 1977).

TWISTON-DAVIES, L AND LLOYD-JOHNES, H J, *Welsh Furniture, An Introduction*, (University of Wales Press, Cardiff, 1950).

WILLIAMS, E, 'Iolo Morganwg in Denbighshire, Extracts from his Itinerary in 1799',*Transactions of the Denbighshire Historical Society*, Vol XVI (1967).

WILLIAMS, G H, 'Estate Management in Dyffryn Conwy, circa 1685',*Transactions of the Honourable Society of Cymmrodorion*, (1979).

WYNN, SIR JOHN, *The History of the Gwydir Family*, (1607), (Woodall and Venables, Oswestry, 1878).

INDEX

People

Places

Subjects

LIST OF SUBSCRIBERS

Harold Aldridge, Llandudno
E R Bowen, Cardiff
T T Braun, Holywell
Mrs L Bryson, York
Clwyd Record Office
E C Davies, Llandudno
G & A Davies, Penrhyndeudraeth
T A Davies, St Fagans
P C Dawson, Colwyn Bay
Dr J C Eisel
Conwy Evans, Wrexham
J Evans, Llandudno Junction
Carole Evans, Cardiff
G L Foulkes, Prescot
Carl Goldberg, Manchester
Michael Goldstone, Bakewell
Gwilym Griffith, Casnewydd
Mrs D E Griffiths, Holyhead
Gwynedd Archives Service
Mrs J V Hadfield, Shepshed
J Haslewood, Cheadle
D R Herbert, Ynys Môn
R Herbert
Paul Hopwell Antiques,
West Haddon
J O Hughes, Betws-y-Coed
R J & B Jackson Antiques,
Llangernyw
Mrs A Jones, Conwy
Aled Jones, Holywell
Mrs B M Jones, Wrexham
Miss D M Jones, Ynys Môn
Mrs E Jones, Bala
In Memory of Mr & Mrs J Jones,
Tan-y-Berllan, Denbigh
J A Jones, Somerset
J A Jones, Whitland
M Jones, Llanrwst
Thomas Jones, Cricieth
W J I Jones, Wirral

Mrs S Kerry, Llanddoged
Mrs Myra Lee, London
D Lindsey, Dunstable
Mrs E Lloyd, St Asaph
Mrs E Lloyd Jones, Ynys Môn
B Loomes, Harrogate
R Luff, OBE, DL, FRSA, Deganwy
J D Luffman, Ludlow
Mrs J Martin, Conwy
Mrs G Mackeson-Sandbach,
Llangernyw
N Morris, Corwen
Mr & Mrs E P Owen, Gwynedd
R Idloes Owen, Chester
Dr W G Owen, Preston
W J Owen, Llanrwst
G Padan, Cerrig-y-Drudion
Mrs M B Padan, Cerrig-y-Drudion
D J Priestnall, Worcestershire
Mr & Mrs G J Pritchard,
Colwyn Bay
Dr W T R Pryce,
Cardiff & Llanfaircaereinion
S H Richards
Miss D H Roberts, Abergele
Miss L M Roberts, Maghull
W T Rowlands, Ynys Môn
R Shenton, Middlesex
Snowdonia Antiques, Llanrwst
P Stogdale, Campbeltown
Mrs D Tennant, Clwyd
R W Ward, MA, MSc,
Hertfordshire
Mrs Eirwen Watts, Johnstown
Welsh Folk Museum, St Fagans
Mrs F M Welsh, Llandudno
Mrs D Williams, Nr Mold
E W Williams, Llandwrog
M O Williams, Llandwrog
Mrs S Williams, Ffestiniog